PARTY Like a
PRESIDENT

True Tales of Inebriation, Lechery, and Mischief from the Oval Office

by BRIAN ABRAMS

illustrated by
JOHN MATHIAS

WORKMAN PUBLISHING · NEW YORK

Library of Congress Cataloging-in-Publication Data is available.

ISBN 978-0-7611-8084-5

Design by Ariana Abud

Illustrations by John Mathias
Background and spot illustrations from Victorian Goods and Merchandising:
2,300 Illustrations by Carol Belanger Grafton/Dover Publications on pages 4–5, 10, 15, 21,
23, 29, 32–33, 39, 46, 53, 70, 82, 84, 88, 94, 108, 113, 117, 118, 123, 126, 133, 140–141, 149,
155, 167, and 178. Background and spot illustrations courtesy of Dover Publications on
pages 6, 14, 25, 29, 37, 44, 58, 86, 95, 137, 142, 153, 159, 161, 170, 185, 199, 202, and 227.

Workman books are available at special discounts when purchased in bulk
for premiums and sales promotions as well as for fund-raising or educational use.
Special editions or book excerpts also can be created to specification.
For details, contact the Special Sales Director at the address below,
or send an email to specialmarkets@workman.com.

Workman Publishing Co., Inc.
225 Varick Street
New York, NY 10014-4381
workman.com

WORKMAN is a registered trademark of Workman Publishing Co., Inc.

Printed in the United States of America
First printing January 2015

10 9 8 7 6 5 4 3 2 1

CONTENTS

To Professor Irwin Corey—
friend, comedy legend, and always
too hip for the room

Which President Would You Have a Beer With?

IN THE TWO YEARS I SPENT RESEARCHING AND WRITING *PARTY LIKE A President*—from reading nothing but political biographies and archived periodicals, to conducting dozens of interviews with presidential museum librarians, university professors, and National Park Service rangers—this was one of the questions that friends wanted me to answer. And why wouldn't they? Such sentiments have plagued elections since 1840. It's perhaps the dumbest thing anyone could contemplate within 300 feet of a polling place's entrance. And yet, Americans are comforted to know that the incoming leader isn't some animatronic black ops experiment—that he or she does, in fact, have an appreciation for a generous pour of 12-year Glenlivet or the salted rim of a margarita glass. We are reassured to learn that they, too, require a stiff one at the end of a long day.

Indeed, alcohol provides a departure from workplace hells—whether one is steaming milk for a teenager's latte or negotiating an armament control treaty. Burdened with establishing precedent at his every move, George Washington plowed through three to four glasses of Madeira during his midday dinners. In the Cold War era, Harry Truman threw back an ounce of Old Grand-Dad each morning "to get the engine going." And let's not dismiss the joys of sex and drugs. John F. Kennedy admitted that he could not "get to sleep" without "a lay." In retirement, an ailing Ulysses S. Grant mixed cocaine with both water and wine to help him finish writing what would become a best-selling memoir. On some level, the fact that even the president of the United States finds sanctuary inside of a bottle or in a mistress's bed might give us a sense of national unity. Or we should elect more responsible leaders. Go figure.

The when, what, and why for each president's need (or aversion) to getting drunk, stoned, and off is pretty much the thesis for this book. Some chapters take a biographical approach to examine the likes of Grover Cleveland's reputation as a soused street fighter and Franklin Pierce's alcoholic depression. Other chapters focus on zeitgeist and culture. (That includes times when they *didn't* partake. Herbert Hoover craved gin as much as the next man, but you'd be damned to find any at his table setting during Prohibition.) Throughout the book, sidebars delve into topics such as the impacts of the beer and wine industries on the eighteenth-century working class and the evolution of health hazards. Cocktail recipes at the end of each chapter should (hopefully) give a sense of fleeting trends, as well as traditions, popularized in U.S. nightlife.

Two years ago, I set out to write a definitive guide to presidents and their vices because I thought that "getting completely blasted is funny." And it is, especially when applied to men of importance who vomited on a horse's mane (Grant) and were soaked with whiskey by a poker-playing monkey (Harding—a man of dubious importance). But my initial interest expanded from collecting fratty anecdotes to presenting these accomplished figures in a more relatable light. I became determined to find the humanity within the most inane subject matter: explicit love letters, slurred speeches, and nude swims at Bing Crosby's house, among other shameless moments.

But which president would you most want to have a beer with? More importantly, why do we care? Because maybe our leaders' vices are just as telling as their accomplishments. After reading the chapter that depicts a hungover George W. Bush regrettably staring at himself in a bathroom mirror, my neighbor put it best: "Presidents, they're just like us." Just like us, as in, *no matter one's IQ score or social status, we're all idiots sometimes?* Yes, I would say that is an accurate assessment. Whether that's a comforting or terrifying realization is entirely up to you.

Brian Abrams
New York City, 2014

PARTY KEY

Here's your guide to the vices, which are noted at the beginning of each chapter. However, the extent to which each president indulged—whether moderately, compulsively, or simply administering illegal substances to interns as if they were lab rats—should be considered on a case-by-case basis.

Ale ale \ˈāl\

It was the joy of working-class America ever since the Framers breathed germs onto the Declaration of Independence. Beginning with hard cider, fermented brew was the country's first successfully mass-produced alcoholic beverage, overwhelming the nation with pride and flatulence. Over time, the basic working recipe branched out to include lagers, pilsners, pale ales, stouts, and pumpkin-honey-mint holiday-flavored atrocities.

Amyl nitrite am·yl ni·trite \ˈa-məl ˈnī-ˌtrīt\

Denizens of the mid- to late-twentieth century's gay underworld might have more familiarity with the term "poppers," a pressurized glass capsule ("pearl") that, when snapped open beneath the nostrils, emits a "pop" and releases the chemical compound of amyl nitrite into the body, giving inflated senses of time and sexual prowess. Send samples to author's attention at Workman Publishing (address, inside front cover).

Champagne cham·pagne \sham-'pān\

Beer may forever hold the honorable title of Choice Beverage in Everyman's public house, but drier varietals of bubbly from European regions have always stocked the cellars of upper-class families. An average bottle clocks a modest 12 to 14 percent alcohol, but rich people do not mind. The effervescent wine still packs enough potency to wreck one's head.

Cigar ci·gar \si-'gär\

Fired up on men's golf courses and at basement poker tables, the flavorful rolled tobacco, popularly grown in the southern United States and Central American regions, continues to symbolize celebration and stature. It also acts as an apparent relaxant before or after meals. Some users prefer a quicker fix by the less distinguished habits of lighting a cigarette or "dipping" a pinch of finely ground tobacco in their lower lip. All are risks actively and joyfully taken, despite the inevitable cancer.

Cocaine co·caine \kō-'kān\

In the late 1500s, South American natives ingested coca and tobacco leaves to get a remarkably tingly, soothing buzz. This recreational habit later expanded across the Earth—and would be administered via snorting; rubbing into the oral tissue; gargling a mixed, water-based solution; and, according to the mythology of Stevie Nicks, blown into the rectal cavity with a straw.

Coitus co·i·tus \'kō-ə-təs\

Simultaneously the great motivator and an Achilles' heel, making whoopee strengthened personal constitutions in several commanders in chief, be it with first wives, second wives, flight attendants, teenage slaves, fanatical admirers, Russian spies, or White House staff.

Gluttony glut·ton·y \'glət-nē\

Before the arrival of television and the twenty-four-hour news cycle that followed, the highly distinguished hungry hungry

hippos of yesteryear could suck down giant slabs of beef with no concern for public scrutiny. Perhaps their impulsive nature helped set a tone for what would become widely accepted as a shameful precedent in U.S. culture. And you wonder why Americans are known for eating like they have five assholes.

Marijuana mar·i·jua·na \mer-ə-'wä-nə\

Sticky icky has inspired and dwarfed American artists for nearly two centuries. As far back as Colonial times, farmers reaped hemp for the purpose of producing paper, clothing, rope, and oakum— whatever "oakum" is. But the percentage of THC content in the hemp would have been too low for recreational use. (Later, more potent leaves from India, Mexico, and the Caribbean would be used for medicinal purposes.) It was not until 1854 that the *New York Times* recognized the "physiological and psychological effects" of the plant in a trend piece titled "Our Fashionable Narcotics."

Martini mar·ti·ni \mär-'tē-nē\

The martini underwent several permutations before arriving at its cleanest form: gin and vermouth with a twist. When the Prohibition era ended, so did the elaborate masking of otherwise gag-inducing moonshine poured into V-shaped cocktail glasses. "With the 1930s, America settled down," according to William Grimes's *Straight Up or On the Rocks*. "The overheated inventiveness of the Jazz Age cooled, the frantic rattling of the cocktail shaker gave way to the gentle clinking of ice cubes in a highball glass and peace settled over the land."

Prescription medication pre·scrip·tion med·i·ca·tion \pri-'skrip-shən me-də-'kā-shən\

If you're trying to find a lenient physician to dole out those coveted medications that double as mind candy, throw a dart. Historically, the dispensing of drugs from licensed practitioners has been, to say the least, liberal. In the late nineteenth century, medical studies reported that female patients were prescribed cordials with 40 to 60 percent alcohol content as well as addictive, opiate-derived elixirs for diagnoses as simple as "being nervous." The pharmaceutical industry has not changed much since.

Punch punch \'pǝnch\

Serving the masses on the cheap? This one's the oldest trick in the bartender's book. In the Age of Discovery, European world explorers stocked up on exceptionally potent, dump-it-all-in-at-once alcohol soups. Batches lasted forever on expeditions, and they cured any ailments (and probably worsened seasickness). One of these butt-kicking concoction's descendants went on to occupy giant bowls at the White House. In the 1880s, journalist Benjamin Perley Poore related "the barbaric reports of former years, when . . . tangle-fast whiskey punch was the fashionable table beverage."

Scotch scotch \'skäch\

In the eighteenth century, aged-oak barrels of Scotland's exhilarating swill first landed ashore from the old kingdom. New Englanders were so taken by its blissful taste, they would try to copy its complexity in their own backyards. Whatever their homemade result, it must have satisfied. Case in point: Farmers became gun-wielding berserkers when George Washington slapped a tax on their precious contraband in 1791.

Whiskey whis·key \'hwis-kē\

The American-distilled beverage made of corn or grain cost next to nothing. High society did not partake in the drink that was commonly and mistakenly called "rum" in texts from these wee olden days; for years it was exclusively considered a signature item on every saloon's value menu.

Wine wine \'wīn\

It remains the only refreshment in history that was endorsed by practically every character in the Bible. Way before the United States was smitten with Alexander Payne's *Sideways* and experimental pinot noirs from Oregon, wealthier settlers relied on overseas shipments from France, Italy, and other old countries with proper vines. Notable Virginian forefathers, such as Thomas Jefferson and James Monroe, gave grape-growing a few whirls. But, like sports cars and *The Office*, their stateside versions did not compare.

The pause between the errors and trials of the day and hopes of the night.

—HERBERT HOOVER,
ON COCKTAIL HOUR

THE HIGH AND MIGHTY GENERAL

APRIL 30, 1789–MARCH 4, 1797

George Washington

INDEPENDENT

Toward the end of Richard Linklater's 1993 stoner mosaic Dazed and Confused, *high school student Ron Slater waxes revisionist on the father of his country.*

"Absolutely, George toked weed," Slater says. "He grew fields of that stuff, man." The scraggly upperclassman goes on to suggest that the first president of the United States and commander in chief of

the Continental Army encouraged marijuana cultivation as "a good cash crop for the Southern states" and that his wife, Martha ("a hip, hip, hip lady"), oversaw horticultural endeavors at the White House and packed "a big fat bowl" for her husband every night.

The mythologizing of George Washington began long ago—before the tall tales of John Henry and Paul Bunyon, before the JFK conspiracy theories, before the unsolved murder of Washington's fellow American hero Tupac Shakur. Entire books have been written on debunking the legend that was not. Young Washington hacked a cherry tree into pieces? False! The general was actually a down-to-earth guy, not some military stiff? True! His dentures were made of wood? False! (See "Washington's Pearly Whites.") As an eighteen-year-old, he was bathing naked in the Rappahannock River when two chicks ran off with his clothes? Er . . . yep! (He went so far as to get the women arrested: Spotsylvania County's courthouse notes that one of the thieves received fifteen lashings on her bare back.)

Even Washington's grandson, a portly college flunkout nicknamed "Washtub," published several half-truths about the old man's war stories. (Tub

Washington's
mythical harvest.

also painted sloppily exaggerated battle scenes of bullets whizzing past his gramps—an eighteenth-century superhero as conceived by a half-wit.) But within the Grand Encyclopedia of Bullshit that circulates in our collective consciousness, Washington's alleged marijuana usage might be the stankiest lie of them all.

Before his service in the American Revolutionary War and his unanimous election to the presidency in 1789, Washington was a Virginia farmer. From 1765 to 1767, of the many crops that sprouted in the fields at his Mount Vernon estate, hemp was indeed in the mix. Those who study this type of thing repeatedly cite a line from Washington's diary in which the green thumb described how he would "separate the male from the female hemp." As readers with lifetime subscriptions to *High Times* and no jobs already know, this would have been for the sole purpose of discerning worthless plants apart from those worth burning.

However, Edward G. Lengel, editor in chief of George Washington's papers at the University of Virginia, has never run across such a line. "People take Washington to be the Johnny Appleseed of marijuana," Lengel said. "You'll see these quotations, and they are partially or entirely fabricated. I don't believe he ever used hemp for anything other than the standard industrial purposes."

Stoner myths aside, Washington did love to party. One might even suggest that, had it not been for the general's inclinations toward whiskey and wine, America might still be part of the British Empire. Lengel maintains that "alcohol helped save the revolution," particularly on account of the relationship that was forged between Washington, then the Continental Army general, and François-Jean de Chastellux, a major-general in the French army. In 1781, Chastellux

WASHINGTON'S PEARLY WHITES

Washington's false teeth were not made of wood, and the fact that the entirety of America believes this to be the case should make us question the gullibility of everybody in the country. In truth, his teeth were a ghastly mix-and-match of ivory and human teeth supported by a metal frame. The inside of his trap looked like a rundown construction site, and probably felt worse. According to biographer Ron Chernow, the false teeth were created after Washington ruined his God-given set from years of afternoon dinners. Wine filled silver cups to the brims, conversation lasted for hours, and the head of the table, against better judgment, snacked from bowls of questionably ripened nuts—effectively ruining his chompers.

acted as liaison between Washington and Jean-Baptiste Donatien de Vimeur, Comte de Rochambeau, aka the leader of the French forces that joined America in the fight against the British and helped win the war. Rochambeau uttered not a word of English, and Washington had a mouth full of bar snacks. Both generals depended on Chastellux to translate their headache-inducing conversations and manage the alliance between the thirteen colonies and France.

Along the way, Washington and Chastellux bonded over booze. During most of the war, according to expense reports, Washington enjoyed more pedestrian drinks such as beer and rum; but, thanks to Chastellux, he discovered a greater appreciation for wine. On July 19, 1781, around the time the Colonial and French armies united, Washington wrote a note to Chastellux thanking him for a barrel of red. "You have taken a most effectual method of obliging me to accept your Cask of Claret," Washington wrote. "I shall, by a refusal, bring my patriotism into question, and incur a suspicion of want of attachment to the French Nation . . . my only scruple arises from a fear of depriving you of an Article that you cannot conveniently replace in this Country." Even a patriot like Washington knew that the Two-Buck Chucks of 1700s Virginia—bleh!— couldn't compete with Chastellux's collection.

Three months later, British army general Charles Cornwallis surrendered his regiment to Washington in Yorktown, Virginia, and the three generals sat down to dinner and exchanged toasts. Rochambeau raised his glass in praise of "The United States!" Washington courteously returned with "The King of France!" When the defeated Cornwallis dedicated a drink to simply "The King!" Washington interrupted, "—of England! Confine him there and I'll drink him a full bumper!"

While president, Washington kept a keen eye on his pocket watch for mealtime. When the first dinner bell rang a little before 3 p.m., Washington would charge his horse back to Mount Vernon. A frequent dish on the menu was fresh catch from the Potomac River, plus the usual three to four glasses of Madeira wine. "Even though he took several glasses of wine with dinner, this was considered acceptable in an age of immoderate alcohol consumption," wrote Ron Chernow in his biography *Washington: A Life*. For the rest of the day, the fishy-breathed, teetering Washington retired to the library before suppertime. The president was tucked in bed by 9 p.m., like a modern-day infant. (In fairness, in a painful schedule later adopted by Howard Stern, Al Roker, and the elderly, he started each day around 4 a.m.)

This might seem like an awfully tame routine for a foulmouthed military veteran and outspoken wine enthusiast who lost his teeth in an eighteenth-century version of happy hour. But by the time Washington entered the presidency, he and his wife of thirty years were determined to show the rest of the nation's leaders that they weren't some couple plucked from the back of the woods. Martha's first husband had died in 1757—Washington swooped in just two years later—and left her enough money to make the new couple wealthy. Still, congressmen and cabinet members considered them hicks.

Biographer W. E. Woodward described Washington as "intensely masculine," with Herman Munster–esque hands and feet. At government functions, Pennsylvania senator William Maclay took note of Washington's tipsy demeanor and also called out the general's awkward manners. "At every interval of eating or drinking," according to Maclay's diary of March 4, 1790, "he played on the table with a fork or a knife, like a drumstick." But, critics be damned, the first couple persisted in their pursuit of social respectability. When not banging on the table like a bored little boy, Washington read books. He cut down on gambling. And while he was known as a first-rate curser, the president held back his vulgarities and attempted to lead by example—all this effort, despite the fact that the majority of newly minted Americans were all defecating in rivers like cavemen. Nevertheless, Southern gentlemen such as Secretary of State Thomas Jefferson—he who famously cavorted with slaves while wearing a wig—still saw the first prez as a bumpkin.

In 1796, Washington decided to step down at the end of his second term, one of many precedent-setting acts that would help define the office. Back at Mount Vernon, he launched a business that actually got people high. He constructed a 75-foot-by-30-foot distillery on his property in which he would process neighboring farms' unused grains into whiskey. In 1798, the former president produced approximately 4,000 gallons of white lightning that sold for 50 cents per gallon. The drink was, according to historians, particularly harsh. Or, as a former associate employed by the Mount Vernon Ladies' Association more politely put it, "a pretty sharp taste." In 2013, Mount Vernon reproduced approximately 1,100 bottles' worth, if you're interested.

MARTHA'S CHERRY BOUNCE

Washington kept a canteen of this brandy-flavored beverage at his side while surveying the Allegheny Mountains in September 1784.

10 to 11 pounds fresh sour cherries, preferably Morello, or 3 jars (1 pound, 9 ounces) preserved Morello cherries

4 cups brandy

3 cups sugar

2 cinnamon sticks

2 or 3 whole cloves

1 piece fresh whole nutmeg

Pit the cherries and place them in a large bowl. Crush the fruit and strain the juice into a jar. Add the brandy and sugar, cover, and refrigerate for 24 hours. Shake the mixture occasionally.

Put 2 cups of the juice in a saucepan over medium heat and add the cinnamon sticks, cloves, and nutmeg. Let simmer for 5 minutes, then strain back into the jar. Store for another 2 weeks. Shake occasionally. Serve at room temperature.

Serves 12

HIS ROTUNDITY'S MORNING ROUTINE

MARCH 4, 1797–MARCH 4, 1801

John Adams

2

FEDERALIST

ohn Adams quenched his thirst with a tankard of hard cider at every breakfast, a habit our second president picked up at age fifteen while attending Harvard. It was cider that helped him choke down school-provided meals. "I shall never forget," he recollected, "how refreshing and salubrious we found it, hard as it often was."

The refreshing habit became the best part of waking up for the rest of Adams's life.

SUNDAY MONDAY TUESDAY

ADAMS IS OFTEN PORTRAYED AS A DISAGREEABLE PUBLIC SERVANT, a wet blanket who found the push-and-pull of democracy to be one giant pain in the hindquarters. True enough, our second president possessed a low tolerance for Oval Office headaches. His feisty, sometimes hostile behavior might have derived from the fact that he began drinking at sunrise and did not take his first cup of coffee until mid-afternoon.

What's more, he succeeded George Washington, who was flawless in the eyes of America. Where Washington was the model patriot and celebrated revolutionary macho, Adams was the cantankerous intellect—a misunderstood wonk, exceptionally schooled in the ways of diplomacy at a time when battle-field heroics captured the imagination of a politically infantile country. It was the presidential equivalent of coming onstage just after Prince.

Prior to his four years as president and eight years as the first vice president, Adams served on ninety different committees in the Continental Congress. The Bostonian was the U.S. ambassador to France, England, and the Netherlands. He once wrote that bars are "the nurseries of our legislators," which likely explains how he cultivated his nickname, "His Rotundity." At a

modest height of five-foot-seven, His Rotundity maintained a beer belly of historic proportions.

Of course, emptying bottles of ale is part of the job for politicians of any era. However, in the late eighteenth century, swilling back the suds was a medicinal necessity as much as it was an occupational obligation. Congress wouldn't pass its first piece of environmental legislation for another one hundred years, and rivers were hardly a trustworthy source for safe drinking water. Garbage mucked up the tributaries that ran through major cities, and wells cost far too much for developing rural areas. So breakfast, for many, was an eye-opener of a meal.

To complement said eye-opener, staff would serve Adams a variety of his native New England cuisine, including poached salmon with egg sauce, toast and apple butter, hasty pudding (porridge), ham steak, "scootin'-long-the-shore" (hash browns cooked in bacon fat with diced onion), and johnnycakes.

Order the John "His Rotundity" Adams Heart-Stopper Breakfast at IHOP today!

HARD CIDER

Back in the early 1800s, before railroads made transport affordable for farmers, New England had more hard cider than it could handle. The massive amounts scrounged from apple orchards resulted in families keeping "a pitcher on every table and a jug in every field," according to W. J. Rorabaugh's *The Alcoholic Republic*. Each year, the average household knocked back fifty-two barrels' worth, and, despite the lack in profits, all that domestic production created a sweet sense of patriotism among Northerners, who collectively regarded hard cider as "the common drink of . . . rich and poor alike." Here's your chance to drink your pride.

1 gallon pure apple juice

half-gallon jug*

1 packet champagne yeast

stopper and airlock*

2 to 3 ounces cheap vodka

plastic tubing*

*Available at any homebrew retailer.

Heat the apple juice on the stovetop to just below boiling point and simmer for 5 minutes. Be sure to sanitize kitchenware beforehand. (Unwanted bacteria may impair the brewing process.)

When the cider cools, shake it in a capped jug mixed with the contents from the yeast packet. Fill the airlock with vodka and replace the jug's cap with the stopper and airlock.

Store for 4 to 6 weeks at room temperature.

Use the plastic tubing to transfer the mixture from the jug into a new container. Refrigerate for a few hours. Drink.

/// **Serves 20** ///

RIDING, DINING, AND A LITTLE UN-BENDING

MARCH 4, 1801–MARCH 4, 1809

Thomas Jefferson

3

DEMOCRATIC-REPUBLICAN

On any given day, the contents of Thomas Jefferson's fridge could blow away that of any Mario Batali restaurant. The president allocated more than $16,500 to wine during his two terms from 1801 to 1809 and, according to the head steward, up to $50 a day for food. (Economists at the U.S. Bureau of Labor Statistics loosely estimate that Jefferson's $16,500 wine bill would run between $300,000 to $350,000 in today's dollars and his $50 daily food allowance close to $1,000.) The kitchen and underground brick wine cellar, nicknamed the "ice house," were replete with partridges, wild ducks, courtyard ducks, venison, squab, goose, pâté, rabbit, squirrel, crabs, and oysters. One of Jefferson's servants back at Monticello, his renowned Virginia palace/slave prison, recalled that Jefferson "never would have less than eight" courses even when dining alone.

His wine collection grew to twenty thousand bottles. A typical monthly order would include 630 gallons of Madeira, one barrel of sherry, 540 bottles of sauterne, and 400 bottles of claret. In 1804, Jefferson's champagne bill alone racked up to nearly $3,000—probably enough to buy five whole black people. But did the president ever reel from sticker shock? "Let the price be what it has to be," Jefferson wrote to a wine merchant.

Smooth operator that he was, the revered "Sage of Monticello" would not allow his weakness for delicacies to contradict his politics. A populist who believed in decentralized government—an agenda contrary to that of his predecessors, George Washington and John Adams—Jefferson recognized the need to rebrand his penchant for loins of veal and 1785 Bordeaux. He influenced American dining trends with a revolutionary atmosphere that didn't call for awkward toasts and uppity dress codes. Imagine a scene comparable to a rustic chic bistro in ritzy modern-day Brooklyn: multiple oval-shaped tables, spread throughout the room and without seating assignments (versus, say, your typical bowling alley–length table, found at WASPy Thanksgivings). Jefferson's guests would serve themselves and clean up afterward, as if dining at a poorly staffed Chipotle.

"He didn't want a servant at every elbow," said Susan Stein, a senior curator at Monticello. "At the president's house and here at Monticello, he had dumbwaiters, which allowed people to remove their own soiled plates and stack them. It was a friendly atmosphere where people commented on the conversation. It was about ideas and discussions. It was about intellectual vitality."

Often clad in his bedroom slippers, Jefferson was known to ladle meals onto his guests' plates, at least for those seated in his immediate area. Whenever a bottle needed opening, he would brandish a custom pocketknife, which included a corkscrew. But don't judge a man by his booze tools. Jefferson's drinking was moderate at best: three glasses per night, or, as New York wine merchant Theodorus Bailey observed, he drank "to the digestive point and no further."

His preference was usually to imbibe *after* the meal—a haughty trick he picked up across the pond.

Jefferson: Virginia locavore.

I N 1784, FIVE YEARS before Washington's inauguration and more than a decade before his own, Jefferson was appointed U.S. minister to France. For five years, the six-foot-two ginger rubbed elbows with Europe's political elite while filling up on fine wines and rich cuisine. As one might imagine, it was not a horrible five years. At the time, Jefferson ate better than pretty much anyone in American history (at least until the advent of truffled macaroni and cheese). He collected silver, paintings, china, and sculptures to adorn Monticello and transformed himself into something of a connoisseur.

Oh, and he appreciated more than just what Europe offered in the way of fine arts. Unlike his prudish colleagues back home, Long Tom didn't get his cravat in a knot at the sight of prostitutes. If anything, the international man of mystery admired those individuals committed to the world's oldest profession.

"St. Paul only says that it is better to be married than to burn," he wrote in 1764. "Now I presume that if that apostle had known . . . to furnish them with other means of extinguishing their fire than those of matrimony, he would have earnestly recommended them to their practice." Fast-forward to 1784, and one can imagine Jefferson's excitement when he discovered the Palais-Royal—Paris's newly renovated entertainment complex, inhabited by cafés, bookstores, gambling, and, when evening came, a pack of hot-to-trot call girls. Jefferson considered it one of the "principal ornaments of the city" and had hopes that the business community of Richmond, Virginia, would replicate it. (If only they had listened! "What happens in Richmond . . .")

Despite his enthusiasm for the sex trade, no evidence suggests Jefferson ever indulged—and why would he bother, when he had a gaggle of comely slave women at his disposal? In 1787, a half-black teenager named Sally Hemings arrived in Paris to serve the forty-four-year-old statesman. Described by Jefferson's grandson as "light colored and decidedly good-looking," Hemings was also the half-sister of Jefferson's wife, Martha, who died from childbirth complications five years prior. The teen slave attended to the widower's daily needs—yes, *those* needs—in exchange for clothing, medical attention, and 12 livres a month, which today could buy you a one-week trial membership to a yoga studio. Upon their return to the U.S., while the diehard romantic would serve presidents Washington and Adams as secretary of state and vice president, respectively, Hemings would bear six (!) of his bastard children. (He also had six children with Martha.)

Indeed, five years in Paris will class up just about any old Southern farm boy.

THE YEARS INSIDE "THE PRESIDENT'S MANSION," AS THE ONE-YEAR-OLD White House was known back in 1801, hardly measured up to Jefferson's good times in the City of Lights or his lavish retirement at Monticello. Hemings did not travel with her master to the city of Washington; she remained in Virginia to care for the plantation and her sextet of illegitimate children. Meanwhile, as commander in chief, Jefferson wrote that he and Meriwether Lewis, his personal secretary, lived like "mice in a church" inside the "great stone house" that was theoretically large enough to fire Munchkins out of a cannon without the neighbors bothering to notice.

Afternoons were quiet enough. Jefferson spent the better part of ten to thirteen hours each day at his writing table, grumbling over policy or, more enjoyably, reading the latest literature on wine or the arts and sciences. Anatomy in particular interested the president. One room in the mansion was reserved for his fossil collection, an assortment of tusks and skulls "spread in a large room," Jefferson once bragged, "where you can work at your leisure." In the evening, he would abandon his desk for "riding, dining, and a little un-bending," successfully avoiding the bear cubs he kept in the yard for a couple of months in 1807. Throw in some Elvis memorabilia and Macaulay Culkin, and Michael Jackson would have felt right at home.

WHITE WINE SPRITZER

During Jefferson's retirement at Monticello, one of his granddaughters recalled a picnic in which he oddly "mixed the wine and water to drink with it." Leave it to one of America's first foodies to experiment with what was presumably a prototype for a light and refreshing summer cocktail.

dried strawberries, chopped

strawberries

white wine (Sauvignon blanc or Gewürztraminer varietals recommended)

soda water

Store the dried, chopped strawberries in the freezer ahead of time to use as ice cubes. Muddle the fresh berries in a bowl with a fork until the consistency is all pulp and juice. Fill a glass halfway with wine, then top with the strawberry pulp, a splash of soda water, and berry ice cubes.

// **Serves 1** //

HIS FINE, PORTLY, BUXOM DAME

MARCH 4, 1809–MARCH 4, 1817

James Madison

DEMOCRATIC-REPUBLICAN

n 1808, Washington City nightlife was a sad state of affairs, as much of the capital was underdeveloped or under construction. State representatives seldom brought their wives or mistresses to the seventeen-year-old town, since they had no decent place to schmooze in the evenings. Unless you happened to know President Jefferson, whose dinners welcomed about a dozen members of the in-crowd every night, the U.S. Capitol building was your way station. The place doubled as both romper room and legislative theater. The congressional sausage fest's more religious members held worship services on the House floor; the postmaster interrupted sermons by shouting mail call across a makeshift pulpit.

Then, on May 31, 1809—two months into their first term—the newest presidential couple, James and Dolley Madison, threw what was essentially the first-ever happy hour at the west end of Pennsylvania Avenue, and government officials finally had a reason to bring a date.

President Madison had little to do with it. A wallflower seemingly born with his nose in a book, the Father of the Constitution typically kept to himself at functions while cautiously sipping a glass of Madeira wine. ("I don't think he drank a quart of brandy in his whole life," one servant remarked.) Credit for the social awakening goes to Dolley Madison, a nineteenth-century first lady with a name fit for a 1980s exotic dancer. Every Wednesday, Dolley's open-invitation drawing room soirees became a reliable standby for firewater, cards, chatter, and nice, long leers at her well-documented curves. Here's why:

☞ SHE ALREADY KNEW THE INS AND OUTS OF THE MANSION

In 1801, Thomas Jefferson, a widower, was in need of a hostess for his nightly dinner parties. James Madison was already his secretary of state, so recruiting his top diplomat's wife was convenient enough.

☞ SHE OPENED CHAMPAGNE BOTTLES LIKE A HELLION

"The cork flew to the most distant corner of the room with an explosion as loud as the sound of a popgun," a land surveyor from Maryland recalled. "The wine seemed to be in haste to follow the cork. She however dexterously filled three large glasses." (Dolley's wonk of a husband filled his glass only halfway. "If you drink much of it," explained the president, "it will make you hop like the cork.")

☞ THE PRESIDENT'S MANSION GOT A MAKEOVER

The Bravo channel could have produced a reality series following architect Benjamin Latrobe during the two years he spent decorating the interior. Between a small upstairs parlor, which initially received these salons, and later the Oval Room after its 1810 unveiling, the opening credits montage alone would look *fabulousssss*. Cut to: sunflower yellow damask and crimson velvet curtains; high-backed sofas; huge mirrors; red-lacquered serving trays; and

D

THE • DOLLEY MAGAZINE

MIX & MATCH
DAMASK, SILK, BROCADE: HOW TO CHOOSE

HIDDEN WASHINGTON

BEST KEPT SECRETS!
Where the eligible bachelors are hiding

LIVE LIFE NOW!

BE EFFICIENT, INDUSTRIOUS, PROSPEROUS & GRACIOUS ALL BEFORE NOON

HOW TO MAKE ANYONE FEEL AT HOME

MY *SIGNATURE* WHISKEY SOUR

Entertain American Style

JULY 1811

Can you believe she put herself on every cover?

silver knives and forks. (Utensils were a rarity for some of the yokels back at the Capitol building.)

☞ YOU COULDN'T TAKE YOUR EYES OFF HER

Every woman was covered in vegetable-dyed earth tones, except the towering first lady. With her ostrich feathers and rose-colored gowns, Dolley lit up the room. Both Madisons stood at five-foot-six-and-a-half, but Dolley's collection of headdresses and high heels gave her a good three inches on her husband—some history books misreported her at five-foot-nine. But, honestly, how could anyone pay attention to such a detail with those low-cut gowns? Socialite Frances Few noted in her diary that Dolley, a veritable Real Housewife, had "the most beautiful . . . neck and bosom . . . I ever saw."

☞ SHE OFFERED ANYONE A PINCH FROM HER SNUFF BOX

That's not a euphemism. Like a minor-league shortstop, the forty-one-year-old was generous with her personal stash of snorting tobacco. "In her hands the snuff-box seems only a gracious implement with which to charm," wrote one scenester.

☞ NOBODY FELT EXCLUDED

The hostess with the mostess went out of her way to make outsiders feel at home. One night, a young man from the backwoods, understandably intimidated by the stuffed shirts and yards of yellow damask, pinned himself against a wall. The first lady introduced herself; he responded by spilling his coffee and dropping his saucer to the floor. Dolley didn't bat an eyelash. She continued to make conversation as if nothing had happened, and the yokel nervously stuffed his empty cup into his breeches.

☞ VIPS DROPPED IN

Up-and-coming short story writer and aspiring office-seeker Washington Irving knew Wednesday nights were ripe with opportunity to engage the sphere of influence. "I emerged from dirt and darkness into the blazing splendor of Mrs. Madison's drawing-room," Irving wrote. "I was most graciously received; found a crowded collection of great and little men, of ugly old women and beautiful young ones, and in ten minutes was hand and glove with half the people in the assemblage. Mrs. Madison is a fine, portly, buxom dame, who has a smile and a pleasant word for everybody."

☞ WORD SPREAD

Dolley achieved celebrity status like no first lady before her. At a time when women's names scarcely appeared in print, she made the cover of Philadelphia's *Port Folio* magazine in February 1818. Upon one occasion, a woman propositioned the first lady: "Perhaps you wouldn't mind if I just kissed you, to tell my gals about."

THE MADISON YEARS WEREN'T ENTIRELY ONE BIG CHILL. THE PRESIdent's second term was consumed by the War of 1812, a land-and-sea military campaign waged against England. For twenty years, the British and French had been at odds; both had long pressured the U.S. to intervene. The nation, no longer a newborn state able to plead isolationism, had to take a position in international matters. (Besides, there was still bad blood from the Revolutionary War that needed spilling.)

The conflict did not end well. British troops sacked ships and burned down several government properties, including the White House in 1814. One upside to the humiliating defeat, if any: It prompted the first lady's most memorable act of her unprecedented tenure at 1600 Penn. With the president already safely out of the city, Dolley and the harried staff, anticipating invasion, prepared to abandon the mansion. Hours before the arrival of the British,

Dolley lit up the room.

a carriage waited outside, but, as described in a letter to her sister, the first lady would not leave the premises without artist Gilbert Stuart's famed 1796 full-length portrait of the first president. "I insist[ed] on waiting until the large picture of Gen. Washington [was] secured," Dolley wrote, "and it require[d] to be unscrewed from the wall. This process was found too tedious for these perilous moments; I . . . ordered the frame to be broken, and the canvass taken out."

There was no reason to argue. The woman knew how to decorate.

MADISON'S WHISKEY SOURS

The name "whiskey sour" itself may not have entered the American lexicon until years later, but "to be fair," according to an assistant curator at Madison's Virginia home, Montpelier, "our modern-day understanding of a whiskey sour is probably similar-ish to the punch served at Dolley Madison's levees." Evidence of this appears in the diary of lawyer Lord Francis Jeffrey, who, in 1813, reported "little cups of what I took for lemonade, but found to my infinite horror was strong punch."

---

1 lemon

4 ounces bourbon

1 teaspoon powdered sugar

ice

Squeeze and strain the juice from the lemon into a bowl. Save the peel. Pour the lemon juice, bourbon, and sugar into a tumbler over ice. Shake well. Serve in a rocks glass over ice. Garnish with the lemon peel.

/// **Serves 2** ///

HOLIDAY ROAD

MARCH 4, 1817–MARCH 4, 1825

James Monroe

DEMOCRATIC-REPUBLICAN

I n the decade that followed the War of 1812—the three-year conflict that culminated in the British army setting the White House on fire—the United States went into healing mode and embraced a newfound nationalism.

Some say this sentiment birthed an easy presidency for James Monroe, a Founding Father who spent the summer of his inaugural year traveling around the northern U.S. and swilling wine like a tipsy Clark Griswold in knee breeches. Monroe's sartorial style was considered passé during this Era of Good Feelings. But the policy wonk and longtime ambassador had advanced in the political scene, not for his fashion-forward wardrobe, but because "people saw some sort of spark in him," said Dan Preston, editor of James Monroe's papers at the University of Mary Washington. "As early as 1802 people talked about him being president."

Monroe did not leave an especially memorable mark on capital nightlife—for one thing, the White House underwent remodeling after the Brits torched the sucker—but his goodwill tour of 1817 made up for it. The four-month, 2,000-mile stretch from Maine to Maryland ultimately served as a publicity campaign to improve relations between federal and municipal governments. The president visited prisons, hospitals, museums, colleges, army bases—you get the picture. (He would do the same in the South two years later.) These days, people are accustomed to seeing their president on television and in news reports several times daily, but it was a rare privilege for nineteenth-century Americans to catch a glimpse of the chief. For that reason alone, the tour was well received. "Avenues, windows, roofs and even chimney tops were thronged with a smiling population," Boston's *Columbian Centinel* reported in July 1817. To fill Monroe's glass in these cities was a big deal—a chance to get a load of the last president to wear a tricornered hat in the Revolutionary War.

"People saw some sort of spark in him."

Every other night, Monroe attended receptions, which lasted from roughly 6 p.m. to midnight and served an unconscionable amount of wine. Nobody was counting calories. Timothy Green of the *Virginia Herald* noted "the glittering 'pomp and circumstance' of courtly parade." Joseph Hopkinson, congressman from Philadelphia, said city officials "pushed the thing to the very borders of the ridiculous." But what could you do? This was tradition, after all, as party-planning committees drafted lists of toasts dedicated to every imaginable toe of government—to each state (there were now nineteen of them), to the nation, to Congress, to the Declaration of Independence, and to any other excuse worth refilling their cups. "They would hit an average of thirty or forty toasts," Preston said. "For each toast, they would drink a glass of wine and sing a song." Fortunately, karaoke machines had not yet been invented.

With each pour approximating 1 to 2 ounces, and Madeira, the most popular varietal back then, containing an overwhelming 20 percent alcohol, you'd expect the average diner would flatline before dessert. One event in New York City, which one hundred guests attended, called for the uncorking of 650 bottles. (Do the math: At four glasses to a bottle, that's twenty-six glasses per head!) One has to wonder if Monroe's generation ever attempted sobriety for the sheer

JAMES MONROE
THE GREAT GOODWILL TOUR
SUMMER '17

BALTIMORE, MD   DOVER, NH
NEW CASTLE, PA   CONCORD, NH
PHILADELPHIA, PA   HANOVER, NH
TRENTON, NJ   NORWICH, VT
NEW BRUNSWICK, NJ   WINDSOR, VT
NEW YORK, NY   WOODSTOCK, VT
NEW HAVEN, CT   MONTPELIER, VT
MIDDLETOWN, CT   BURLINGTON, VT
HARTFORD, CT   LAKE CHAMPLAIN, VT
DEAF & DUMB ASYLUM, CT PLATTSBURGH, NY
SPRINGFIELD, MA   SACKETTS HARBOR, NY
NEW LONDON, CT   NIAGARA, NY
STONINGTON, CT   BUFFALO, NY
NEWPORT, RI   DETROIT, MI
PROVIDENCE, RI   LANCASTER, OH
BOSTON, MA   ZANESVILLE, OH
CHARLESTOWN, MA   CANONSBURGH, PA
SALEM, MA   PITTSBURGH, PA
NEWBURYPORT, MA   HAGERSTOWN, MD
PORTSMOUTH, NH   FREDERICK, MD
PORTLAND, ME

What a long,
strange trip that
must have been.

thrill of it. "I don't know," Preston admitted. "Were they slightly inebriated all the time because people were drinking so much? Was everyone going around in a perpetual alcoholic haze? They operated in it because it was normal."

One thing is for certain—most people felt like shit more often than not. Monroe permanently suffered bouts of fever after a bullet was lodged in his shoulder during a Revolutionary War battle. In the pre-antibiotic days, medicines were weak, predominantly herbal; the most one could do was numb the pain. Trade with China was booming and opiates were readily available. Even as far back as 1790, an entry in President George Washington's diary mentions "excruciating tooth pain" and a "swelled and inflamed gum" that was later treated with laudanum. And if such a fearless warrior required loads of dope to mollify a toothache, one can speculate the amounts of Madeira needed to tuck in a wounded Monroe at midnight. Maybe this was the "spark" they saw in him.

///

SYLLABUB

The syllabub reigned supreme among those with sweet tooths until ice cream came to power in the nineteenth century. Recipes varied—Monroe preferred nutmeg to whipped cream—but here's the more common mixture for all you dessert junkies.

⅔ cup white wine

⅓ cup sherry

2 tablespoons grated lemon zest

¼ cup lemon juice

⅔ cup sugar

2 cups heavy cream

fresh mint sprigs and berries for garnish

Mix the wine, sherry, lemon zest, and lemon juice in a bowl. Stir in the sugar until dissolved. In a separate bowl, whip the cream until the mixture forms into medium-size stiff peaks. Then, combine and stir with the wine mixture. Scoop the mixture into wineglasses. Cover the glasses and chill in the refrigerator for at least 12 hours. When ready to serve, top with the mint and berries.

/////////////// **Serves 8** ///////////////

GAMBLING FURNITURE

MARCH 4, 1825–MARCH 4, 1829

John Quincy Adams

DEMOCRATIC-REPUBLICAN

At five-foot-seven and pushing 180 pounds, John Quincy Adams maintained a remarkable exercise regimen. An early riser, he started the day at 5 a.m. with a four-mile walk or, weather permitting, a swim in the Potomac River. (Make that a naked swim in the Potomac River.) In the evening, Adams's athleticism continued in the form of bar sports. In his first year at the White House, the fifty-seven-year-old found solace in a formerly vacant room that he outfitted with game room staples, such as chessmen and a billiard table purchased secondhand from a Washington storekeeper in 1825—

basically it was his own private precursor to Chuck E. Cheese's. Every night until midnight, Adams pounded port and bank shots to escape the hell that was his presidency.

He was doomed from the start. The political parties were at war, largely due to a November 1824 backroom handshake that secured Adams's victory in a highly contested election. The republic grew resentful upon learning of this so-called corrupt bargain (see box), which would haunt Adams throughout his one-term presidency and turn military celebrity/campaign rival Andrew Jackson into his arch nemesis.

THE CORRUPT BARGAIN OF 1824

In the election of 1824, Andrew Jackson won the popular vote, but none of the four candidates accrued a voting majority in the Electoral College. In accordance with the Twelfth Amendment, the decision was turned over to the House of Representatives. Adams prevailed by the slightest margin, thanks to (as legend has it) a promise to Speaker of the House Henry Clay to make him secretary of state if Clay could coerce enough legislators to vote Adams into office.

Adams was not the only miserable soul who slept at 1600 Penn. "There is something in this great, unsocial house which depresses my spirits beyond expression," First Lady Louisa Adams wrote. Her sole purpose, it seemed, was to "cook dinner, wash his clothes, gratify his sexual appetites." Between an obstructionist Congress and an unhappy marriage, the tainted president accomplished little. Some say he suffered from depression during his stint in office. While Adams was moping around his game room, Action Jackson's minions on Capitol Hill seized every opportunity to frame the president as snobby and dishonest. Newspapers supporting Jackson piled on with a deluge of scathing attacks, some libelous.

Strangely enough, it was that secondhand billiard table in the president's game room that launched a four-year-long campaign to run Adams out of town. The barrage began a year into Adams's presidency, when Representative Stephen Van Rensselaer of New York submitted a routine inventory of recently purchased White House furnishings to Congress. Items on the list, prepared by Adams's son and private secretary John Adams II, included a billiard table for $50; a green felt cover for $43; cues for $5; and three sets of billiard balls at $6 each.

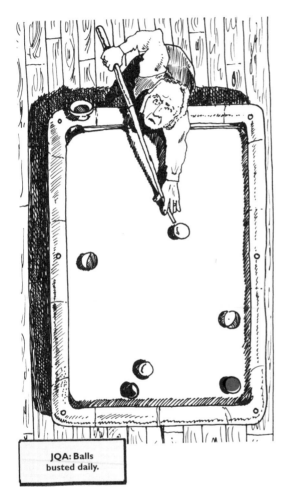

JQA: Balls
busted daily.

Adams's rivals went to town. "Is it possible to believe," Representative Samuel Carson asked the House floor, "that it ever was intended by Congress, that the public money should be applied to the purchase of gaming tables and gambling furniture?" Washington's *United States Telegraph* erroneously reported that the billiard table cost $500. Frankfort, Kentucky's *Argus of Western America* fanned the flames: "If the people tolerate the trifling expense of a billiard table, balls, and chessmen out of the public funds, what may they next expect?"

In rural areas, voters required an explanation as to what the hell a billiard table was in the first place. In 1827, the editor of Woodstock, Virginia's *Sentinel of the Valley* wasted a great number of column inches on describing this unknown pastime. The hillbilly readership may not have comprehended the purposes of its "frame of mahogany" or "beautiful ivory balls," but lightbulbs probably went off when they were told the purchase "amounted to as much as would buy a brace of wagon horses." Other publications expanded their inquiry into the president's questionable lifestyle on the nation's dime, including arranging prostitution services for the czar of Russia.

None of the press's claims were proven true. Supporters of the administration argued that whatever these extravagances—even if they were on the government's tab and were frowned upon by the church—were a necessity of political life. How else should the executive mansion entertain wealthy and

powerful visitors from around the globe? This defense didn't help. In 1828, Jackson won in a landslide—no tiebreaker decision from Congress necessary.

There were shades of Larry David in Adams's lame duck presidency: a disagreeable, middle-aged bald man who fell victim to an unruly mob of his own making. His denials of excessive "gambling furniture" fell on deaf ears, and he would be dogged by criticism of the Corrupt Bargain of 1824 for the rest of his life. Just imagine if he been caught during one of those skinny-dips in the Potomac. Seriously: Have you *seen* a portrait of John Quincy Adams? A nation shudders.

HOT MULLED CIDER

Like father, like son: John Quincy Adams also appreciated seeing apple orchards put to good use.

---

2 quarts apple cider

½ cup light brown sugar

pinch of salt

¼ cup unsalted butter

2 cups dark rum

ground cinnamon

8 cinnamon sticks for garnish

Warm the cider in a pot on the stove. Remove the cider from heat and stir in the sugar, salt, and butter until dissolved. Wait 5 minutes, then stir in the rum. Serve the cider in heated mugs. Sprinkle the ground cinnamon on top and add a cinnamon stick.

/////////////// **Serves 8** ///////////////

ANIMAL HOUSE

MARCH 4, 1829–MARCH 4, 1837

Andrew Jackson

DEMOCRAT

Andrew Jackson's inaugural reception inside 1600 Penn on March 4, 1829, was that rare White House celebration that anybody could attend. While hardly the executive mansion's first open-to-the-public function, it was the only one that let in any piece of riffraff. Are you a filthy vagrant reading this book after waking up inside a Dumpster behind Urban Outfitters? Congratulations! You're probably dressed for the occasion.

Historians often refer to Jackson's inauguration as "the People's Day." As the first Washington outsider to be elected president—not to mention the first tobacco-chewing, foul-mouthed Tennessean without a college education—his victory certainly felt like a coup for the everyday schnook. But even rich folks were fascinated by the president.

The most shameful block party in pre–Gathering of the Juggalos era America.

Jackson's time as a major-general in the War of 1812 had turned him into some kind of Colt revolver–carrying superstar. (Before the wonders of Hollywood, a general in the United States Army was roughly equivalent to a Bruce Willis or George Clooney. In President Benjamin Harrison's case, maybe Jason Statham.) Everybody wanted to meet this guy.

People of all races and classes crossed state lines to witness "Old Hickory" take office. Every hotel room in town was booked, some sleeping five to a bed. Boardinghouses price-gouged to $20 a week—three times the going rate. In protest, many slept on tavern floors and in open fields. It was a miserable means of lodging, to be sure, but those dedicated constituents would soon have the pleasure of taking part in what was possibly the most shameful block party in pre–Gathering of the Juggalos era America.

Despite the general's hospitable reputation, Jackson did not stand in the White House entrance hall handing out koozies to every slack-jawed yokel. Since the passing of his wife, Rachel, the depressed president-elect (who, at six-foot-one, weighed a sickly 140 pounds) wasn't exactly up for company, not even a low-key event intended only for those "officially and socially" qualified to join the new president indoors for cake, ice cream, and orange punch—a barn-burning recipe for moonshine that smacks sweet on one's lips before tearing out the lining of one's stomach. But, in the month leading up to Inauguration Day, his personnel failed to coordinate the reception for the swearing-in. Jackson and his predecessor, John Quincy Adams, hated each other (see "Some Heavy Beef" on page 33) and no communication was attempted between the two presidents' camps, which resulted in zero White House security measures put in place the morning of the inauguration.

AT 11 A.M. ON MARCH 4, JACKSON LEFT HIS WIGWAM SUITE AT JOHN Gadsby's National Hotel and set out on foot to his new home. Clad in a black suit and no hat, he was accompanied by a military escort along the main road to the White House. A wagon full of gawking females slowly trucked alongside, like groupies escorting Led Zeppelin to the Fillmore. The streets were full, and the area surrounding the East Portico was jam-packed.

As Jackson approached the dais, a marching band beat their drums and soldiers fired an honorary twenty-four rounds into the air. (Members of Adams's caravan, just outside the city at this point, overheard those shots as the former president bitterly headed east.) Only the people in Jackson's immediate vicinity could hear his soft-spoken inaugural speech. According to mortified congressman James Hamilton Jr., as Jackson made his way inside the White House, "the mob broke in . . . [t]housands poured in one uninterrupted stream of mud and filth, among the throngs many fit subjects for the penitentiary."

The public, no longer interested in the newly sworn-in president, darted for the kitchen doors with a collective bull's-eye target on waiters pushing barrels of orange punch into the reception area. Thirsty ruffians and scalawags, their priorities in order, shoved the waiters to one side. A few barrels tipped over in the process, spilling their contents onto White House carpets and floors. Thousands of dollars' worth of crystal and china were flung off serving trays, smashing in tandem with the pool of orange that was already tarnishing the White House marble. Shards of glassware stuck to men's work boots in the State Dining Room, and imprints from their mud-caked soles stained the damask satin–covered chairs as they tried to get a better view of the new president. And what a sight to see: the man of the hour, manhandled and, in the words of one eyewitness, "nearly pressed to death and torn to pieces."

The whole scene resembled a party thrown by the "bad" fraternity in a movie made by baby boomers. One "stout black wench" decided to raid the White House pantry and was found eating from a jar of jelly with a gold spoon. A mother and father supposedly lost their daughter, whom they later found jumping on a couch in Jackson's private quarters. "Just think," the girl told her mother. "This sofa is a millionth part mine!"

The joint reeked of whiskey and anarchy. Fights broke out, and noses were bloodied. As the White House continued to fill up with lowlifes who were very likely the ancestors of Rick Perry—the Texas governor's kinfolk lived in Tennessee at the time—reporters struggled to break through the crowd to question Jackson. The White House cooks, jaws dropping as they peered out of the kitchen doors, decided it would be best to keep the cake and ice cream in the freezer.

At some point in all the madness, a group of civilians noticed that the president was nearly suffocating from the barrage of drunken celeb stalkers and forged a ring of arms around him. At the same time, the distressed kitchen staff came up with a brilliant idea for how to get rid of bad company. "Tubs of punch and pails of liquor were transferred to the lawn outside," according to Jackson biographer Robert Remini, "and all the windows were thrown open to provide additional exits for those anxious to keep up with the refreshments." The mob followed the complimentary booze out the windows in lumbering zombie-walk fashion. The president even used the same exit to flee the scene and take in some fresh air.

The White House cleared, and everyone began to breathe easier. "I never saw such a mixture," recalled Joseph Story, associate justice of the Supreme Court. "The reign of King Mob seemed triumphant. I was glad to escape from the scene as soon as possible."

SOME HEAVY BEEF

Throughout Adams's presidency and a nasty 1828 reelection bid, the opposing candidates got personal. Jackson claimed that Adams scored prostitutes for a Russian czar and used government dollars to purchase a billiard table. Adams's people questioned the general's possibly unlawful marriage to a "profligate woman" named Rachel. (When the Jacksons were joined at the altar, Rachel was still married to another man in Kentucky, a knot she had hastily tied at the age of eighteen.)

But no matter: Old Hickory legitimately snagged both the popular and the electoral votes in 1828. He would ascend to the presidency in March, but not before sixty-one-year-old Rachel—traumatized from mudslinging and public humiliation—collapsed and died in their Tennessee home on December 22, 1828.

The last person he probably felt like dealing with was President Adams—the cue ball–headed rival who, meanwhile, expected the president-elect to kiss his ring upon arriving in Washington. When that failed to happen, Adams decided to skip town the day of the inauguration.

As King Mob stumbled off the White House lawn and went its separate ways, the well-to-dos continued the celebration deep into the night at the Inaugural Ball. The saloon inside the Washington Assembly Rooms counted around 1,200 dapper folk, just drunk enough to dance without embarrassment until around 2 a.m. Meanwhile, the president, ragged out from the afternoon and still

grieving over the loss of his wife, convalesced at Gadsby's before a quiet sirloin steak dinner with Vice President John C. Calhoun. He went to bed early.

The man of the hour.

WHAT WENT DOWN AT 1600 Penn that day may not have been intended by the administration, but it certainly set the tone for the sort of open-container antics that ensued during Jackson's two terms. Washington colleagues, cabinet members, and reporters frequently misconstrued the president's fiery temperament for belligerent and drunken behavior. Yet while Old Hickory would pound his fist against his desk in meetings and shout like a madman to intimidate and guilt colleagues, he could hold his liquor. "Jackson was a volcanic personality at times," historian and Jackson expert H. W. Brands said. "Some people could attribute his outbursts, not infrequently calculated, as evidence of too much booze, but I never read accounts that made me believe his judgment was impaired. He didn't lose control of himself."

The same cannot be said for White House staffers during work hours. The president was famously charitable to his guests and committed the bulk of his $25,000 annual salary toward keeping the address party-ready—and that included making liquor cabinets and wine stock accessible to anyone on the premises. Château Margaux and Château Lafitte flowed at dinners and functions, and the place was always stocked with gin, rum, brandy, whiskey, beer, ale, and porter. Reportedly, the president's doorman, Jimmy O'Neal, was always so drunk that he failed to complete his primary task of answering the doorbell.

During his last month in office, in celebration of George Washington's birthday, Jackson ordered a 1,400-pound wheel of cheese to be placed in the entrance hall for guests and passersby. It took nearly two years for company to eat the wheel, and, as a result, the executive mansion reeked of cheddar throughout most of Martin Van Buren's presidency.

ORANGE PUNCH

The archivists at Andrew Jackson's Hermitage estate in Nashville do not have the recipe for the fabled White House punch, but a number of nineteenth-century cookbooks suggest this version for large crowds.

9 cups orange juice

3 cups lemon juice

3 cups mulled orange syrup

3 cups maraschino liqueur

3 cups Cognac

6 cups soda water

ice (divided)

Angostura bitters

Pour all the ingredients except the bitters into a high school prom–size punch bowl and mix with ice. Serve each cup over crushed ice. Add a dash of Angostura bitters.

Serves 25

MARTIN VAN RUIN

MARCH 4, 1837–MARCH 4, 1841

Martin Van Buren

DEMOCRAT

A fter Andrew Jackson's 1829 inaugural free-for-all and the steady stream of houseguests in the eight years that followed, 1600 Penn looked like an auditorium after a *Sledge-O-Matic Gallagher performance.*

Cheese stuck to carpets like gum wads on the undersides of elementary school desks. Cups were chipped. China was cracked. The second floor's Oval Room was such a mess that it got an entirely new paint job and was rechristened "the Blue Room." Martin Van Buren, Jackson's hand-picked successor, likely spent more energy overseeing the reupholstery of ratty furniture than sampling drams from the brandy cabinet.

The republic would not have tolerated another rip-roaring White House. Van Buren took office five weeks into the Panic of 1837, when most Americans were either unemployed or breaking their backs in factory hellholes that made today's Walmart jobs seem the stuff of privilege. Sensitive to the economic turmoil, Van Buren put the kibosh on high-profile functions. The Democrat cut out food and liquor at open-to-the-public events. On the infrequent occasion that he would invite VIPs for elegant affairs, staff did their best to minimize press exposure. With roughly one-third of New York City's workforce going without pay, there was no sense rubbing it in the mugs of manual laborers that the eighth president was polishing off bowls of turtle soup and bottles of Madeira.

One could argue that wining and dining was something of an obligation to those in high office, especially when convincing foreign dignitaries that the United States was not entirely populated by tar-spitting hicks—a continuing struggle. Thanks to a shrewd Whig Party opposition set on squandering the Democratic president's reelection chances in 1840, word inevitably spread of Van Buren's private dinners. By the end of his first term, voters resented the president for what was, ironically, his attempt at being understated. As far as the middle class was concerned, whatever functions the White House quietly hosted might as well have been Caligula's orgies.

HISTORIANS MARK 1840 AS THE YEAR OF OUR NATION'S FIRST MODERN election. Political mudslinging evolved into sophisticated media spin. The Whigs successfully painted MVB as an entitled clotheshorse who preferred a wine flight to beer. (Like today, beer was the patriot's drink because, unlike wine, it was often manufactured in the U.S. See "Morale Booster" on page 40.) His opponent, William Henry Harrison, adopted a blue-collar, Springsteenian image to win over Joe Six-Pack. Coined the "log cabin and hard cider" candidate, the former army general and war hero (given the moniker "Old Tippecanoe" for battling Native Americans in 1811) took his first breath not inside some storied

MORALE BOOSTER

Colonials prided themselves on their newfound success in the barley business. To stimulate growth in the following decades, manufacturers pushed the idea that beer was "the most wholesome beverage," a hearty libation that kept workers energetic and in good spirits. Puckering one's lips to a frosty mug after hours on the job soon became American tradition.

Wine, however, was hardly received with the same enthusiasm. In the 1830s, annual consumption rounded to three-tenths of a gallon per person. Resented by everyday alkies for its higher cost and, perhaps, because it was a reminder of the Old World from which their fathers once rebelled, the imported beverage was served mostly at upscale dinners. The American elite figured the yokels just didn't have the palate for it.

log cabin but inside a brick mansion on the family estate. Cider rarely touched his adult lips. Most bizarre, he wore a toupee—not because he was balding but rather, as the sixty-six-year-old explained in 1839, so "those red men don't take one hair off of my head." (Years later, John Travolta would employ similar logic.)

Van Buren, on the other hand, came from truly modest beginnings. Born inside his parents' one-and-a-half-story wooden tavern—making him the first United States president to be born inside a bar—he shared a roof with fifteen others. He learned English as a second language (his family spoke Dutch) before quitting school at age thirteen. Inside his combination dive bar/motel birth-place, the child watched his mother wait on travelers passing through his rural hometown of Kinderhook, New York, where the family inn prevailed as a convenient pit stop for politicians in between Albany and New York City. One of these was Aaron Burr, a famed office holder and notorious womanizer who was rumored to have been the kid's real father.

In his memoirs, Van Buren remembers that Burr, in the years before he became Thomas Jefferson's vice president, paid "much attention" to the young tavern boy. Despite their matching receding hairlines and the fact that Burr was an unmitigated horndog who likely would not have resisted a romp with an upstate beer wench—slaves bore at least two of Burr's illegitimate children—academics generally doubt the possibility of his impregnating Mother Van Buren. Even so, speculation about parentage would haunt Van Buren in 1840 when he was battling Whigs for reelection. Had MVB known the torment that was to come, maybe he would've selected another line of work altogether.

But he didn't. In 1807, twenty-four-year-old Van Buren married Hannah Hoes, another upstate New Yorker with a Dutch accent. They had four sons. Twelve years later, while Van Buren presided as state attorney general, Hannah, thirty-five, died of tuberculosis. Documentation does not suggest the widower feeling one way or another about his loss, as he did not discuss Hannah in speeches or memoirs (his autobiography rarely addresses personal details). Van Buren remained committed to his career in law and public service—and spending an inordinate amount of time in pubs. But he wasn't drowning his sorrows; he was networking. "He was developing a useful skill for a politician," Ted Widmer wrote in his biography *Martin Van Buren*, "the ability to walk into a tavern and hold an enormous amount of alcohol without any sign of impairment."

In a little more than twenty years, Van Buren held practically every major public office imaginable. After his stint as attorney general, the five-foot-six bar crawler took the New York governor's office, then became U.S. senator of New York. In Washington, President Jackson appointed his well-dressed confidant to U.S. secretary of state and minister to England, where Van Buren spoiled himself rotten with a variety of ales. During Jackson's second term, he served as vice president and, in 1836, received the necessary endorsement from a retiring Old Hickory that clinched the presidency.

Nicknamed "the Little Magician," Van Buren was without a doubt the ultimate political insider. Still, given his modest background and progressive

Who's your daddy? No, really, who is he?

platform, he must have understood the everyman's plight. As president, Van Buren signed an executive order to cap federal workers at ten-hour workdays and took a public stance against slavery, going against members of his own party. (His vice president, Richard Johnson, had consensual relations with "a buxom young negro," according to the postmaster general. Southern Democrats, including Jackson, wanted Johnson removed from the reelection ticket, but Van Buren refused.) Post-presidency, MVB continued to promote abolitionism and helped push the subject into the national discourse. If that weren't enough, he even introduced his hometown to the concept of indoor plumbing. At Lindenwald, Van Buren's retirement home in Kinderhook, the Little Magician's luxurious new-fangled toilet could make shit disappear like none of the locals had ever seen. (See "The Democratic Potty.")

Despite all of his accomplishments, Van's sharp tongue and penchant for fine clothes may have been effective at dinner tables and bar tops throughout his political ascension, but those qualities did not appeal to the working man.

AT HARRISON RALLIES, GLEE CLUBS DISTRIBUTED COPIES OF *THE LOG Cabin Songbook: A Collection of Popular and Patriotic Songs* for Whigs to belt out their hatred of the president and appreciation for Old Tippecanoe. (The lyrical agitprop ranged from "Let Van from his coolers of silver drink wine/And lounge on his cushioned settee/Our man on a buckeye bench can recline/Content with hard cider is he" to "Farewell, dear Van/You're not our man/To guide the ship/We'll try old Tip.") E. C. Booz, a Philadelphia distiller whose last name is supposedly the origin for what is now household slang, donated cases of his Old Cabin Whiskey. At Booz-sponsored events, the gimmicky bottles, shaped like log cabins (the pattern on their necks resembled a chimney), provided incentive to see Old Tip on the stump. Well, it was at least one incentive. "I am sorry to say that I have seen ladies too joining in with them," Vice President Johnson said, "and wearing ribands across their breasts with two names printed on them." A voluptuous Harrison supporter verified this in a June 1840 editorial: "We would indeed be traitors to our sex if our bosoms did not thrill at his name."

All this talk of bottles and bosoms probably frustrated Van Buren. Whatever happened to the destitute masses in no mood for a White House kegger? ("We have fallen, gentlemen, upon hard times," shouted a supporter at one Harrison rally, "and the remedy seems to be hard cider!") The incumbent, who came to be known as "Martin Van Ruin"—a name fit for an obscure Batman villain—displayed the political acumen of a piece of plywood. The president simply decided to stay off the campaign trail whenever possible to avoid the Whig onslaught. Davy Crockett, who had renounced his wild frontier crown to become an illiterate congressman from Tennessee, authored (with the assistance of somebody who could read and write) *The Life of Martin Van Buren*, a 200-page hatchet job that accused the book's subject of abandoning "sons of little tavernkeepers" and "all his old companions and friends in the humbler walks of life." Crockett also questioned Van Buren's sex on account of all those fancy clothes.

In a speech titled "The Regal Splendor of the Presidential Palace," U.S. representative Charles Ogle criticized Van Buren on the House floor for three days. On April 14, 15, and 16, 1840, Ogle's attack

THE DEMOCRATIC POTTY

Located twenty-seven miles south of Albany, Lindenwald was the president's getaway for fishing, horseback riding, and, conceivably, eating plenty of roughage. His sons encouraged him to purchase the home during his hellish term in Washington, as they knew Father would need a place to convalesce. After the beating taken in 1840, the former president turned his full attention to the 220-acre estate, where he spent the last twenty-one years of his life.

Van Buren's throne—Kinderhook's first indoor commode—still remains tucked away on the first floor in a closet-size room inside the beautifully battered landmark preserved and cared for by the U.S. National Park Service.

focused exclusively on a $3,665 allocation for White House upkeep, line items of which included "expensive imported wines" and "golden spoons" purchased with public funds. Other items cited by the Pennsylvania congressman ranged from dinnerware, groundskeeping services, and furniture to liquor stands,

golden chains to dress the necks of wine decanters, and "hundreds of dollars in supplying his toilet with Double Extract of Queen Victoria." The spendthrift allegedly rubbed his red and gray whiskers in the brand-name cologne.

"The remedy seems to be hard cider!"

That Jackson's wear and tear on the mansion might have made these purchases necessary was never considered, but another Whig congressman, Levi Lincoln, brought to his colleagues' attention that $3,665 was walking-around money compared to other presidents' personal spending.

No one cared.

Van Buren, an oenophile and connoisseur of brew, truly appreciated the barroom bachelor lifestyle, yet it was his supposed cider-loving rival, a teetotaling silver spoon prude, who clobbered at the ballot box: Van Buren picked up sixty electoral votes in the November 1840 tally and won only six states, not even his own New York or Jackson's Tennessee; Harrison garnered 234 votes.

TURN BACK THE CLOCK!

IT'S 1840 ALL OVER AGAIN WITH 22 GOLDEN GREATS CAPTURED ON THIS DELUXE TWO-ALBUM SET!

Get *The Log Cabin Songbook: A Collection of Popular and Patriotic Songs* at the special introductory price of $18.99 for double LP record or $9.99 for double cassette or compact disc (plus shipping & handling).

SO MANY OF THE HITS YOU LOVE, INCLUDING:

The Log Cabin March • Van, Van, He's a Used-Up Man
Let Van from His Coolers of Silver Drink Wine
Tippecanoe Quick-Step • Harrison Hoe-Down
We've Tried Your Purse-Proud Lords Who Live in Palaces to Shine
I Love the Rough Log Cabin • Farewell, Dear Van
The Plain Fare of Old Tippecanoe • Van Buren! There He Goes! Put It
to Him! • No Ruffled Shirt, No Silken Hose
Old Tip, He Wears a Homespun Coat
and more!

NOT SOLD IN STORES. ALLOW 3–4 WEEKS FOR DELIVERY.

//

THE VAN BUREN

In 2013, Robert C. Mack, a mixologist at Albany's Speakeasy 518, named a drink after the man with the red and gray whiskers. "The Van Buren" is more or less the same recipe as the classic El Presidente, the signature drink of Manhattan's Club El Chico in the 1920s, but, rather than using three fingers of rum, Speakeasy 518 provides its own stock of a barrel-aged cocktail—a mixture of rum, vermouth, and curaçao aged in a charred white oak bourbon barrel for thirty days. For those fresh out of charred white oak bourbon barrels, here's a more pedestrian version that should do the trick.

ice

dash of orange bitters

2 ounces high-quality aged rum

½ ounce sweet vermouth

¼ ounce curaçao

¼ ounce simple syrup

orange peel for garnish

Put the ice and orange bitters in a rocks glass. Pour the rum, vermouth, curaçao, and simple syrup on top. Stir. Garnish with the orange peel.

// **Serves 1** //

32 DAYS

William Henry Harrison

WHIG

O n January 26, 1841, William Henry Harrison boarded
The Ben Franklin *steamboat in North Bend, Ohio, where
hundreds of Old Tippecanoe fans—some tossing hats and
handkerchiefs, others blasting celebratory ammunition—gathered
to bid farewell to their Washington-bound president-elect.*

*Before shoving off on the Ohio River, the sixty-seven-year-old
offered parting words that, given his fate a short time later, now
seem a little on the ominous side.*

*"Perhaps this may be the last time I may have the pleasure of
speaking to you on Earth or seeing you," Harrison shouted over a
brass band and cannon fire. "I will bid you farewell, if forever, fare
thee well."*

MARCH 4, 1841

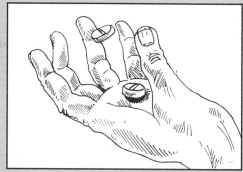

3 WEEKS LATER...

APRIL 4, 1841

I WISH YOU TO UNDERSTAND THE TRUE PRINCIPLES OF GOVERNMENT . . . NOTHING MORE.

HIS ACCIDENCY

APRIL 4, 1841–MARCH 4, 1845

John Tyler

WHIG

What people remember about John Tyler, when they bother to remember him at all, is his status as the first vice president to move into 1600 Penn without an election (thanks to William Henry Harrison's status as the first commander in chief to die in office). For that, the Virginia gentleman, unflatteringly dubbed "His Accidency"—and not because he fathered fifteen (!) children—was resented by legislators throughout his lame duck presidency.

Congress temporarily cut off appropriations for the White House. It was a petty yet effective power move by Capitol Hill. In turn, Tyler caught hell from the press for neglecting the executive mansion, "its virgin white sadly sullied," as the

New York Herald reported, "the splendid drapery falling in tatters all around time's rude hand." Washington correspondent F. W.

1842 was not his year.

Thomas added that "many of the chairs in the East Room would be kicked out of a brothel." To make matters worse, Letitia Christian Tyler, his wife of twenty-nine years, died seventeen months after Tyler assumed office. Nope, 1842 was not his year.

A president who was both a Washington pariah and alone in the bedroom—a dilapidated one at that—could at the very least try to find love. It didn't take long. Just months after burying his beloved Letitia in the cold, cold ground, Tyler pursued the sexy Julia Gardiner—thirty years his junior and daughter of a former New York State senator. At a George Washington birthday ball in 1843, the widower asked the twenty-two-year-old nymphet for her hand in marriage. "I said 'No, no, no,' and shook my head with each word," Gardiner later recalled, "which flung the tassel of my Greek cap into his face with every move. It was undignified but it amused me very much to see his expression as he tried to make love to me and the tassel brushed his face."

For those keeping score, at twenty-two she was the same age as Monica Lewinsky during her internship. Yet Gardiner didn't come as easy. In fact, it took multiple gory deaths, including that of her poor father, to bring her into the presidential bed.

The bloodbath went down on February 28, 1844, when President Tyler—accompanied by Gardiner and her father, multiple cabinet members, former first lady Dolley Madison, and 350 others—boarded the USS *Princeton* to view the steam frigate's new cannons, the "Oregon" and the "Peacemaker." Robert Stockton, the *Princeton*'s hawkish commodore, couldn't wait to weigh anchor from the Washington Navy Yard and brandish the ship's new toys on the Potomac. Armed with champagne flutes and top hats, dignitaries awaited the captain's demonstration—save President Tyler, who was preoccupied below deck with bottles of bubbly. Fifteen-year-old P. Y. Pember remembered the afternoon vividly. "[A]lthough the President had been twice summoned and his Cabinet awaited him," she wrote decades later, "his voice could still be heard through the skylight, laughing and talking with Secretary [of War William] Wilkins over their wine . . . Tyler still lingered in the cabin till a third message reached him, and then he laughingly called out, 'Tell Stockton to go ahead; neither Wilkins

A not-so-fantastic voyage.

nor I like firearms.'" Pember could hear the two men popping champagne corks like it was target practice.

As Stockton readied its third round of fire, the Peacemaker self-destructed, sending fragments of searing metal into the crowd. Dozens of spectators were injured; six were killed. Stockton's "head [was] saturated with blood," according to Pember. "His full black whiskers meeting under his chin were burnt to a crisp, and for many weeks he was not willing to be seen." Fatalities included Secretary of State Abel P. Upshur, Secretary of the Navy Thomas W. Gilmer, and Julia Gardiner's father.

According to Tyler biographer Edward P. Crapol, the *Princeton* episode "cemented" the romance between the president and Gardiner. Four months after the explosion, Tyler eloped with young Gardiner, now twenty-four and, perhaps, in need of a new father figure. The youngest first lady in history retired the Greek cap with the tassel and sought the president's constant attention in the White House—to the point that he called her a "spoilt child."

"Tone down the lovemaking!" Gardiner's mother wrote to the randy young bride. "Let your husband work during all business hours. Business should take the precedence of caressing—reserve your caressing for private leisure and be sure you let no one see it unless you wish to be laughed at."

They found enough private leisure. Together, the president and Gardiner managed to beget seven children, the last of whom was born in 1860 when her parents had reached the ages of seventy and forty.

//

MINT JULEP

In 1984, the *Washington Post* interviewed President Tyler's grandson Harrison Tyler. With an assist from his wife, Paynie, Harrison transformed the president's Sherwood Forest plantation into a Virginia tourist attraction. When not hosting buffet dinners for suckers with Sony cameras around their necks, the entrepreneurial kinfolk enjoyed grilling hamburgers out back and "swimming naked in the goose pond" with neighbors, Paynie told the paper. And, though her husband was "more partial to vodka," she did stumble across the herb patch near the stables where President Grandpappy grew mint, a staple ingredient for his preferred cocktail on the porch at nights.

This recipe dates back to 1828.

3 sprigs fresh mint

1 tablespoon white sugar

2½ tablespoons water

ice

orange slice, assorted berries

2½ ounces bourbon whiskey

In a tall glass, muddle the mint sprigs in the sugar and water. Fill the glass with ice. Garnish with more sprigs in the glass, stems down. Add the fruit. Pour the whiskey. Dust more sugar on top. Get a straw.

// **Serves 1** //

WORKAHOLIC

MARCH 4, 1845–MARCH 4, 1849

James K. Polk

DEMOCRAT

For many a nineteenth-century president, accepting an audience with even the lowliest of callers was just part of the job. For James K. Polk, however, it was nothing but a distraction. In 1849, a gentleman named Lawrence entered the chief's chamber to request an office appointment for a friend. For some reason, Lawrence—perhaps the most presumptuous man to ever live—attempted to sell the president of the United States wine. The visit was brief. "I made short work of it with him," Polk wrote in his diary. "It is not the first time that the same person has annoyed me about matters in which neither the public nor myself could have any interest."

Call him a killjoy, but Polk ran arguably the most intense and effective single term in presidential history.

Polk and his wife, Sarah, moved into the mansion at the ages of forty-nine and forty-one—spry enough to lead Washington's social scene without concern for bedtime or adult diapers. But firsthand accounts suggest that an evening at the Polk White House was about as much fun as an afternoon at a monastery. One visitor recalled the vibe as "dull and pinchpenny." Another found its anterooms "large, cold and dreary." The first couple, devout southern Presbyterians, scratched hard liquor, music, dancing, and even food from public receptions, which were routinely scheduled at early hours on Tuesdays and Fridays.

The first lady banned pretty much any food more interesting than bread. Come feed time, one could not anticipate zesty flavors or rich sauces but constipating farm-style fare (fried country ham, cornpones). Ushers managed to liberate wine and cider from a battened-down dark cellar, but the firm head of the table rarely indulged. (The president's diary notes that he took part in the occasional toast, although he often requested coffee when others imbibed.)

The wife of a U.S. congressman described the spread from a December 1845 affair: "Pink champagne, gold sherry, green hock, Madeira, the ruby port [and] sauterne formed a rainbow round each plate with the finger glasses and water decanters." Polk likely scoffed at said display. With a perpetual sneer at the social calendar, the exec chained himself to his desk as much as possible. It was as if he were burdened with the responsibility of running some sort of global enterprise. Loser.

The no-nonsense attitude should not have come as a shock to anyone. At a pre-inauguration

Also available on cassette.

☑GETTING ☑THINGS ☑DONE

JAMES K. POLK
Former President of the United States

sit-down with Secretary of the Navy George Bancroft, Polk made his intentions clear. "There are to be four great measures of my administration," declared Bossypants, while slapping his palm against his thigh like the headmaster of a

Polk had his work cut out for him.

school for ill-behaved children. "The settlement of the Oregon question with Great Britain, the acquisition of California and a large district on the coast, the reduction of the tariff to a revenue basis, [and] the complete and permanent establishment of the Constitutional Treasury." Everybody got that? According to Bancroft, annexing the state of Texas was also tacked on by the meeting's end.

Like all president-elects, Polk had his work cut out for him. Unlike most president-elects, this one managed to accomplish everything that he promised—meaning that it was this stuffed shirt who brought Venice Beach, Portland, and Austin into America's fold. If it weren't for the unfortunate fact that he backed the expansion of slavery, Polk might today be hailed as one of the greats—an American pioneer for Getting Things Done. And he didn't even want the job.

In May 1844 at the Democratic National Convention, Polk, a former governor of Tennessee, had his sights set a touch lower, aspiring to the vice presidency. For president, many delegates were gunning for Martin Van Buren, campaigning in his first of two (failed) attempts to win back the White House. But there was not a consensus.

It took days to agree on a ticket. Eight ballots later, Van Buren's chances had faded, and Polk emerged as the dark horse for the presidential nomination. He accepted, albeit reluctantly. "It has been well observed that the office of the president of the United States should neither be sought nor declined," Polk wrote on June 12. "I have never sought it, nor shall I feel at liberty to decline it, if conferred upon me by the voluntary suffrages of my Fellow Citizens." (Can't you feel the warmth and excitement?) In addition, the note declared his "settled purpose of not being a candidate for reelection."

It would be a busy four years.

In 1846, President Polk reinstated the Independent Treasury, which essentially permitted the government to manage its own money. (Andrew Jackson's decentralization of the federal banking system fourteen years earlier caused financial panic.) That same year, Polk pushed legislation through Congress

that lowered tariffs on imported luxury items (save tobacco and alcohol). The decrease in taxes stimulated international trade and alleviated tension across the pond. This would assist Polk in his next order of business: the Oregon Treaty of 1846, resolving boundary issues between the U.S. and Great Britain along the 49th parallel. The administration expanded the U.S. to epic proportions—approximately 525,000 miles for twelve states. Polk even wagered and won a war against Mexico to strong-arm negotiations for new territory. Was there nothing this man could not do? "The only thing wrong with Polk," quipped Texas senator Sam Houston, "was that he drank too much water."

Indeed, these days fell on the lamer side of White House social history. In an effort to avoid ethical quandaries (or, perhaps, human interaction), the president would not accept gifts. When a high-priced saddle or wines by the caseload landed on the front steps, Polk would request an invoice or that the parcel be returned to its rightful donor. In the evenings, Washington socialites ditched functions early and skipped across Lafayette Park to Dolley Madison's residence. Now in her eighties, the former first lady showed them a better time than President Polk, who decreed that no company was welcome on the Sabbath. To anyone who spent time with Mr. Antisocial, it would come as no surprise to learn he was outshined by an octogenarian widow.

RASPBERRY SHRUB

Sarah Polk, along with many women in the late 1840s, kept Mrs. A. L. Webster's *The Improved Housewife* cookbook on her shelf. (To this day, an 1847 copy remains among memorabilia at the Polk Home in Columbia, Tennessee.) The Raspberry Shrub was a disgusting concoction that Webster heartily endorsed: "Two spoonfuls of this mixed with a tumbler of water is an excellent drink in fevers."

3 quarts raspberries

1 quart vinegar

6 pounds sugar

brandy

Let the raspberries sit in the vinegar for 24 hours. Strain. Add the sugar. Skim it clear, while boiling for about half an hour. Let cool. Add 2 wineglasses of brandy for each quart of "the shrub."

////////////// **Serves 15** //////////////

THE HAZARDS OF A TEETOTALER LIFESTYLE

MARCH 4, 1849–JULY 9, 1850

Zachary Taylor

WHIG

12

After decades of chin-rubbing and grave-digging, academics cannot pinpoint what foul fare was responsible for taking Zachary Taylor's life. There are those in the historical community who do not think food- or drink-poisoning was the culprit; rather, they blame festering piles of excrement, politely referred to as "night soil," which White House staff had the privilege of schlepping seven blocks downstream on a daily basis. (As recently as 2014, researchers argued this breeding ground for deadly microbes was the reason for William Henry Harrison's death, not the largely accepted diagnosis of pneumonia.) Oh, to have been a White House intern before Washington's sewer system was developed in the 1850s.

Other scholars attribute Taylor's passing to a single pitcher of iced milk, something of a luxury in the mid-nineteenth century. At 12 cents per quart, the refreshment cost more than whiskey and came with the tremendous risk of puking your guts out. Refrigerators would not become a common household appliance for another sixty years, and thus methods for dairy storage, especially while in transport, were unreliable. What's worse, a toxin in white snakeroot—a weed grazed upon by pasture-fed cattle—led to the sometimes-fatal condition popularly known as "milk sickness." (This disease put quite a few innocents in the dirt, including Abraham Lincoln's mother.)

CONNECT THE DOTS

Uncover what pernicious and foul fare killed our twelfth president!

Only the bravest of individuals did not fear the cow's teat. This may have been because these people were uninformed or had faced greater threats on the battlefield. Or maybe they swore off alcohol and had little alternative at the dinner table? President Taylor could stand behind all three reasons. The war hero only received a grade-school education and never registered to vote. He saw so much action in battles against Native Americans and Mexico that he acquired the nickname "Old Rough and Ready," which also aptly described his surly mug and vulgar appearance. (Had it been up to Washington rumor-mongers, the moniker could have just as easily been applied to his better half.

THE FIRST LADY'S CORNCOB PIPE

Margaret Mackall Smith Taylor did not assume hostess duties and lived as a recluse, perhaps because the sixty-two-year-old was exhausted from raising six children and living in barracks with her military hubby. Some whispered that the president kept her in seclusion to conceal her impoverished appearance and off-putting corncob pipe habit. In truth, she did not smoke and came from an upstanding family in Maryland. Likely, after thirty-eight years of marriage to a war hero, the president's wife had probably grown sick of public service.

See "The First Lady's Corncob Pipe.")

The nation respected and elected General Taylor for his bravery and military service. He trembled at nothing—certainly not a glass of 2 percent—with the sole exception of God's law, which apparently influenced him to forgo alcohol. Thanks to a teetotaler diet, the sixty-five-year-old's term at the White House—and on Earth—concluded only sixteen months after he was sworn into office. In 1850, to commemorate Independence Day, which landed on a miserably humid Thursday afternoon, Senator Henry S. Foote delivered the keynote at the laying of the cornerstone for the Washington Monument. Flanked by cabinet members, Old Rough and Ready patiently observed a marathon of boring speeches while battling potential sunstroke for three hours. But neither the high temperatures nor the agonizing blather killed him.

Taylor returned to the mansion around 4 p.m. To ward off the sweltering heat, he gorged on iced cherries, milk, and green apples. Ever the risk-taker, he also "drank immoderately of water," noted Senator Willie P. Mangum, "nearly two gallons before dinner." The North Carolina senator recalled the president "dined perhaps immoderately—eating vegetables of all sorts—especially those the very worst and most pernicious—cabbages and cucumbers—made for four-footed animals and not bipeds."

Whatever queasiness Taylor sustained that evening worsened in the following days. That Saturday, he sought a doctor. By Sunday, he knew

Death is a bowl of cherries.

the end was near. On Wednesday, July 9, the president spoke his last words: "I am not afraid to die. I have done my duty. My only regret is leaving those who are dear to me."

Taylor's physician chalked the whole thing up to acute gastroenteritis, known then as cholera morbus. Denizens of Washington, albeit saddened by the loss, became equally concerned for their own lives. "Everyone here begins to fear the cholera," a distressed Mangum wrote to his wife. "The utmost care in diet ought to be observed. Avoid vegetables and fruits of all kinds . . . Attend to the bowels. This must not and cannot be neglected with prudence or safety."

Yeah, and when you're done, leave your mess down by the creek near the White House.

WAS IT POISON?

In June 1991, a former professor at the University of Florida suspected foul play, specifically arsenic, and convinced the Jefferson County coroner in Kentucky to exhume Taylor's corpse for sample testing. "The exact cause of death cannot be said," the chief medical examiner reported, "but he definitely was not poisoned."

PINEAPPLE AND SAGE MARTINI

In the 1840s, sage had its own entry in the United States pharmacopoeia, which recognized the herb's benefits for indigestion relief. (Sage oil thins mucus—gross but good to know.) So maybe drink this the next time a pernicious snack wreaks havoc on your tummy.

4 sage leaves

ice

3 ounces pineapple juice

2 ounces vodka

Muddle the sage leaves in a tumbler. Add the ice, pineapple juice, and vodka. Shake well. Strain into a martini glass.

Serves 1

CULT OBSCURITY

JULY 9, 1850–MARCH 4, 1853

Millard Fillmore

WHIG

A historical footnote[1], our thirteenth commander in chief Millard Fillmore left a minuscule mark in the annals of the United States. Best remembered for not being remembered at all, he was the stuff ironic legends are made of. As he had no significant accomplishments to mount above the fireplace or words of wisdom to recite inside elementary school classrooms, more than 120 years would pass before Americans congregated to mockingly celebrate the smorgasbord of blah that was his presidency.

[1] When President Zachary Taylor died unexpectedly sixteen months into his term, some constituents would have rather kept the cholera-ridden corpse in the big chair, but, as the Constitution would have it, Taylor's veep Fillmore ascended. Supposedly, a White House attendant called Fillmore "a secondhand president" to his face—a fitting insult. During those three forgettable years, the walking doormat asserted no social or political identity, said nothing of importance, and did nothing worth noting. Fillmore prohibited the use of alcohol and tobacco in the executive mansion, a real treat for out-of-towners, and stepped lightly around the matters at stake on Capitol Hill. He conceded to congressional pressure to support the expansion of slavery, thereby exacerbating the events that triggered the Civil War.

There is so little to report on Fillmore that historians, desperate for color, have roundly convinced them-selves of fabricated stories. In 1917, H. L. Mencken wrote a satirical column in the *New York Evening Mail* on the genesis of the modern bathtub, asserting that "Millard Fillmore, even more than the grudging medical approval, gave the bathtub recognition and respectability in the United States." Nine years later, Mencken clarified that the story was "a piece of spoofing to relieve the strain of war days," but the *Onion*-like essay had already corrupted a naive academic community. A biography published as recently as 1981 references Fillmore's cast-iron installation

Millard Fillmore
Birthday Party
Society.

as a White House first. (However, the existence of a White House tub was previously mentioned in 1840, when U.S. Congressman Charles Ogle berated the sophisticated Martin Van Buren for being "the first president" to indulge in "the pleasures of the warm or tepid bath" alongside other "proper accompaniments of a palace life.")

Several unaffiliated chapters of tongue-in-cheek barroom fan clubs have honored the Whig's mediocrity. The Millard Fillmore Society "is dedicated to the principle that Millard Fillmore was the most incompetent non-entity ever to hold the position of president," according to one woman, who requested a membership application in the 1970s. "When I expressed my interest, I was told that I had just disqualified myself."

Around the same time, Phil Arkow, then a newspaper reporter in Colorado Springs, launched an outfit with bowling alley buds called the Society for the Preservation and Enhancement of the Recognition of Millard Fillmore, Last of the Whigs (SPERMFLOW). Inspiration came in part, Arkow said, after paying a visit to Fillmore's birthplace, a "pile of rubble" that sat next to the town dump. In 1972, the Millard Fillmore Birthday Party Society (MFBPS) threw one of its liquid luncheons in Spring Valley, New York. While there, members considered endowing a college scholarship in Fillmore's name, to be given to students with C averages. It was a grand idea for sure, and appropriately enough, it never came to fruition.

HERO OF MANY A WELL-FOUGHT BOTTLE

MARCH 4, 1853–MARCH 4, 1857

Franklin Pierce

14

DEMOCRAT

Franklin Pierce learned to enjoy a stiff one at an early age. Alcoholism came from his mother's side, the president would claim in later years, but a glimpse into his childhood leaves one the impression that the entire family did a number on him. In 1804, the year he was born (as the sixth of nine siblings), his father, General Benjamin Pierce, built a homestead on a cheap piece of property in southwest New Hampshire. The Revolutionary War

Pierce: Season-ticket holder, drunk.

hero and future governor of the Granite State converted the farmhouse into a tavern, where the old man tossed back "whiskey with his guests," according to Peter A. Wallner's two-volume biography, and "laced conversations with profanity while spraying listeners with tobacco juice." The potty-mouthed general's wife, Anna Kendrick, drank more than her share and wore "a short gown that showed her ankles encircled with red ribbons."

With drinking vessel in hand (presumably spiked by one of his three older brothers) toddler Pierce witnessed his model parents in action. Dear ol' dad would exchange handshakes and favors with bloated patrons. Having inherited the glad-handing gene, Pierce entered law practice and local politics after college. He had an excellent memory, a knack for recalling the names of every juror who ever sat on one of his cases, and could give thirty-minute-long speeches without notes. At twenty-six, he was elected New Hampshire's speaker of the house, the youngest ever to run the state's congress. By the time he was thirty-one, his good looks and charm had won him a seat in the U.S. Senate, and in 1847, Pierce followed his father's footsteps by serving as a brigadier general in the Mexican-American War.

But it was during the 1830s and early 1840s that the raven-haired senator gained status within the Democratic Party. In Washington, the ever-popular "Handsome Frank" led a loyal following of congressional peers—mostly into restaurants and hotel bars. A night at the theater often involved the pre-ritual of brown-bagging wine. Bottles no doubt clanked and rolled down the aisle as Pierce rapidly garnered a reputation around town as a nightlife champion. One champagne-goggled evening resulted in a member of his entourage (who also happened to represent the seventh district of Indiana) drawing a pistol on an army lieutenant in the street. This incident turned into quality fodder for the opposition during the presidential election of 1852. Whig Party members smeared Pierce as a "Hero of Many a Well-fought Bottle," a deadbeat lush who allegedly abandoned the U.S. Senate in 1842 "because he was almost continually intoxicated." These were the good times.

"I think he was a happy drunk up until his presidency," Wallner said. "He wasn't drinking out of any kind of remorse in the beginning. In later years, his drinking became more of a crutch from suffering too much from various defeats. He was a sick man, an alcoholic."

Prior to his election, Pierce was no stranger to tragedy. But who wasn't back then? Before the miracle of science put a halt to waterborne epidemics, Las Vegas could have run numbers on the national infant mortality rate. Chlorinated waters weren't regularly used in a local drinking supply until 1908; prior to that, diarrheal disease took the lives of thousands of newborns each year. In 1900, the United States Census Bureau listed upward of 18,000 deaths related to typhoid fever alone. So, if Zachary "Old Rough and Ready" Taylor supposedly croaked from bogus milk or veggies at the ripe age of sixty-five, how could poor little bambinos with vulnerable immunities survive a world overrun with contaminated food and faulty sewage systems?

Pierce and his wife, Jane, found out the hard way. The couple buried two sons—their firstborn not three days old in 1836, the other before his fifth birthday in 1843—both of whom contracted fatal illnesses. The charismatic politician and introverted homemaker forged ahead with family life, but, in the first year of Pierce's presidency, they were broken by the death of Benny, their third and final child.

On January 6, 1853, two months shy of Pierce's inauguration, the future first family boarded a 1 p.m. train from Andover, Massachusetts, to return home to Concord. One mile outside of the Andover station, the sole passenger car's rear axle broke, causing the train to derail and rattle down a 20-foot embankment.

Seated next to Jane, the president-elect grabbed his wife to protect her as they tumbled down the hill. He extended an arm toward Benny, who was seated alone on the bench behind his parents, but could not reach him. The train car crash-landed on its roof. As another passenger, a minister from Manchester, recalled standing "amid a mass of broken glass and splintered wood, and groaning men and women," Pierce found his eleven-year-old son lying dead on the ground. The back of his skull was split in two. To shield his wife from the horror, Pierce threw his coat over the body.

Jane stayed in Andover. She did not attend Benny's funeral in Concord nor her husband's March 4 inauguration. In a letter to her deceased child dated January 23, Jane said how forever the "ride in those rail cars [will be] agonizing to my soul." She was in no condition to rub elbows in the capital. Her aunt, Abby Kent Means, arrived in Washington City to act as surrogate hostess for public functions. The first lady remained in seclusion for nearly two years and continued writing letters to Benny. She did not make a public appearance until a New Year's reception in 1855. One guest described her as the "very picture of melancholy."

FROM THE DIARY OF CLEMENT MARCH

Friday, October 23, 1857

"The general and I dined at the Tremont at one o'clock, a glass of brandy and water before, a pint of champagne at dinner, went to the Fair Grounds and returned to the Tremont at 5, drank brandy and water till 7½, supped at Parker's on broiled oysters, beefsteak, and Pomy's Claret, went to the Theatre, and saw Fanny Kemble and her daughter in a private box by mistake, returned to Parker's and drank some very old brandy in his private room, went back to the Theatre and took possession of our 'proscenium box,' then again to Parker's and had raw oysters and a bottle of Stein Wine, then to the General's room, drank two pint bottles of champagne, took a stroll about the Streets, and made a call in Fruit Street, where we disbursed some thirty dollars, and at 4 o'clock repaired to our rooms at the Tremont."

President Pierce minimized his alcohol intake inside the White House; elsewhere was a different story. Ida Russell, a socialite who kept a gossipy journal (as most socialites do), deduced that his apparent sobriety was on account of "a bad wife" who required that the henpecked president's wineglass be turned upside-down at dinner "as a constant advertisement that he has weaknesses," Russell wrote, "placing him in a position degrading to his self-respect." Shows what little Russell knew. Pierce indeed had his fill, mostly when traveling. Friend/enabler Clement March, who elaborately catalogued his nights out with New Hampshire's first commander in chief, recorded a Boston getaway in which March experienced "the greatest frolic of my life." He also wrote how, at some point between said frolic and the next morning, an anvil might have dropped on his head. (See "From the Diary of Clement March" on previous page.)

Before the Election of 1856, the Democratic Party nominated former Secretary of State James Buchanan for the November race and sent the Pierces packing for New England. Jane died seven years later from tuberculosis, leaving the grieving widower to spend his remaining years alone, bedridden and crawled inside a whiskey bottle. One visitor wrote how Pierce became "very weak" from a case of bilious fever and looked "fearfully wasted, but not blue" and could barely sit upright. In a diary entry marked July 30, 1869—three months before his death, caused by cirrhosis of the liver—March reported that Pierce "still drinks."

///

HOT RUM PUNCH

Although evidence points to Madeira wine as Pierce's drink of choice—he imported casks from Europe—cohorts observed the president's consumption of champagne, whiskey, and brandy. (Wallner: "He would drink anything.") Presidential cookbook author Poppy Cannon claims Pierce's "partiality" to hot rum punch, the recipe for which can be found in several nineteenth-century texts.

---

1 cup lemon juice

2 cups dark rum

2 teaspoons sugar

2 ounces boiling water

fresh grated nutmeg for garnish

4 cinnamon sticks for garnish

Mix and stir the lemon juice, rum, sugar, and water in heated mugs until the sugar dissolves. Top with fresh grated nutmeg and use the cinnamon sticks for garnish.

/////////////// **Serves 4** ///////////////

BOSOM BUDDIES

MARCH 4, 1857–MARCH 4, 1861

James Buchanan

DEMOCRAT

15

When newspaperman John W. Forney spent the summer at Wheatland, James Buchanan's farm in south central Pennsylvania, he couldn't keep up with his hangover-immune host. We're talking two or three bottles of brown at each sitting, plus an inexorable amount of grape juice for grown-ups. And each and every time, Buchanan woke up feeling no pain. "The Madeira and sherry that he has consumed would fill more than one old cellar," the journalist later boasted. "The effect of it! There was no headache, no faltering steps, no flushed cheek . . . All was cool, as calm and as cautious and watching as in the beginning."

For Forney, these swilling sessions were "ambitious." For Buchanan, they were "Tuesdays."

Several factors could have contributed to Buchanan's habit. A piss-poor four years in the White House, leading to the Civil War,

He remained a bachelor for his entire life.

surely reduced the president to a Bukowski-esque ball of self-pity. But, more than likely, a woeful case of survivor's guilt combined with his own closeted homosexuality prompted Buchanan to drink his feelings.

All the rainbow flags are there. He remained a bachelor for his entire life. In Washington, he rented a room with Senator William Rufus King, and the two maintained a loving, supposedly platonic relationship for twenty-three years. Fellow congressmen addressed the pair as "Buchanan and his wife," among other homophobic, pre–Andrew Dice Clay epithets. But no extant evidence confirms whom the fifteenth commander in chief took to bed. "There's no smoking gun that says 'A-ha! This guy was leaning toward the same sex,'" Wheatland director Patrick Clarke said, "and, frankly, it's just not there for the opposite sex either."

In 1809, when Buchanan moved to the town of Lancaster, Pennsylvania, the Dickinson College graduate practiced law and signed up for city services—specifically at the Union Fire Company, where he volunteered as ladder man more than 150 years before the Village People cut their first LP. As his nephew and personal secretary, James Buchanan Henry, would later describe him—towering at six feet with a large, fleshy head and broad shoulders—he fit the part. Just imagine back at the Union No. 1, the fabulous Uncle James snapping a pair of red suspenders, whipping his hair to one side, and hefting that ladder at the alarm bell's first ring.

There was also the matter of his engagement to Anne Coleman in the summer of 1819. Coleman, another lawyer whom he met at Lancaster's White Swan Inn, came from one of the richest families in the state. An unmarried twenty-three-year-old woman was a rarity, but this brunette had devoted herself to her career. Far from unattractive, she had "dark, lustrous eyes," according to Philip S. Klein's encyclopedic *President James Buchanan: A Biography.* "She was by turns proud and self-willed, tender and affectionate, quiet and introspective, or giddy and wild." She also did not possess the male anatomy and thus probably would not find a soul mate in James Buchanan, Esquire.

The burning
hot heroes of
Lancaster, 1809.

AUGUST

Sunday	Monday	Tuesday	Wednesday	Thursday	Friday	Saturday
		1	2	3	4	5	6
7	8	9	10	11	12	13
14	15	16	17	18	19	20
21	22	23	24	25	26	27
28	29	30	31			

Her father, Robert Coleman, suspected the worst; he thought the future son-in-law nothing more than a gold-digging opportunist. Also, back in the day, the iron mine millionaire sat on the board of trustees at Dickinson, a bad coincidence for Buchanan, who, around the same time, had been expelled for misconduct. (The school principal readmitted him after one year.) In a matter of months, Anne would become equally displeased with her petty suitor, not for his lazy right eye but because he preferred the company of others. When returning from out of town on business or the County Courthouse—which, for all we know, was the name of an underground leather bar—Buchanan called upon friends before seeing to her. Like a Meg Ryan movie played backward, a fed-up Anne broke off the engagement and moved to Philadelphia to live with her sister's family. Just after midnight on December 9, 1819, Anne overdosed on laudanum. Her parents blamed the death on Buchanan, who was not welcome at the funeral.

When Buchanan joined the ranks of the U.S. Congress two years later, whispers about the Coleman episode spread among the maids and matrons of Washington City. (They did not hold the ladder boy responsible but rather pitied him for his loss.) Save a two-year stint while serving as U.S. minister to Russia, Buchanan put in nearly twenty-five years on Capitol Hill. That's ample time to woo widows along the East Coast; however, the extent of the heart-breaker's trysts with members of the opposite sex is questionable. There are letters from Buchanan to Congressman Thomas Kittera, who lived with his aunt and niece, with vague postscripts such as "my love to my intended" and requests to please send regards to "my portion of the world's goods." Perhaps Buchanan was hedging bets with both of Kittera's housemates; maybe all three of 'em.

There's no sense in trying to solve the mystery. By 1836, forty-five-year-old Buchanan had moved into a boardinghouse with William Rufus King. Five years Buchanan's senior and described by a colleague as "unobtrusive, retiring [and] gentle," the hospitable Southerner acted as something of a mentor to his room-mate. "King was part of this circle of 'dandies,' they called 'em," historian Jean H. Baker told the History Channel in 2005. "There certainly was some sense in this group of men that they were having homosexual relations." Legislators called the senators "Siamese twins." President Andrew Jackson nicknamed them "Miss Nancy" and "Aunt Fancy." A New Hampshire newspaperman would say about King, who, in 1852, was elected Franklin Pierce's vice president, "You know he is

Buchanan's bosom friend." Historian Daniel F. Brooks, the leading authority on King, who believes himself to "know more about his personal life than anyone," said that the Alabama senator was "not attracted to women."

As to the particulars of Nancy and Fancy's nightly whereabouts, i.e., salons attended and games of leapfrog won or lost, little is on the books. Whether the two were lovers or a nineteenth-century version of *The Odd Couple*, they certainly cared for each other. King was "among the best, purest, and most consistent public men I have ever known," wrote Buchanan, adding that he was "a sound judging and discreet fellow" and a "very gay, elegant looking fellow."

After King was appointed U.S. minister to France in 1844, the separated Siamese twins exchanged the kind of sap that wears off for your average newlywed couple in the first eight months. "I am selfish enough to hope you will not be able to procure an associate," King wrote, "who will cause you to feel no regret at our separation." King's wish was granted. "I am now solitary and alone, having no companion in the house with me," Buchanan confided in a letter to the wife of a New York judge. "I have gone a wooing to several gentlemen, but have not succeeded with any one of them."

KING DIED OF TUBERCULOSIS FOUR YEARS BEFORE BUCHANAN WAS elected president. At the inaugural ball on March 4, 1857, caterers poured $3,000 worth of wine and shucked 400 gallons of oysters. The rest of the spread featured 60 saddles of mutton, 500 quarts of chicken salad, and 125 beef tongues, as one can never have too many beef tongues.

Buchanan's niece, Harriet Lane Johnston, assumed the role of first lady during his administration, a stressful and socially low-key four years for her uncle, who was unable to pacify a nation on the brink of civil war. The attitude and spirit of Buchanan behind closed doors remains unknown. Wheatland's Clarke argues that the supposed cagey atmosphere was actually savoir-vivre. "Whenever he had a gathering, he followed along the guidelines that were pretty typical of anyone living

> **"You know he is Buchanan's bosom friend."**

at that time," Clarke said. "Big parties of fifteen, twenty people were considered in poor taste."

French-service dining, popular in the 1850s, was more about the presentation of food than the efficiency of serving a hot meal. Every course would be presented at once, so unless you wanted entrées to go cold, hosts would generally invite a smaller number of guests—a custom, which, conveniently, would have made the perfect cover for White House After Dark.

///

BOURBON CRUSTA

When supplies ran low at Wheatland, Buchanan used his Sunday ride to First Presbyterian Church as an excuse to hit up Jacob Baer's whiskey distillery. Every week, he would pick up a 10-gallon cask of Old J. B. Whiskey. Guests thought the initials stood for "James Buchanan," which he liked.

But what of those guests incapable of guzzling spirits directly from the barrel? Here's a popular bourbon cocktail from the era with a sweeter finish.

2 ounces bourbon

3 dashes simple syrup

½ ounce orange liqueur

½ ounce lemon juice

dash Angostura bitters

ice

Pour the ingredients over ice in a tumbler. Shake well. Strain into a cocktail glass.

/////////////// **Serves 1** ///////////////

A HOUSE IN DISARRAY

MARCH 4, 1861–APRIL 15, 1865

Abraham Lincoln

REPUBLICAN

Every president is encouraged to decorate and entertain at their new digs. White House upkeep, after all, is a line item in the national budget. So when Abraham Lincoln and his emotionally unhinged wife, Mary Todd, dragged luggage through the North Portico entrance in March 1861, Congress approved its standard allotment of $20,000 for the next four years.

It doesn't sound like much, does it? In 2014 alone, the president required an estimated $750,000 for repairs and restoration. To be fair, inflation notwithstanding, 150 years' worth of festivities have probably taken a toll on the joint. But, in 1861, the sixteenth president had no plans to bulk-order Silly String and piñatas or have the carpets shampooed. As far as Lincoln was concerned, there was little reason to celebrate or spruce up.

The United States was on the brink of the most devastating crisis in its history. One month after the inauguration, hundreds of thousands of Americans would begin killing each other, and half of the population continued to treat black people almost as well as livestock. With the nation's weight on his shoulders, a burdened Lincoln couldn't stomach three square meals per day, let alone new duvet covers and shams.

At lunchtime, the president would force down an apple with a glass of milk. He'd often skip dinner, and, despite an astronomical endorsement offer from Gillette, the six-foot-four Republican stopped shaving altogether. Even when an aide suggested a press reception with tea and cakes to express gratitude to them for covering one of Mary Todd's military hospital visits, Lincoln shot down the idea. The social calendar was demanding enough with receptions for the son of Napoleon Bonaparte or Princess Clotilde of Italy and other visiting European royalty.

If Lincoln had one guilty pleasure, it was attending the theater, a pastime that didn't pan out too well for him. His emotional state, fluctuating between drowning sorrow and piping-hot rage, seemed akin to that of a fifteen-year-old aficionado of The Cure. To battle depression, he was rumored to have taken "blue mass"—prescription pills that, in 2010, the Royal Society of Chemistry determined had been riddled with harmful amounts of mercury, and were likely the reason for Lincoln's chattering teeth, shaky hands, and unpredictable fits of anger.

But mercury overload couldn't have triggered Lincoln's ailments on its own. Lincoln would press flesh with anybody and everybody at public events, sometimes thousands in a row and always without a bottle of Purell. On January 1, 1863, hours before signing the Emancipation Proclamation, his mitts took a beating in the Blue Room during a New Year's Day reception. With his right hand covered in blisters, Lincoln worried that a sloppy autograph on the crowning achievement of his presidency would be misconstrued for hesitation or doubt.

As for Lincoln's temper, let's recall that four-year $20,000 allotment for the arguably debilitated mansion: Within the first few months of White House life, and against her husband's wishes, Mary Todd surreptitiously blew the entire budget and then some on home furnishings and other necessary fixer-uppers. In the first lady's defense, President James Buchanan's salons didn't exactly leave things tip-top, but to hide this shopping spree from your pill-popping husband? Nine out of ten

Lincoln couldn't stomach three square meals per day.

marriage counselors agree this is not the best strategy. Benjamin Brown French, Lincoln's appointee for commissioner of public buildings, wrote in his diary that "it would stink in the land to have it said that an appropriation of $20,000 for furnishing the house had been overrun by the President when the poor freezing soldiers could not have blankets."

Lincoln gave the first lady hell, but, by February 1862, the point became moot. After losing their third son, eleven-year-old Willie, to typhoid, Mary Todd neither possessed the inclination to maintain an elegant home nor host events for several months. Plus, her husband's generous open-door policy left the mansion in shambles. Tourists and passersby would tear off pieces of fabric and pickpocket makeshift souvenirs. Basically the White House looked like a Greyhound bus station without the vending machines. "By late November 1864," according to Elizabeth Smith Brownstein's 2005 biography, "carpets, upholstery, drapes, and even the wallpaper and fixtures in the public rooms had been cut up, ripped off, wrenched out and carted away."

LINCOLN WASN'T ALWAYS SUCH A DRIP. DECADES BEFORE DONNING THAT goth stovepipe hat and signature chinstrap beard, the Great Emancipator tended bar.

Too preoccupied with making ends meet to pursue an interest in national affairs, the twenty-four-year-old opened a grocery in January 1833 with army buddy William F. Berry. (Previously, Lincoln volunteered about thirty days in a U.S. militia and held a series of agonizing odd jobs that included store clerk and flatboat guide; were he twenty-four today, he would likely be folding sweatpants at Old Navy.) Aptly named Lincoln and Berry, the emporium offered its partners a fulfilling, albeit brief, sense of entrepreneurship. They secured provisions such as bacon, guns, and beeswax—essentials for any homemaker—as well as a liquor license, registered in Berry's name, which permitted the outfit to sell French brandy by the half-pint for $0.25, among other spirits. Another $0.25 would afford an out-of-towner lodging for the night.

Villagers of New Salem, Illinois, frequently patronized Lincoln and Berry for bottles of rum, whiskey, and brandy to help them tolerate their drafty cabins and grisly wives. It's unclear whether they poured by the glass inside those four walls; since the business went belly-up within a matter of months, not much is known about its daily operations. Though there was this one time . . . The biographer Carl Sandburg, he who questioned the president's sexual orientation after characterizing a former roommate of Lincoln's possessing "a streak of lavender" and "spots as May violets," documented the most macho and

I hate Mondays.

homoerotic act in all of Abe's life. To settle a financial dispute between store employee Bill Greene and a local gambler, the six-foot-four shopkeeper promised the latter one of the store's fur hats unless Lincoln "could lift a barrel of whiskey from the floor and hold it while he took a drink from the bunghole." In which case, the gambler would pay Greene.

Lincoln performed the stunt with superhuman strength in a tactical squat position, and the stranger forked over the dough. Unfortunately, the strongman showcase did not draw much attention from the community, and resulted in no extra business for the struggling store.

Berry died two years later, and it took Lincoln as long as fifteen years to pay off the grocery's debts. Fortunately, by 1848, he had found a more fitting career: law and politics. He served in the Illinois state legislature for eight years, plus another two years in the U.S. House of Representatives. But the failed endeavor would come back to haunt him during his 1858 run for senate. In a series of debates, incumbent Stephen A. Douglas exposed Lincoln's past life as a "flourishing grocery-keeper in the town of [New] Salem" who could down "more liquor than all the boys of the town together." Lincoln refuted the claim.

It was times like these that one could use a hearty slug of whiskey from the barrel's bunghole.

69ᴛʜ **REGIMENT PUNCH**

This tart cocktail, presumably served on rainy nights in honor of the scrappy Irish New Yorkers who sent Confederate soldiers running, may cause drowsiness. "Blue mass" could intensify this effect.

2 ounces Irish whiskey

1 ounce scotch

1 teaspoon sugar

2 ounces hot water

1 lemon wedge

Stir the whiskey, scotch, sugar, and water in a heated mug until the sugar dissolves. Add the lemon wedge.

// **Serves 1** //

IN THE FACE OF MY NATION

APRIL 15, 1865–MARCH 4, 1869

Andrew Johnson

DEMOCRAT

17

I t's not every four years that a vice president–elect knocks back three belts of whiskey before his inaugural ceremony.

Already something of a Washington outcast, Andrew Johnson remained the only legislator from a secessionist state who did not join the Confederacy. The Tennessean lingered in the senate as a Southern apologist who pleaded sympathy for slave owners. (In the Bloody Sixties, there was not a more effective way to isolate oneself in a Northern-dominated Congress.) Even with his permanent scowl and unfavorable nickname, "the Grim Presence," Johnson was seen by Abraham Lincoln as a symbolically unifying figure who would help secure his second term. The president tapped the fifty-five-year-old Democrat as his running mate for the 1864 election—replacing sitting Vice President Hannibal Hamlin, a Republican from Maine.

On March 4, 1865, their inaugurations were scheduled one after another—Johnson's, then Lincoln's. The ceremony was originally set outdoors, but expected scattered showers moved the proceedings inside the Senate chamber. Cramped as they were, suits and civilians considered it an honor to crowd shoulder to shoulder on such an important day at the historic Capitol building: "a sanctuary," Aaron Burr once boasted, "a citadel of law, of order and of liberty." For Johnson that day, the venue might as well have been the patio at Señor Frog's. The vice president–elect "bellowed for half an hour the idiotic babble of a mind besotted by a fortnight's debauch," the *Cincinnati Gazette* reported. "He dragged its proudest ceremony into the slough of his degradation and turned it to shame and mortification."

Too much hair of the dog, it seems, prompted the catastrophic gaffe. After a whiskey-drenched night, Johnson entered Hamlin's chamber with bloodshot eyes and a face as flushed as a baboon's ass.

"Mr. Hamlin," the vice president–elect intruded. "I am not well and need a stimulant. Have you any whiskey?"

"No," Hamlin answered, "but if you desire, I will send across the street for some whiskey."

Delivery was arranged without hesitation. Some suspect the outgoing vice president rubbed his hands with glee as his usurper, not thinking twice, slugged two shots and took a "third tumblerful," according to Hamlin's family papers, "without any water."

Minutes before noon, Johnson was escorted by Hamlin arm-in-arm into the Capitol. With good book in hand, Chief Justice Salmon P. Chase of the Supreme Court waited beside the dais to administer the oath of office to a man who looked like he just came from a Jimmy Buffett show. Everyone, President Lincoln included, watched in horror as the man of the hour snatched the Bible from Chase, held it in the air, and shouted, "I kiss this book in the face of my nation of the United States."

In earshot of several reporters, Johnson continued to rant for what felt like days, and failed to properly name fellow members of the Cabinet. (He was heard whispering, "Who is the secretary of the Navy?" to a nearby colleague.) Senator Charles Sumner of Massachusetts practically banged his head on his

desk. The *New York Herald* called the blathering speech "disgraceful." Senators covered their mouths like Japanese schoolgirls as they giggled at the speaker's wobbly posture. Another respectable bystander, Attorney General James Speed, shut his eyes in disbelief, praying that his memory of the entire ceremony would wash away. Unfortunately, the attorney general—and everyone else in attendance, for that matter—could still hear the hiccups and slurs emitting from Johnson, who made such a drunken spectacle that newspapers demanded that the statesman resign immediately. A hangdog Lincoln nudged U.S. Marshall Ward Lamon to obstruct the vice president from further remarks outside the chamber. Clouds parted as the veep's address wrapped, and the president's ceremony relocated to the Capitol's East Portico.

The more generous biographers cite typhoid fever as Johnson's reason for the pre-inaugural bourbon bath. But neither diaries nor medical records support this claim. In fact, Johnson was such a loner in both public and private life that his drinking habits were seldom documented. Colonel W. H. Crook, Johnson's bodyguard, claimed that Johnson "never used tobacco in any form, and seldom touched alcoholic beverages." Treasury Secretary Hugh McCulloch "never saw him when under the influence of liquor." Two days after the inauguration, Lincoln assured colleagues, "You need not be scared, Andy ain't a drunkard."

Gossip spread anyway. "Drunken Andy Johnson" was one of many tarnishing pet names bestowed upon the vice president, who disappeared for two weeks after his swearing-in. He had supposedly gone on a bender, or so folks in the capital wished to believe. (Colleague Francis Blair later vouched for his stay on his family's estate in Silver Spring.) Johnson's social status worsened over time, especially after an unexpected promotion six weeks later. On April 15, Lincoln was pronounced dead from an assassin's bullet, and the newly appointed President Drunken Andy Johnson— and his Confederate-sympathizing policies—would only bring more humiliation to the country.

//

SANTA CRUZ SOUR

In the 1860s, mixology pioneer Jerry Thomas opened his first establishment in New York City. As Manhattanites exited from (or made their way to) Laura Keene's New Theatre, they would pop into the bartending legend's shack for one of several experiments, like this one.

---

ice

1 teaspoon sugar, dissolved in seltzer water or club soda

3 dashes lemon juice

1 wineglass Santa Cruz rum

berries for garnish

Load a tumbler or tall glass with the ice, sugar, lemon juice, and rum. Shake well and strain into a cocktail glass. Garnish with berries.

//////////////// **Serves 1** ////////////////

A NATURAL CRAVING

MARCH 4, 1869–MARCH 4, 1877

Ulysses S. Grant

18

REPUBLICAN

Ulysses S. Grant may not have been the biggest drunk of 'em all, but he was the most reckless. From childhood to deathbed, Grant's lifelong habit put an incredible strain on an accomplished career in public service, not to mention his health—and he had the bumps and bruises to prove it.

The love-hate affair between Grant and the bottle began early in Brown County, Ohio. The son of an entrepreneurial father and a pious mother who raised her children to abstain from dancing or gambling, young Ulysses would wait for his parents to go to church before raiding Dad's stash in the storm cellar—casks of blackberry cordial, acquired for the sole purpose of preventing cholera. It was a home remedy even teetotalers Jesse Root Grant and Hannah Simpson Grant could abide.

The young man didn't seem to mind self-medicating. While his folks were in town praying, he would bring friends downstairs for a nip. "I don't know whether we took it right or not," recalled one of Grant's friends, "but certain it is that we did not take the cholera."

Our eighteenth president was an adolescent numskull. His marks in school were nothing brag-worthy. The boy did not attend church—oddly, he wasn't even baptized—and showed no interest in his father's tannery business. Grant was considered an introvert during these teenage years. He occupied himself with chopping firewood out back and seeing after that precious storm cellar. Unimpressed, the old man called in a favor to their congressman and got his seventeen-year-old accepted into the United States Military Academy at West Point.

As a young cadet, Grant may as well have been the inspiration for Bill Murray's *Stripes* character. He racked up a wealth of infractions, mostly for sloppiness and tardiness. He played penny-ante games (forsaking one of his mother's cardinal rules) and would escape academy grounds to the neighboring Highland Falls for drinks at Benny Havens' Tavern. As was tradition among the slackers of West Point, Grant cut through upstate New York's heavy woods and skated down icy rivers to sear his lips on a "hot flip," Benny's candy-like house special: rum, whipped eggs, sugar, and spices, scalded in a giant metal pitcher with a hot fireplace poker.

In 1843 he finished twenty-first in his class, which sounds impressive until you take into account that there were only thirty-nine students. The U.S. Army sent the graduate to the Fourth Infantry at Jefferson Barracks, near St. Louis, where Grant courted his West Point roommate's sister, Julia Boggs Dent. Soon Ulysses and Julia were engaged, but before they had a chance to tie the knot, the second lieutenant was commissioned to military bases in Louisiana and Texas. In 1846, he became an infantryman in the Mexican-American War—aka President James K. Polk's ploy to bully Mexico into selling the United States a chunk of real estate.

During the advance on Monterrey, one of many battles fought by Grant, our indifferent soldier stuck out his twenty-four-year-old neck "when it was discovered that our ammunition was growing low," Grant described in his

Personal Memoirs. "I volunteered to go back to the point we had started from . . . I adjusted myself on the side of my horse furthest from the enemy, and with only one foot holding to the cantle of the saddle, and an arm over the neck of the horse exposed, I started at full run . . . I crossed at such a flying rate that generally I was past and under cover of the next block of houses before the enemy fired. I got out safely without a scratch."

We'll never know where his battlefield courage came from—maybe he was drunk—but it was this edge that eventually projected him into military stardom. Biographer Edward G. Longacre noted "stockpiles of whiskey and wine" that Grant kept among his provisions on the other side of the Rio Grande. A drum major in the Fourth was eyewitness to the "pretty good whiskey he had." In May 1848, Captain John W. Lowe of the Second Ohio Volunteers squealed to his own wife about his army buddy's debauchery and Billy Gibbons–length facial hair. "I fear he drinks too much," Lowe wrote, "but don't you say a word on that subject."

WHEN THE WAR HERO RETURNED HOME, HE MADE AN HONEST WOMAN of Julia. The two would have four children over the next six years and when possible, she accompanied her groom wherever the army would transfer him. But the military would soon take its toll on Grant, who always over-indulged when he missed his Julia.

In July 1851, hubby was assigned a rough ride down the Atlantic coast on the overcrowded USS *Ohio*, where he paced on deck until 3 or 4 a.m. A sympathetic captain permitted the seasick soldier access to his cabin's liquor stash. "Every night after I turned in," the captain recalled, "I would hear him once or twice, sometimes more, open the door quietly and walk softly over the floor, as not to disturb me . . . Then I would hear the clink of the glass and a gurgle, and he would walk softly back."

Two years later, Grant was transferred to Fort Humboldt in California. He could not afford to relocate his wife and children across the country on an officer's salary, so they stayed back at the farm outside St. Louis. Besides, Fort Humboldt was not family-friendly. Considered "the most dreary and isolated billet in the Nineteenth Century army," according to Longacre, the camp was essentially a government-run institution that encouraged alcohol abuse. It was

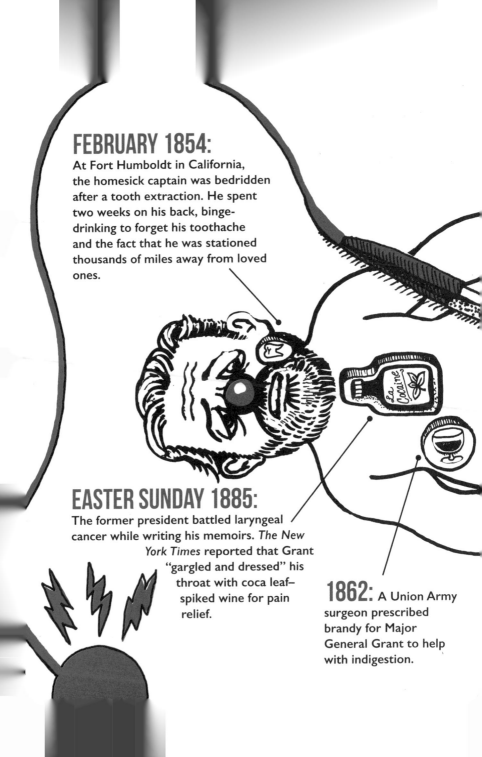

FEBRUARY 1854:
At Fort Humboldt in California, the homesick captain was bedridden after a tooth extraction. He spent two weeks on his back, binge-drinking to forget his toothache and the fact that he was stationed thousands of miles away from loved ones.

EASTER SUNDAY 1885:
The former president battled laryngeal cancer while writing his memoirs. *The New York Times* reported that Grant "gargled and dressed" his throat with coca leaf–spiked wine for pain relief.

1862: A Union Army surgeon prescribed brandy for Major General Grant to help with indigestion.

JULY 1851: On the USS *Ohio*, a seasick Grant paced on deck until 3 or 4 a.m. A sympathetic captain allowed the soldier access to the liquor stash in his cabin. "Every night after I turned in," the captain recalled, "I would hear him once or twice, sometimes more, open the door quietly and walk softly over the floor, as not to disturb me . . . Then I would hear the clink of the glass and a gurgle, and he would walk softly back."

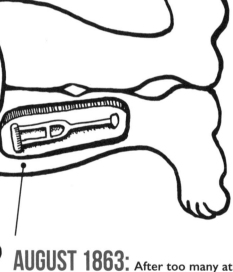

AUGUST 1863: After too many at a celebration for the siege of Vicksburg, the Union Army victor was New Orleans–bound when a passing train spooked his horse. "The horse . . . fell, probably on me," Grant recalled. "When I regained consciousness . . . my leg was swollen from the knee to the thigh, almost to the point of bursting." Grant was on crutches for two months.

built on the side of a cliff, for God's sake! "Grant got to drinking on the Coast very hard," according to one infantryman. "[He] used to go on long sprees [until] his whole nature would rebel and then he would be sick."

The soldier was more than likely referring to Grant's inability to hold his liquor (you'll see), but, in February 1854, Captain Barfman also contracted migraines and a case of the chills, possibly malaria. Then, after a tooth extraction (it was not a good month), he spent the next two weeks bedridden and depleting jugs of liquor to forget his pains, not to mention the fact that he was stationed thousands of miles away from his beloved. "You do not know how forsaken I feel here!" he wrote to Julia.

Months later Grant resigned from the U.S. Army, which took effect July 31, 1854. He returned to the Midwest to humbly work at his father's hardware store, among other odd jobs, and join Julia in rearing the kids. That is, until the Civil War broke out.

PRESIDENT LINCOLN WOULD OVERLOOK THAT DEGENERATE STINT BACK in California. In the mid-nineteenth century, the United States had no standing army; the president needed volunteers, and, as far as military experience went, Grant's was at the top. He was due for a historic comeback, and, in an army made up of amateurs and half-pints, the general didn't have to hide his shameful, alcoholic past. "I have a natural craving for drink," Grant told one of his subordinates.

With no Julia around to keep him in check, Grant emptied plenty of bottles on secession state battlefields. It was almost as if he was better at commanding while wasted. What other American general in recent history could successfully outfox his foe while nursing from a canteen of liquid courage? Officers recollected the general taking three slugs at a time.

Everybody knew. Major General Benjamin Butler recalled Grant "in a most disgusting state" while swilling whiskey during an inspection tour one afternoon, causing him to projectile-vomit onto his horse's neck and shoulders. Newspapermen reported on Grant's "staggering in gait." In 1862, a surgeon prescribed Major General Grant brandy to help with his indigestion. It had the adverse effect of enabling our man to mount his horse and recklessly gallop through ditches and piles of fallen logs. One of his wife's cousins, who dined with Grant that day, noted, "The doctor was a fool to have given him as much medicine as that." In August 1863, after too many at a celebration for the siege of Vicksburg, the Union Army victor was New Orleans–bound when a passing train spooked his horse. Failing to bridle his steed, Grant found himself on crutches for two months. "The horse . . . fell, probably on me," the general said. "When I regained consciousness . . . my leg was swollen from the knee to the thigh, almost to the point of bursting."

ACCORDING TO REPORTS, "every kind of intoxicating liquor had been excluded" from Grant's 1869 presidential inauguration, so none of the six thousand attendees would get out

---

MISQUOTED

A piece of hearsay about Grant and Lincoln remains in the ether. On November 26, 1863, the *New York Herald* reported that a temperance committee requested the sixteenth president relieve Grant of his duties because he "drinks too much whiskey." Lincoln's fabled reply? "Well, I wish some of you would tell me the brand of whiskey that Grant drinks. I would like to send a barrel of it to every one of my other generals."

Lincoln would agree that the Civil War myth perfectly captures his approval of the Union Army commander. "I didn't happen to say it, but it's a good story, a hardy perennial," the president responded to the *Herald*. "I've traced that story as far back as [eighteenth century's King] George II and [British Army] General Wolfe. When certain persons complained to George that Wolfe was mad, George said, 'I wish he'd bite some of the others!'"

---

of hand. Or maybe it was a precautionary measure taken by the president himself. Our conquering hero stabled his sordid behavior after assuming office, likely on account of political pressures as much as the comfort of having the first lady by his side. Those eight years in the White House were the longest they spent living together, and they lived them well.

"There are a couple of descriptions of maybe getting tipsy at the dinner table, but nothing happened on the streets," said biographer Brooks D. Simpson. "They weren't nearly as exciting or colorful reports as earlier. He changed from hard liquor of an uncertain quality to fine wines. He was not drinking as much to get intoxicated."

No horses were vomited upon during Grant's presidency, but Ol' Lyss did bring a taste of his past life into the executive mansion. He briefly employed his former quartermaster as head chef, but the bland Army chow wouldn't fly. First-rate cooks and hoteliers took over food and drinks operations, at the behest of Julia, who, after years of dragging army brats across state lines with her slovenly dressed husband, now had the opportunity to entertain with twenty-one-course meals and a fully stocked wine cellar. Back in the day, field rations kept the five-foot-seven general at a waifish 135 pounds; after the election, Grant packed on at least 25 more. Thankfully, the added weight and better-grade booze helped the president absorb alcohol more efficiently and with far less embarrassment.

DESPITE THE SELF-INFLICTED ACHES AND PAINS ON THE BATTLEFIELD, IT was not the drink that killed him.

After decades of hoovering snuff and cigars for breakfast, Grant, in his twilight years, picked up an agonizing case of throat cancer. In 1885, the retiree spent his last days in New York, where he worked on a multivolume autobiography that Mark Twain was set to publish under his short-lived Charles L. Webster & Co. imprint. To power through eight-hour writing sessions, the dying general numbed his larynx with cocaine, providing much-needed relief. The man couldn't even open his gullet for water, not that he cared much for H_2O in the first place. "If you can imagine what molten lead would be going down your throat," the invalid wrote, "that is what I feel when swallowing."

The sixty-three-year-old didn't kneel in a bathroom stall with a rolled-up $50 bill. Throat specialist Dr. John Hancock Douglas bathed the general's tongue in mixtures of the narcotic with disinfectant. Some afternoons, Douglas's "cocaine water" would come in the form of a spray; other times, as the *New York Times* noted on Easter Sunday 1885, the president's throat "was gargled and dressed in cocaine."

In addition to doctor's orders, Grant ingested a particular coca leaf–spiked wine—bottles of vin Mariani French tonic, each containing six milligrams of cocaine per fluid ounce. It's unclear who obtained the tonic for Grant, but Twain, whose publishing house was in its first year, later admitted to aspirations of becoming something of a drug kingpin. In Twain's autobiography, published in 1910, he shared that he had "a longing to ascend the Amazon. Also with a longing to open up a trade in coca with all the world."

Grant died on July 23, 1885, leaving his fifty-nine-year-old beloved Julia approximately $450,000 in royalties from the cocaine-fueled and critically acclaimed bestseller *Personal Memoirs of Ulysses S. Grant*.

MERINGUE AND ROMAN PUNCH

Valentino Melah, Grant's chief steward, came from an extensive background of premier hotels and introduced the White House to meringue-and-Roman punch, a digestif served for years in the executive mansion as a mid-dinner refresher course.

juice of 2 oranges

8 ounces champagne

8 cups rum

2 ounces orange liqueur

1 quart lemon sherbet

2 egg whites

5 drops lemon juice

3 cups powdered sugar

ice

Stir the orange juice, champagne, rum, and orange liqueur into the lemon sherbet. Store in the fridge. For the meringue topping, beat the egg whites and lemon juice together in a separate metal bowl for 5 minutes until the mixture forms stiff peaks; then carefully mix in the powdered sugar for another 5 minutes. Bake the meringue mixture in a 350-degree preheated oven for 10 minutes. Pour the cocktail punch into glasses over ice and top with the meringue.

///////////// **Serves 10** /////////////

THE WATER FLOWED LIKE CHAMPAGNE

MARCH 4, 1877–MARCH 4, 1881

Rutherford B. Hayes

REPUBLICAN

After the Civil War, metropolitan areas experienced spikes in public drunkenness in the streets and unsanctioned wrestling matches in the home. Long-suffering wives, failing to recognize the possibility that they simply married a bunch of assholes, targeted alcohol as the social culprit. In the hopes of deterring future would-be Maury Povich guests, the Women's

Christian Temperance Union lobbied for legislation against saloons and liquor stores in multiple states and pushed an agenda that favored family values. (The crusade was also timely. Since duties from alcohol imports were no longer required to finance the war, Big Booze lost significant political leverage.) Community drinking fountains became available as an alternative to liquid lunches. (See "Water Works.") Schools taught classes about the negative effects of drinking. Coffeehouses began to sprout up.

With registered voters influenced by the likes of teetotalers and religious zealots, it's no coincidence that, in the 1876 presidential election, the nation pulled the lever for a bland and bearded churchgoer with a squeaky-clean first lady at his side.

WATER WORKS

Toward the end of the 1800s, bubbling fountains replaced the well and bucket because experts (wrongly) believed that drinking from a communal well caused the outbreak of a certain airborne-transmitted disease. "There was a huge scare around tuberculosis, in passing it and getting it," according to a medicine and science curator at the Smithsonian Institute. "No-spit-on-sidewalk laws were put into effect. Communion cups were replaced by individual, eyeball-size glasses." Eggheads might have initially dropped the ball on how TB actually spread, but at least regulations in filtration systems and bacterial testing made water supplies less of a health risk.

One never had to worry about the conduct of Rutherford B. Hayes. The Harvard Law graduate and three-term Ohio governor, who could have dressed as Gandalf for Halloween, upheld a studious, morally upstanding image. The press thought him simultaneously a comfort to the people and a bore to insiders. "The kind of neutral man," wrote Charles A. Dana of the *New York Sun*, "who is always taken when the powerful chiefs can only succeed in foiling each other." Journalist Henry Adams described the nineteenth president as "a third rate nonentity, whose only recommendation is that he is obnoxious to no one." Hayes's wife, Lucy, nicknamed "Lemonade Lucy," was the morally upstanding icing on the cake. The devout mother of eight (three of whom died in infancy) banned wine and liquor from White House public functions. According to Attorney General William Maxwell Evarts, "The water flowed like champagne."

But Evarts must have not been in the know, for one item quietly served at events would always fly off the sideboard: hollowed-out oranges, filled with sorbet, and spiked under the noses of lawmaking prudes. "Waiters were kept busy

Lemonade Lucy, do your worst!

to seated guests in a hot and timely fashion—exactly like the service at contemporary restaurant chains—except in a hot and timely fashion.

///

SPIKED SORBET

The Hayeses claimed to have known all about the sly rum. "The joke . . . was not on us but on the drinking people," wrote the uptight president, insisting the oranges had "not a drop of spirits in them" but "the same flavor that is found in Jamaica rum."

1 quart lemon sorbet

4 ounces rum

4 ounces Cognac

1 ounce orange liqueur

8 ounces champagne

4 oranges, sliced in half with fruit scooped out and discarded

Mix the sorbet, rum, Cognac, and liqueur in a container and freeze overnight. At serving time, add the champagne. Pack the frozen mixture into the scooped-out oranges.

/////////////// **Serves 8** ///////////////

replenishing salvers upon which the tropical fruit lay," recounted newspaper correspondent Benjamin Perley Poore. "Concealed within the oranges was a delicious frozen punch, a large ingredient of which was strong old Santa Croix rum."

Meanwhile, Lemonade Lucy minded her pristine table settings: elaborate centerpieces for state dinners, fresh roses picked from the conservatory, boutonnieres tucked inside men's napkins. Meals were served à la russe, or "Russian style," in which staff hand-delivered individual courses from a service station

UNDOING THE HAYES BAN

James A. Garfield

REPUBLICAN

When teetotaler Rutherford B. Hayes didn't run for reelection in 1880, the Women's Christian Temperance Union and similar organizations kept fingers crossed that the next president would continue to set an example and maintain a dry White House. They also had high hopes that his first lady would carry on Lemonade Lucy's tradition of inviting congressmen to Sunday evening hymns.

James A. Garfield had a different agenda.

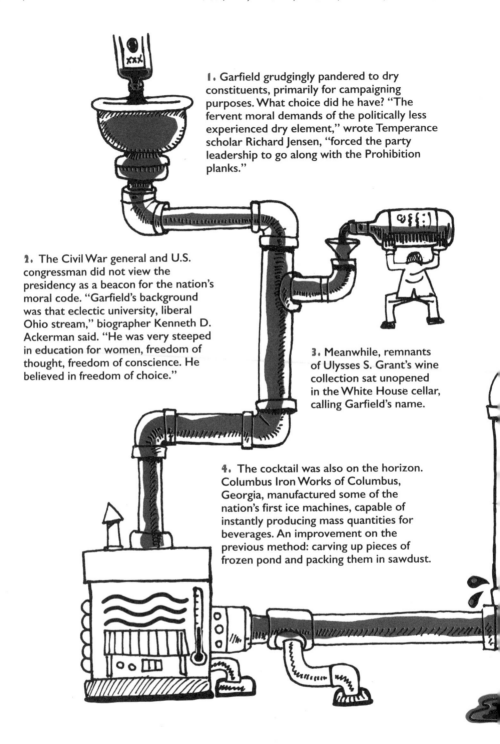

1. Garfield grudgingly pandered to dry constituents, primarily for campaigning purposes. What choice did he have? "The fervent moral demands of the politically less experienced dry element," wrote Temperance scholar Richard Jensen, "forced the party leadership to go along with the Prohibition planks."

2. The Civil War general and U.S. congressman did not view the presidency as a beacon for the nation's moral code. "Garfield's background was that eclectic university, liberal Ohio stream," biographer Kenneth D. Ackerman said. "He was very steeped in education for women, freedom of thought, freedom of conscience. He believed in freedom of choice."

3. Meanwhile, remnants of Ulysses S. Grant's wine collection sat unopened in the White House cellar, calling Garfield's name.

4. The cocktail was also on the horizon. Columbus Iron Works of Columbus, Georgia, manufactured some of the nation's first ice machines, capable of instantly producing mass quantities for beverages. An improvement on the previous method: carving up pieces of frozen pond and packing them in sawdust.

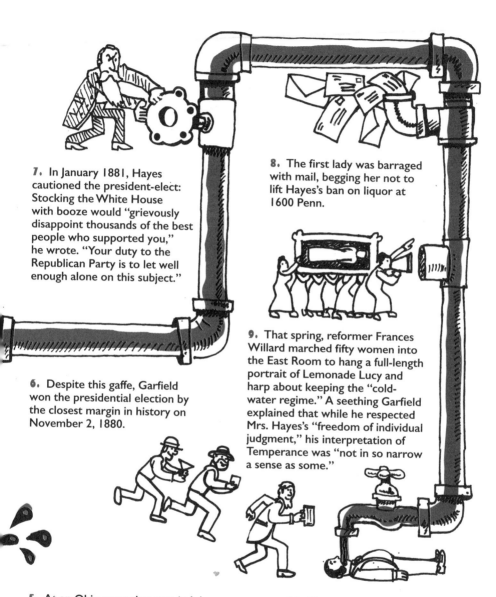

7. In January 1881, Hayes cautioned the president-elect: Stocking the White House with booze would "grievously disappoint thousands of the best people who supported you," he wrote. "Your duty to the Republican Party is to let well enough alone on this subject."

8. The first lady was barraged with mail, begging her not to lift Hayes's ban on liquor at 1600 Penn.

9. That spring, reformer Frances Willard marched fifty women into the East Room to hang a full-length portrait of Lemonade Lucy and harp about keeping the "cold-water regime." A seething Garfield explained that while he respected Mrs. Hayes's "freedom of individual judgment," his interpretation of Temperance was "not in so narrow a sense as some."

6. Despite this gaffe, Garfield won the presidential election by the closest margin in history on November 2, 1880.

5. At an Ohio campaign stop in July 1880, Lucretia Rudolph, Garfield's wife and mother of five, let slip that "the general does not believe in total abstinence." News rang through the prudish heartland.

10. Treasury Secretary John Sherman advised a way to reintroduce liquor while minimizing backlash: Turn on the taps for guests, but make everyone in the room aware that the first couple would abstain. Ever the martyrs, the Garfields complied.

THE SWINGING GARDEN OF BABYLON

SEPTEMBER 19, 1881–MARCH 4, 1885

Chester A. Arthur

21

REPUBLICAN

A former White House clerk once said of his employer that President Chester A. Arthur "never did today what he could put off until tomorrow."

The mutton-chopped leader maintained a workweek that could qualify for part-time status. Staffers witnessed Arthur carry a "property basket" that was, according to Thomas C. Reeves's definitive *Gentleman Boss: The Life of Chester A. Arthur*, "filled with official-looking documents which he brought with him to appointments to create the appearance of industry." It was a trick out of the George Costanza playbook. And the slacker routine was no secret. In its February 1882 edition, the satirical *Puck* magazine ran a cartoon titled "King Chester Arthur's Knight(cap)s of the Round Table," depicting the president and cabinet members clad in pajamas while napping on the job. The following month, an editorial in the *Chicago Tribune* said, "No president was ever so much given to procrastination as he is."

Just who was this amazing mortal? A modern-day teenage stoner somehow beamed into the nineteenth century? Slacker genius . . . or pompous fool?

ANYONE WHO LIVED IN A MAJOR AMERICAN CITY AT THE END OF THE nineteenth century was bound to cross paths with a particularly obnoxious subset: an entitled breed that thrived on business monopolies and cronyism and, for a brief period, managed to keep the nation's wealth among themselves. This group would be practically unrecognizable in modern America. Literary circles coined the era as the "Gilded Age," a time when showboating jackasses who prioritized style over substance blew stacks of cash at lavish bistros and private clubs (and more on trimmings than on the actual cuisine). One Manhattan restaurant that took full advantage of these big spenders was Delmonico's, which hosted high-dollar banquets with diners' names embroidered on silk cushions, menus hand-lettered in gold on satin pages, and swans paddling around a 30-foot lake that encircled the tables. (The perfect setting for the birthday party of a newly minted twelve-year-old millionaire.)

An exemplary specimen of this ilk was Chester A. Arthur, an indulgent New Yorker who could not refuse a department store charge account or an overpriced meal. Proof is in the potbelly. In the 1870s, the civil rights attorney's "figure was full and commanding," according to an eyewitness, "but he was laced up as to conceal his tendency to corpulence." That corpulence blubbered up to around 225 pounds. For those keeping score with a body mass index, Arthur stood at six feet. Which is to say that, in the medical parlance of the day, he was a disgusting pig.

Blame rich foods and restaurant wine cellars for Arthur's paunchy frame, plus the fact that he consumed mass quantities late at night. The sideburn-sporting gent was always "the last man to go to bed in any company," one drinking buddy said.

Arthur's busy week.

After-hours romps often culminated at his brownstone apartment—and tormented Ellen Lewis Herndon Arthur, his wife. (Divorce was taken into consideration.) Grieving the death of her firstborn infant with two more kids yanking at her skirt, "Nell" had little room to abide a gluttonous husband who was pulling all-nighters downstairs. But that first floor at 123 Lexington Avenue served a greater purpose than a parlor for practicing smoke rings and producing bourbon stains on the sofa. "Dinner, drinks and cigars were not just diversions," according to Zachary Karabell's 2004 biography, *Chester Alan Arthur*. "They were tools of Arthur's trade."

Arthur developed relationships with operatives who ran the Stalwart faction in the Republican Party. In 1871, the counselor was appointed collector of the Port of New York. A decade later, he somehow was elected vice president under James Garfield. It was also in his first-floor stomping ground that, on the morning of September 19, 1881, at 2 a.m., Vice President Arthur was alerted to the passing of President Garfield, who had been slowly dying of infections after taking a slug in his back from an assassin's pistol. (See "Garfield's Death.") Arthur was to become the twenty-first commander in chief.

He immediately tackled the important issues. Upon inspection of the executive mansion, President Arthur noted that the "badly kept barracks" resembled more of an

GARFIELD'S DEATH

On July 2, 1881, a deranged job-seeker, who previously visited the White House with hopes of an ambassadorship, gunned down President Garfield at a railroad station. The wounded president spent his last weeks convalescing while a team of doctors took turns pumping him full of chicken broth and morphine. He never got to polish off Grant's leftovers in the wine cellar.

intensive care unit than a luxury residence for the nation's leader. Its tattered interior and drafty corridors had long been critiqued by first families, but Arthur, with his low tolerance for bad living, was the first to actively protest its condition. "I will not live in a house looking this way," he said, acting like the Dan Aykroyd character in *Trading Places* more than a man who just accidentally ascended to the highest office in the land. "If Congress does not make an appropriation, I will go ahead and have it done and pay for it out of my own pocket. I will not live in a house like this." It was nice to see Muttonchops so worried about his new job: running the United States of America.

The government footed the bill for a complete renovation while the first family—at the time consisting of the president, his ten-year-old daughter Nellie, and Princeton-bound son Allan (his wife had died of pneumonia the year before)—shacked up at Nevada senator John P. Jones's house for three months. Meanwhile, Arthur commissioned thirty-three-year-old designer Louis Comfort Tiffany, heir to specialty retailer Tiffany & Co., to do his bidding. First order of business: twenty-four wagonloads of objectionable furniture and other household items were removed from the presidential property.

One would think that such a treasure chest of items would be stowed away and preserved for future generations. Instead, it was fed into a giant yard sale, subject to public auction. Items included a birdcage that belonged to Ulysses S. Grant's first lady; a pair of Abraham Lincoln's trousers; and Lemonade Lucy Hayes's sideboard, a gift from the Women's Christian Temperance Union. (A saloonkeeper on Pennsylvania Avenue acquired the sideboard and stocked it with bottles of liquor.) Oh, what the *Storage Wars* folks would have made of this! Put it in the woodpile, for all Arthur cared; he was busy transforming the residence into a Gilded Age McMansion.

On December 7, 1881, Arthur quietly celebrated his first evening at 1600 Penn with close friends, but such low-key dinners would be few and far between. "The Gentleman Boss," as was his nickname, stocked his wardrobe with English tweeds, frock coats, silk scarves, and never-ending rows of pants. (Arthur, obviously very busy running the country, would try on twenty pairs at a time before deciding on the right ones for that evening's affair.) His carriage was lined with lacy upholstery embossed with his monogram. *The New York Times* hailed it as "the finest which has ever appeared in the streets of the capital." Dinnertime, pushed back until later in the evenings, promised fourteen-course meals with eight varietals of wine and a new glass for each varietal. Like a cheesy wedding reception, the centerpiece displays even had themes. One twenty-one-course meal shared the tablecloth with "The Swinging Garden of Babylon," a bouquet of roses, carnations, and honeysuckle freshly picked from the conservatory.

Rutherford B. Hayes, who banned alcohol during his four years in the White House and was ostensibly repulsed by the stench of new money, alleged there was "nothing like it ever before in the Executive Mansion—liquor, snobbery and worse." The former president's opinion did not seem to coincide with that of Washington. With the exception of smaller dinners reserved for unmarried and widowed congressmen, an Arthur function typically crammed up to three thousand guests in the East Room. The general of the U.S. Army, Philip Sheridan, and his wife once had to squeeze through an open window to get into the damn place. At a New Year's reception, the U.S. minister from the Kingdom of Hawaii dropped dead. Now *that's* what Chester A. Arthur called a party!

SHOCKINGLY, THE REPUBLICAN PARTY CHOSE NOT TO NOMINATE ARTHUR for reelection in 1884.

This may not have been his biggest problem. In 1882, the president had been diagnosed with Bright's disease, now known as lupus. By the end of his term, his health had deteriorated. Besides, he obviously hated his job. "You have no idea how depressing and fatiguing it is to live in the same house where

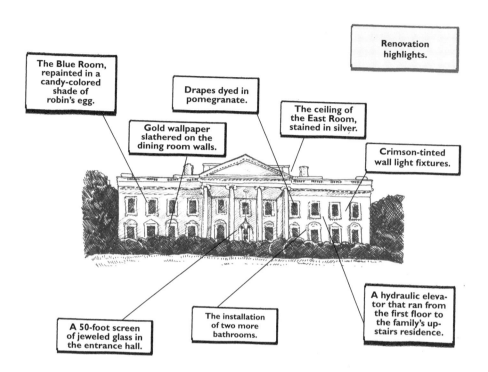

Renovation highlights.

The Blue Room, repainted in a candy-colored shade of robin's egg.

Drapes dyed in pomegranate.

The ceiling of the East Room, stained in silver.

Gold wallpaper slathered on the dining room walls.

Crimson-tinted wall light fixtures.

A 50-foot screen of jeweled glass in the entrance hall.

The installation of two more bathrooms.

A hydraulic elevator that ran from the first floor to the family's upstairs residence.

you work," he told the *New York World* in 1884, bringing the concept of White People Problems to heights never attained since.

Two years after his presidency, the fifty-six-year-old widower spent his final days bedridden at 123 Lexington Avenue, surrounded by his sister and children. In 1944, an Indian grocery took over the square footage that was once the president's first-floor parlor. Decades later, there are still great deals on dried fruits and falafel. The other floors are leased for residential and office space. A small bronze plaque hangs next to the upstairs front entrance to commemorate the former tenant. In 2005, a realtor told the *New York Times* that "people who live there just kind of giggle when you point it out." President Arthur would have been proud.

CURAÇAO PUNCH

A reflection of its times, the restaurant scene had a lesser appreciation for the taste of alcohol itself. Saccharine liqueurs and mixers busied up glasses to excess with flavors and overtones reminiscent of everything but the booze that was ordered. Granted, some were definitely worth sampling. Harry Johnson, "the Dean of Bartenders," was one of the first to publish extensive guides for his bottle-swinging colleagues. In 1882, his *New and Improved Bartender's Manual* included this sweet taste of hellfire.

½ tablespoon sugar

2 to 3 dashes fresh lemon juice

1 ounce soda water

shaved or crushed ice

1 ounce brandy or Cognac

2 ounces orange curaçao

1 ounce Jamaican rum

handful of strawberries and blueberries and/or lemon wedge

In a glass or goblet, combine the sugar, lemon juice, and soda water and stir until the sugar is dissolved. Fill the glass with finely shaved or crushed ice. Add the remaining ingredients. Stir well. Garnish with the fruit.

// **Serves 1** //

SHERIFF JUMBO

MARCH 4, 1885–MARCH 4, 1889

Grover Cleveland

DEMOCRAT

22

he hollow decorum of the Gilded Age did not consume every commander in chief. In fact, one president in particular fit in about as well as Rodney Dangerfield on the fairway at Bushwood Country Club. An overweight son of a New Jersey minister, Stephen Grover Cleveland preferred a knife to a fork when shoveling food into his gape. As a president who remained unmarried until the age of forty-nine, Cleveland bartered chef-prepared meals for the servants' corned beef and cabbage. Once at a charity gala, the gassy bachelor was coerced onto the

GROVER CLEVELAND IS

SHERIFF JUMBO

FEATURING

Lyman K. Bass   Louis Goetz   Oscar Folsom   Maria Crofts Halpin

dance floor, and the crowd made so much fun of his ballroom waddle that he never again attended such a highbrow affair.

The natural-born plumber felt at home in less pretentious settings, such as Buffalo, New York, where he spent four years studying law. Off-hours, his ass crack hung off the side of a barstool. S. Grover Cleveland, or "Big Steve" as friends called him, eventually gained notoriety as a city official and even more so as an enthusiast of pale lagers and high-calorie platters. He would soon drop the "S" from his signature and gain roughly 100 pounds of man-flesh in a matter of fifteen years, a stint that biographers deem mostly insignificant to his political career.

But, for the sake of tavern folklore, those fifteen years made history.

THE EXTRA MEAT IN THE SEAT WAS NOT A GLANDULAR ISSUE, FOR Cleveland was merely a victim of the predatorily cheap moonshine and greasy bar food of the mid-nineteenth century. In Buffalo, saloon grub barely met the nutrition standards of a modern-day Arby's. Many of the seven hundred or so establishments served heavily salted sandwiches at no charge, leaving patrons little choice but to douse themselves with schooners of beer. (Hence the origin of the maxim "there's no such thing as a free lunch.") Mark Twain described the city as a "sink of iniquity," a salacious mecca in which prostitutes lay on their backs seven days a week. "Big Steve" supposedly kept his distance from women in general—but not because he wanted to spare them trips to the chiropractor. If someone brought up the subject of marriage, the stud muffin winced. "The more I think of it," he told family members, "the more I think I'll not do it."

Bavarian-German beer gardens, rather than brothels, took priority. He "drank stein after stein of beer," according to Rexford Guy Tugwell's *Grover Cleveland*, "and he loved the hearty food . . . the sausages and sauerkraut, the thick stews and the immense cuts of meat." After the usual triple-flusher that followed, the carnivore sought out the best happy hour in town. "Everything about saloons he found irresistible," wrote Charles Lachman in *A Secret Life: The Lies and Scandals of President Grover Cleveland*, "the lusty male camaraderie, the thick fog of cigar smoke, and the crunch of sawdust under his boot."

At age twenty-eight, Cleveland shared a room with Lyman K. Bass, an attorney of the same age and alcohol tolerance yet with a much thinner frame. Inside the Southern Hotel, the two lived in filth. When they weren't in their flophouse cluttered with empty beer bottles and filled ashtrays, they were probably tapping a keg at one of the nearby pubs. Take your pick: There was the Shades, a hole-in-the-wall that ran on the honor's system and lacked a bar top, stools, and staff. Then you had Gillick's, a popular armpit that was frequented by lawyers on the prowl for paid sex and nightly specials. For a more exclusive vibe, an intimate haunt called Boas's was in possession of five chairs and an owner who discouraged customers from using them.

In the same year, Cleveland and Bass pitted against each other for another sort of seat to call their own: district attorney of Erie County. Coinciding with the friendly competition, the roommates obliged to reduce their suds consumption, just enough to manage their campaigns without slurred speech. Their pact—limiting nightly drinking to four glasses of beer—was broken in a matter of days. They soon agreed that if one was still thirsty, either party could "anticipate," or borrow against, the previously agreed upon four glasses and cut back on another day. That didn't work, either. "Grover," Bass said one week later, "do you realize we have by now anticipated the whole campaign?"

The next evening, they discovered a loophole in their pointless gentleman's agreement: Commit to four glasses but use 48-ounce tankards. This equaled approximately one gallon of beer per candidate each night, an acceptable allotment in a town that prides itself as the origin for deep-fried hot wings.

On Election Night, the first round was on Bass, winner of the county seat by the slightest margin. The new district attorney went on to become a U.S. congressman, while other young clerks of Buffalo's legal firms grew in age and maturity, and found themselves in bigger jobs, marriage, even fatherhood. Not Cleveland. "Big Steve" became known as "Uncle Jumbo," a nickname to simultaneously acknowledge his body mass and his vague tavern wisdom. In other words, it was the nicest way for the next generation of nighthawks to pay respects to a middle-aged barfly with a hairy gut and no family.

At 250 pounds, Cleveland was not a man you wanted to insult. Or so attorney Mike Falvey discovered. A liveryman recalled an evening in 1873 when Cleveland dragged the unfortunate big-mouth onto the wooden sidewalks and "landed the first punch." No one really knows why. "Whatever the start may have been," said the livery proprietor John C. Level, "the finish began when . . . Cleveland banged him into the gutter near Seneca Street." The fight stopped when both men lost their breath. According to eyewitnesses, the drunken brutes wiped the dirt from their clothes and shook hands. A truce was concluded inside Gillick's, as they convalesced over buckets of brew, the Neosporin of its day.

At 250 pounds, Cleveland was not a man you wanted to insult.

Around the same time, the brawling Cleveland was somehow elected sheriff of Erie County. Unsurprisingly, his two-year term has never been optioned by Clint Eastwood's production company. More useful to taverns as a customer than a peace officer, Sheriff Jumbo put away so much beer that he would sometimes "lose a day." On those lost days, it would not be inconceivable to find his badge at home while the lawman led Blume's Saloon in a sing-along. One proprietor, Louis Goetz, was often terrorized by his antics. This included one instance, around midnight, as the barkeep was napping on the job, the on-duty sheriff set the barroom clock ahead by two hours (last call was 1 a.m.). He then woke Goetz and cited him for keeping open past operating hours, a prank Cleveland revealed only after the Dutchman went ballistic.

This is what happens when you elect one of your regulars to a position of power.

THE CITY SURVIVED CLEVELAND'S SINGLE TERM AS SHERIFF. SOON AFTER, he opened a legal practice and found himself in, as he would later call it, a "woman scrape." Enter Maria Crofts Halpin, a thirty-three-year-old widow who bore a son on September 14, 1874. The department store clerk named her boy Oscar Folsom Cleveland, implicating the thirty-seven-year-old attorney as his father. Without fuss, Cleveland provided financial support. Details are hazy, but the allegation was that on December 15, 1873, a "persistent" Cleveland forced himself upon Halpin after dinner at the Ocean Dining Hall & Oyster House, his treat. (Curiously, the mother also named the child after Cleveland's law partner, Oscar Folsom, which raises suspicion that Cleveland's intention was to take the fall in order to protect his colleague, who was already married.)

Within a year of her son's birth, Halpin was briefly committed to Providence Lunatic Asylum for psychiatric evaluation; little Oscar was sent to an orphanage. *A Secret Life* author Lachman, also longtime producer of the tabloid *Inside Edition*, suggests this was "an abuse of power by political elites" to erase a smudge in Cleveland's past and advance him to the governor's mansion. Almost a decade later, the alleged date-rape incident surfaced and ironically improved Cleveland's chances in the presidential election. "A Terrible Tale: A Dark Chapter in a Public Man's History," read the July 1884 headline in the *Buffalo Telegraph*. The author, a Baptist minister, elaborated that Cleveland's apartment was "a harem." Perhaps he meant a harem of turkey legs?

Cleveland responded to the accusations. He owned up to the bastard child, which, in some beautifully sinister PR spin, built his reputation as an "honest" politician and ultimately clinched a November squeaker for the White House. He wedded his former law partner's twenty-one-year-old daughter, Frances Folsom, during his second year in office. At age fifty-four, he fathered his first legitimate child. *The New York Tribune* famously nicknamed her "Baby Ruth" . . . anticipating Jumbo would get hungry.

//

APRÈS SOUPER

Doubtful that Cleveland would have tipped back this one, but a bartender named "The Only" William Schmidt noted in 1892's *The Flowing Bowl: When and What to Drink* that the Gilded Age's "After Dinner" was likely customary among the president's more mild-mannered peers.

---

ice

2 dashes simple syrup

1 ounce crème de menthe

½ ounce maraschino liqueur

3 ounces brandy

Fill a tumbler with ice. Pour all the ingredients inside and stir. Strain into a cocktail glass.

//////////////// **Serves 2** ////////////////

THE PIOUS MOONLIGHT DUDE

MARCH 4, 1889–MARCH 4, 1893

Benjamin Harrison

REPUBLICAN

During the four years wedged in between Grover Cleveland's two nonconsecutive terms, an exceptionally less gregarious and gluttonous individual sank his backside into the White House furniture.

Benjamin Harrison, a former Union Army general and Indiana senator who married a preacher's daughter, demonstrated

A loving family's concerns, up in smoke.

June 5, 1850

Pa thinks you are a very young gentleman to be acquiring so bad a habit.
Love,
Anna

July 23, 1848

We feel constantly anxious about you... I hope you will be prudent in your diet and that Benja may abstain from cucumbers.
Mary Jane

November 4, 1850

A sainted mother, once made of you the request to make the sacrifice for her, to induce you at once to say, "I have smoked my last cigar," and adhere to it....
John Scott Harrison

July 1848

Pa is quite hurt to think that he still continues to eat cucumbers notwithstanding his advice....So if he wants to please his father, he will change in this respect.
Sallie

December 10, 1849

You are now exposed to many temptations incident to a college life.
John Scott Harrison

incredible restraint when it came to social conduct—in other words, the five-foot-six Presbyterian was a world-class stick in the mud. Harrison considered a "drunken revel" to be "disgusting" and believed that uncorking a bottle was suitable during a "pleasant, cheerful dinner of the kind where only wine enough is taken to give vivacity to the mind." During the Civil War, he banned liquor from his brigade in the hopes of converting his troops into lean, mean sobriety machines. Enlisted men griped about their superior in letters home.

As an impressionable young coed, Benjamin Harrison, grandson of tee-totaler President William Henry Harrison, happened to cultivate one vice that stuck with him for life. While attending Farmers' College outside Cincinnati with older brother Irwin, the fifteen-year-old "Benja" received several grating letters from his churchgoing kinfolk about his taking up cigars and—paging Dr. Freud—eating cucumbers, a vegetable the parental units deemed "forbidden." (Live a little, wild child—eat the cucumber!) The honor roll student might as well have rolled up and smoked his family's entire correspondence, for he did not quit the lung-tarring pastime.

Harrison's future wife didn't seem to mind. After transferring to Miami University in Oxford, Ohio, for his final two years, Harrison spent a great deal of time on the front porch of a particular boardinghouse for the neighboring Oxford Female Institute. One of the boarders was Caroline Scott, a painter and musician whose father

THE GOURD OF DOOM

Around the time that Mary Jane Harrison penned her brothers in the hopes that they "may abstain from cucumbers," one senator speculated that President Zachary Taylor was killed by the same snack—apparently, "the very worst and most pernicious" side dish one could serve. What the hell? "People thought they created intestinal stress," said Phyllis D. Geeslin of the Benjamin Harrison Presidential Site. "I think that's why a burpless cucumber was developed."

Oh really? According to a cucurbit expert at North Carolina State University, the burpless cucumber is certainly easier on the stomach than your typical variety; but, in regard to its origins, the jury is still out. "They probably arrived in America some time in the 1800s," said Dr. Todd C. Wehner, Department of Horticultural Science. As for the alarming letters, "I don't know why they would implicate one fruit or vegetable over another. The only real culprit is how workers handle them. Fecal bacteria are almost always the problem. Cucumbers by themselves are pretty clean."

was a minister and the institute's president. A courtship began. Innocent activities between Ben and Caroline consisted of afternoon buggy rides and evenings on that porch, but the couple "did not dance," according to a family scrapbook, because "[i]t was considered a great sin at Oxford." Judging by word around campus, however, sweet nothings must have been exchanged. Why else did classmates refer to our well-behaved suitor as "the pious moonlight dude"? (Yes, they really called him that.)

The Presbyterian was a world-class stick in the mud.

The minister's daughter married Harrison in 1853. They spent the next thirty-nine years rearing children in Indiana, where he practiced law and, after the Civil War, served the Hoosier State in the U.S. Senate.

Predictably, Harrison's stint in the executive mansion was G-rated. He reintroduced morning prayer and was the first president to dress an indoor Christmas tree. Its branches held lit candles in the second floor's Oval Room, which doubled as an office and, sometimes, a sitting room for his family. And about that family of his—nine members of the Presbyterian clan came to Washington to live with the president and first lady.

In addition to Caroline, the president put up his father-in-law, two children, their two spouses, four grandchildren, and a pet goat named Old Whiskers. One of the grandchildren, Benjamin Harrison "Baby" McKee, was spoiled rotten with goat-drawn carriage rides and bonbons. On his fourth birthday, cake was served in a dining room furnished with fifteen high chairs. (Does it say something about President Harrison's hedonism that the craziest party on his watch was thrown for a toddler?) As for the adults who came to visit, Caroline wasn't stingy. Guests gulped down oysters on the half shell followed by an ice cream with fruit compote. Cognac and wine were served at state dinners. After said dinners, the president preferred Daniel Webster cigars or the occasional Havana. There is no word regarding his old cucumber habit.

Between the daily grind of civil service and the bedrooms occupied by the would-be cast for a bad TGIF sitcom, the first lady was gunning for an overhaul. None too thrilled with bathing and breakfasting at the same address where her husband ran the country, Caroline commissioned architect Fred D. Owen for multiple renovation plans. One design included an entirely separate residence built for the Harrisons, a proposal Capitol Hill politely declined. Instead, Congress appropriated enough scratch to install electric lights and additional bathrooms. In 1891, the Edison Illuminating Company took four months to replace gas chandeliers with a wiring system controlled by wall switches. A typical pair of country folk reluctant to embrace technology, neither of the Harrisons ever touched the switches—no doubt out of a fear that Jesus would smite them. The president had already pressed his luck by eating those diabolical cucumbers.

MARYLAND EGGNOG

In 1890, Caroline Harrison rounded up more than two hundred recipes from Washington wives for her cookbook, *Statesmen's Dishes; and how to cook them*, "to promote the development of pleasant social intercourse," as she wrote in its introduction. "The result is that the art of entertaining is carefully cultivated, and all that is pleasant and graceful in the science of the table—which must always play so important a part in hospitality—receives its highest development." The wife of a Supreme Court justice contributed a festive Christmas beverage that should make the holiday season a little less painful.

1 dozen eggs

1 cup sugar

1 nutmeg, grated

1 pint brandy

1 pint rum

1 gallon milk

Separate the egg yolks from the whites. Whisk the egg whites and set aside. Whisk the yolks and add the sugar and nutmeg. Gradually add the brandy and rum. Continue beating and stirring until light. Pour the gallon of milk into the mixture. Cover with the whisked egg whites. Chill.

//////////// **Serves 24** ////////////

STEALTH OPERATION

MARCH 4, 1893–MARCH 4, 1897

Grover Cleveland

DEMOCRAT

24

I n 1893, the first year of his second term, decades of throwing back beers and chomping on stogies caught up with President Grover Cleveland. On May 5, he detected what felt like a patch of sandpaper on the roof of his mouth, a creepy swelling on the "cigar chewing side." The fifty-six-year-old blew it off for many reasons. An economic crisis was at hand. His wife, Frances Folsom Cleveland, was scheduled to give birth to their second child. Breakfast was getting cold. "The woman he brought from Albany knows exactly what he likes," wrote journalist Frank Carpenter. "She cooks for him oatmeal, beefsteak, eggs or a chop, with coffee to wash it down."

In all fairness, Cleveland took only fifteen minutes to inhale the average meal, "sometimes with wine," Carpenter noted, "and sometimes without," but surely the twenty-fourth president, elected

"I'd have it removed at once."

to an unprecedented nonconsecutive second term, could have made time for a doctor to examine the piece of nasty in his snack hole. The suspicious lesion "often caused him to walk the floor at night," according to the first lady, and would eventually prompt him to seek medical attention. Burrowed on the left side near his molars resided a form of varicose carcinoma—cancer cells associated with poor diet, consumption of alcohol, tobacco, and venereal disease. (At times like these, one begins to wonder whether those Buffalo prostitutes kept diaries.) The tumor measured approximately the size of a quarter. New York's Dr. Joseph Bryant called it "a bad looking tenant." He added, "Were it in my mouth, I'd have it removed at once."

The specialist's advice was taken to heart. But, considering the pressures of a Wall Street on the brink, Cleveland insisted the surgery be conducted in secret. (For the public to discover that the president of the United States had a life-threatening disease could have sent the marketplace into hysterics.) So, on July 1, he borrowed his friend's yacht, the *Oneida*, and shoved off from Manhattan's East River to the open waters of Long Island Sound. Six doctors were aboard the ship, and, in a confined space below deck, they set up a surgery room loaded with the essentials for your average night at a Slovakian brothel: ether and nitrous oxide for anesthetic, chisels and forceps for carving, gauze and morphine for recovery. However, with no suction device to clear airways or intravenous transfusion to make up for blood loss, the inventory was questionable at best, even for 1893.

"You see this time and again in American history," said Matthew Algeo, author of *The President Is a Sick Man*. "Presidents who have some kind of illness or disability don't get the best treatment because their doctors acquiesced to the patient's demands instead of doing what is best for the patient, medically, or physically."

It doesn't help when the patient is a chimney. On the *Oneida*, Cleveland smoked cigars hours before the operation, which took approximately ninety minutes. Bryant successfully extracted the tumor, but not before removing

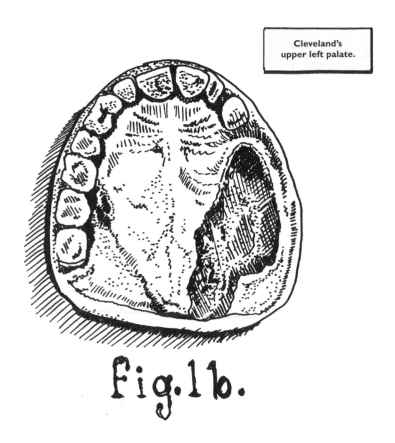

Cleveland's
upper left palate.

Fig.1b.

pieces of the president's upper left palate and several teeth along with it. For the next few days, an overmedicated President Jumbo went into hiding to let his newly deformed face heal. After the July 4 holiday, he returned to shore. If anyone asked why the president wasn't his usual oratorical self, they were told that a dentist removed two teeth, a minor operation.

In roughly three weeks, Cleveland would go under the knife once more. A prostheticist removed two more teeth to make room for a piece of vulcanized rubber that Algeo likened to the size of a hockey puck. (Fig. 1b. depicts a mold of Cleveland's mouth, taken before surgery and used to fashion the prosthesis.) The synthetic-jawed president was basically transformed into an evil henchman from the James Bond series. But, on the bright side, Cleveland's facial hair went unharmed. He and his walrus mustache would live together happily until his death in 1908 at the age of seventy-one.

THE MARTINEZ

In the 1890s, variations of the martini began to appear in both name and recipe on cocktail lists and bar guides.

At San Francisco's Occidental Hotel, one could order a "Martinez," named after a nearby town. Heavy on the vermouth, the Martinez delivered less bite than what more contemporary lushes would wash down during the Prohibition era. The saccharine beverage has been described by dining historian William Grimes as "a molten gumdrop."

1 ounce gin

1½ ounces sweet vermouth

dash maraschino liqueur

dash of orange bitters

2 lumps ice

lemon or orange peel for garnish

Fill a mixing glass with the gin, vermouth, liqueur, and bitters, then add the ice. Stir for 30 seconds. Strain into a cocktail glass. Garnish with the lemon or orange peel. Serve.

///////////////////////////////////// **Serves 1** /////////////////////////////////////

FRAT BOYS TAKE THE STAND

MARCH 4, 1897–SEPTEMBER 14, 1901

William McKinley

REPUBLICAN

T he social life of William McKinley proved so excruciatingly dull that conspiracy theorists surely wondered: When the president was assassinated at a Buffalo recital hall in 1901, perhaps it was a hit that he put on himself.

Just how boring was a night on the town with the big-business Republican? Save the occasional cigar and scotch before bedtime, his idea of leisure was a carriage ride at dusk. Granted, the commander in chief had an ambitious agenda. Expansion in trade and victory in the Spanish-American War advanced the U.S. as an international force. The efforts of his administration arguably

The state of Ohio vs. Todd.

afforded the nation's future leaders a permanent seat at the table of world superpowers—but when it came to cutting a rug in the East Room or blasting a fart at dinner for comic relief, McKinley was not your man.

Blame his parents. "Dancing, cards and theatrical entertainment had been as rigidly forbidden in his strict Methodist home as those other snares of Satan, wine and tobacco," according to Margaret Leech's *In the Days of McKinley*.

One highlight of McKinley's prudish ways happened in 1869. Four years out of law school, he served a single term as prosecuting attorney of Stark County, Ohio. The hardworking sprout, still living with siblings, advocated stricter alcohol licensing laws as well as complete abstinence. It was an effective way to move up the ranks: Stark County was mostly a Democratic-leaning county at the time, and the twenty-six-year-old stumped for the reelection of Governor Rutherford B. Hayes, fellow Republican and heavyweight champion of the temperance movement. McKinley ended up carrying the county for the triumphant governor in a squeaker of a race.

"He and Hayes had been very close in the Civil War together," said Lewis L. Gould, author of *The Presidency of William McKinley*. "There would have obviously been an element of calculation in McKinley's temperance efforts, but it would have fit ideology and expediency at that time. There was a huge emphasis on closing businesses on Sundays, Bible-reading in schools, stuff like that. Republicans tended to take the evangelical, pietistic point of view."

Indeed, the pill was seemingly put on this Earth to discourage any sort of decent pastime that involved catching a buzz. During his two-year term, the Stark County prosecutor secured indictments against bar owners for allegedly strong-arming college kids into purchasing liquor. Coeds were summoned to the courtroom to recollect what must have been a traumatizing experience. Philander C. Knox, law student at Mount Union College (class of '72), gave elaborate testimony that convicted several saloonkeepers.

The suck-up tore a page right out of McKinley's opportunism manifesto. After graduation, Knox moved to Pittsburgh and became a fund-raiser for the president. He was appointed U.S. attorney general in 1901.

///

FREE SILVER FIZZ

When McKinley ran for a second term in 1900 against William Jennings Bryan, GOP rallies chanted, "McKinley drinks soda water/Bryan drinks rum/McKinley is a gentleman/Bryan is a bum!" This was, in the eyes of McKinley's constituents, somehow an item for the plus column?

Meanwhile, Democrats enjoyed this beverage that, according to William Grimes's *Straight Up or On the Rocks*, "gave liquid expression to Bryan's political platform."

2 ounces dry gin

1 ounce lime juice

1 teaspoon sugar

1 egg white

ice

club soda

Pour the gin, lime juice, sugar, and egg white into a tumbler with ice. Shake well and strain into a cocktail glass. Top with the club soda.

// **Serves 1** //

THE MIGHTY LORD OF THE WILDERNESS

SEPTEMBER 14, 1901–MARCH 4, 1909

Theodore Roosevelt

REPUBLICAN

26

I n 2006, psychiatrists at Duke University Medical Center concluded that several presidents struggled with symptoms related
to bipolar disorder. Chief among these illustrious head cases
was Theodore Roosevelt, an alpha male whose contemporaries
attributed his eccentric behavior to drunkenness, which was simply not true. The twenty-sixth president barely touched the stuff.

OFFICE SPACE

In the summer of 1902, Roosevelt managed what previous tenants such as Chester A. Arthur and Caroline Harrison could only dream of: a White House expansion that would separate the first family's private quarters from the daily grind. By November, the completion of the West Wing provided enough square footage to relocate the residence upstairs while making room on the first floor for cloakrooms and storage for administrative staff.

At White House dinners, guests were bathed in fine wines such as a Marcobrunner or a Château d'Arsac Grand vin Le Montiel 1893, a great year, but Roosevelt refrained. Save the rare occasion for a mint julep or glass of white wine diluted with sparkling water, he mostly harbored a thirst for the blood of large animals.

From the 1880s, when he served as a New York State assemblyman, to post-presidency decades later, the strapping marksman traveled the globe to track big game. In *Hunting Trips of a Ranchman: Sketches of Sport on the Northern Cattle Plains*, one of several memoirs on his adventures in wildlife, Roosevelt detailed a remarkable slog through the Northwest—in the Bighorn Mountains, specifically, where he first encountered the grizzly bear. "It gave me rather an eerie feeling in the silent, lonely woods," Roosevelt wrote, "to see for the first time the unmistakable proofs that I was in the home of the mighty lord of the wilderness." Evidently navigating his hunting party around piles of paw-printed excrement, the ranchman soon enough met his match: a nine-foot-tall silvertip, weighing more than 1,200 pounds. The beast was conquered, as were others by the author, who was clearly not vegan. "On this trip we killed five grizzlies with seven bullets," he continued. "The flesh of the little black bear . . . tasted like that of a young pig."

The carnivorous escapades went international in 1909. After two terms in the White House, Roosevelt was commissioned by the Smithsonian to spend a year in Uganda and present-day Kenya to collect specimens. Accompanied by his son Kermit and an 1895 lever-action Winchester rifle, the fifty-year-old developed an amazing tan but rarely imbibed—not even when ill. "There are differences of opinion as to whether any spirituous liquors should be drunk in the tropics," reasoned Roosevelt. "Personally, I think that the less one has to do with them the better . . . when feverish or exhausted by a hard day's tramp, hot tea did me more good than brandy."

East Africa Protectorate

Hunter's License

Season No 190 _2_

DESCRIPTION:

Age __50__ years   Height __5__ feet __10__ inches
Weight __200__ pounds   Complexion___Wht___
Color of Hair___brn___   Color of Eyes___blue___

This Certifies That _Theodore Roosevelt_
a resident of _United States_, State of___New York___ has
complied with the law authorizing the issuance of
hunting licenses to nonresidents of the East Africa Protectorate and
is hereby licensed to hunt as such for the period of one year from the
date of this license.

WITNESS: _____

this _21st_ day of ___Feb___ 190_2_

Indeed, the teetotaling psycho showed exemplary restraint while slaughtering hundreds of endangered species for sport. In no way did this trouble the local authorities. In fact, they recommended a special hunting permit for killing an unlimited amount of exotic animals that, if given the choice, would have much preferred a zoo cage. Roosevelt declined the generous offer and instead went with the standard license, the Noah's Ark Massacre Special, which

BODY COUNT

Don't feel bad if you cannot identify most of the following species that TR slayed on the Dark Continent. They're probably extinct by now anyway.

buffalo (6)	guinea fowl (5)	pelican (1)
bushbuck (6)	hartebeest (33)	python (3)
bustard (5)	hippopotamus (7)	reedbuck (10)
crane (2)	hyena (5)	rhinoceros (13)
crocodile (1)	impala (7)	roan (4)
dik-dik (1)	klipspringer (1)	steinbok (4)
duiker (3)	kob (14)	stork (5)
eland (6)	lechwe (3)	topi (12)
elephant (8)	lion (9)	warthog (8)
francolin (1)	monkey (6)	waterbuck (11)
gazelle (28)	oribi (18)	wildebeest (5)
gerenuk (3)	oryx (10)	zebra (20)
giraffe (7)	ostrich (2)	

allowed the kill of two of each kind. He would surpass that number by quite a bit.

SO, WAS THE STONE-COLD SOBER

successor to William McKinley naturally wired, overly caffeinated, or completely mental? Long before the aforementioned Duke University study, scholars roundly debated this nonsense about Roosevelt, easily the manliest president to ever run the country. Known as "TR," because nothing says macho more than reducing one's given name to initials, the iconic bro possessed an explosive persona—one with the manic energy to achieve radical social change (e.g., Big Business trust-busting; labor and health reform); laser-focused determination to bring new levels of authority to the presidency; and a Nobel Prize–worthy mustache that was forever sculpted into Mount Rushmore.

But how many of these accomplishments are indebted to something as rudimentary as coffee? Rumor had it that the cousin to future president FDR drank more than a gallon per day, and rumor became corporate myth after one supposed breakfast in 1907 at Nashville's Maxwell House Hotel, where the president remarked that the blend of bean at the inn was "good to the last drop." Years later, the coffee giant would attach the catchphrase to their logo and dubiously credit TR as its origin.

Bottomless cups of joe are cited in several journals and biographies, but that's hardly an explanation for his active lifestyle. The restless New York native preoccupied himself with boxing, wrestling, swimming, rowing, and horseback riding. Even then, his intensity did not fade. He sought action in the most relaxed of settings. A downstairs neighbor once recalled our subject sitting by the fireside and deeply engrossed in a book while showing no concern for his feet's proximity to the burning kindling. The bookworm did not adjust his reclined position until the soles of his boots were ablaze.

For Roosevelt, the campaign trail might as well have been a scene from *Die Hard*. Running for a third presidential term, he famously gave a speech to voters in Milwaukee just moments after an assassin's bullet struck him below the rib cage. (The assailant, John F. Schrank, believed that the ghost of McKinley told him to seek vengeance; he spent the rest of his life in an asylum.) "I have just been shot," Roosevelt told the crowd after approaching the podium, where he remained for ninety minutes. "The bullet is in me now, so that I cannot make a very long speech, but I will try my best."

Since he was not coughing up blood, the candidate ascertained that the wound was not fatal. Instead, he recognized an opportune moment to display his bravery. Or insanity. You choose.

//

HOT MILK PUNCH

In May 1913, the former president filed a libel lawsuit against the editor of *Iron Ore*, the weekly newspaper of Ishpeming, Michigan, after an article characterized him as a tippling degenerate who "gets drunk, and that not infrequently, and all his intimates know about it." Roosevelt testified that he had "never been drunk or in the slightest degree under the influence of liquor."

The court ruled in TR's favor, but not before he admitted to having a "measured spoonful of brandy" in a glass of milk before bedtime. Here's a more potent version, courtesy of the legendary *Jerry Thomas' Bartenders Guide: How to Mix Drinks*, published in 1862.

2 to 5 ounces hot water

3 ounces whole milk, heated

2 ounces Cognac brandy

1 ounce Santa Cruz rum

pinch of grated nutmeg

Heat a glass by filling it with the hot water. Let it sit for one minute. Empty the water from the heated glass. Fill it halfway with the hot milk, then add the brandy and rum. Stir. Top with the nutmeg.

//////////////// **Serves 1** ////////////////

CONTINUOUSLY HUNGRY

MARCH 4, 1909–MARCH 4, 1913

William Howard Taft

27

REPUBLICAN

I n Cincinnati's boom years, journalists and slaughterhouse
workers jokingly referred to the meatpacking epicenter of the
Midwest as "Porkopolis," a suitable moniker for a snout-filled
city that, in 1857, produced one of American history's most iconic
gluttons. It's no secret that William Howard Taft, born inside his
parents' home one mile north of downtown, never met a meal that
he didn't demolish, but he grew up with just as much ambition
for an education and a career. The Yale Law School graduate was
a nonsmoker who eschewed vulgarities and heavy drinking and,
before age thirty, was appointed a judge on the Superior Court

of Cincinnati. Two decades later, he won a presidential election while maintaining an exquisite handlebar mustache. Want more? After the White House, he taught at his alma mater, and at sixty-three years old was confirmed chief justice of the Supreme Court, the first (and only) president to hold such a seat.

Of course, such accomplishments are not realized without a modicum of anxiety. Over the years, Taft's weight yo-yoed due to emotional eating, and for most of his adult life, he appeared as if he had just been hooked up to a tire pump.

At six feet tall and ballooning up to 350 pounds with a waistline that measured an impressive 54 inches—your standard department store size for window drapery—Porkopolis's hometown hero was the punchline to a lifetime's worth of fat jokes. In his teen years, classmates called him "Big Lub." When he served in President Theodore Roosevelt's cabinet, subordinates at the War Department frequently teased that Taft gave up his streetcar seat for three ladies. A personal physician wryly suggested that he reduce the usual 12-ounce breakfast steak to 8 ounces.

At twenty-nine, Judge Taft married Helen "Nellie" Herron, a twenty-five-year-old intellectual equal and lover of booze and smoke. Back in college, when a unitard-clad Taft joined the Yale wrestling team, his future wife joined her hellion friends in mixing whiskey with milk and playing poker for cash. She could roll tobacco like a Cannabis Cup winner. Leading up to their wedding day, however, Nellie's nights of chugging hard dairy and choking on cigs softened into weekend salons. The sweethearts engaged thirtysomething neighbors in discussions related to politics and Shakespeare while noshing on strawberries and oysters. It was a sophisticated, affectionate partnership that continued for forty-four years until Taft's death in 1930.

AS TAFT'S CAREER EXPANDED, SO DID THE ELASTIC IN HIS PAJAMA bottoms. Assigned to a U.S. Circuit Court in 1892, he was always traveling, and hotel meals were the easiest resort—and they weren't "nearly as healthful . . . as those at home," he confessed to Nellie in a letter dated February 1894. "We have lunch late, and I eat too much." He also picked up an addictive taffy habit and tipped the scale to 325 in the next ten years. Nellie tried to help Judge Big Lub control the impulse. "Keep quiet if you do not feel alright in your

"I will not give up my favorite decoration."

stomach," she wrote. "For my sake, darling, do send out for a sandwich or go and get a glass of milk, and eat less at the other two meals."

As President Roosevelt's handpicked successor, Taft made efforts to lighten his load during the 1908 presidential election. The secretary of war admitted that he was "continuously hungry" to a nutritionist, who prescribed a sensible regimen: modest pieces of meat and fish, cooked vegetables without butter, salads, fruit, a glass of wine at lunch. Golf became a routine exercise, an excruciating activity for any man capable of losing spare change in his love handles—and this particular pork chop didn't even touch wine or liquor for one year. Between dieting and hitting the links, Taft lost 60 pounds in six months. He gained some weight back before Inauguration Day but still proudly flaunted a 300-pound

Executive Mansion Dining

Menu

Breakfast

Grapefruit, potted partridge, grilled partridge, venison, sour milk waffles, hominy, rolls, bacon, beefsteak, oranges, coffee

Lunch

Smelts, lamb chops, salted almonds, deviled almonds, lobster stew, roasted wild turkey, lobster a la Newburg, salmon cutlets, tenderloin, cold tongue, ham, terrapin soup, Billi Bi, peach salad with cream cheese, persimmon beer

Dinner

Back Bay plant oysters, turtle soup, radishes, green olives, celery, filet of Pompano, cucumbers en gelée, filet mignon of mutton, tomatoes stuffed with corn, fritters, grilled sweet potatoes with rice, lettuce and artichoke heart salad, cheese biscuits, lobster liver, vegetable salad, salmon salad, baked ham

Dessert

Ice cream, bonbons, coffee, four-color cream, fruit pie

What Taft ate.

frame on the dais. Though, once in the hot seat, his girlish figure would not last. To keep stress levels on an even keel, White House troughs were filled with lobster stew, stacks of bacon, cheese biscuits, hams, and an array of comfort foods.

For the most part, the president continued to stick with nonalcoholic beverages, such as persimmon beer, a fruity refreshment that he used to wash down possum at a banquet thrown by the Atlanta Chamber of Commerce in 1909. "The best dish I have tasted in weeks," the human garbage disposal told the *New York Times*. It would come as a surprise to no one if he said that after every meal.

The question still stands: How much did his binge-eating hinder the administration? An aide remembered how "he pants for breath at every step." Senator James Watson recalled that Taft looked perpetually exhausted, which was later ascribed to sleep apnea. The medical community could not

THE TUB

In January 1909, a pre-inaugural Taft set sail for Central America to review construction of the Panama Canal. To accommodate El Presidente Gordo, the captain of the USS *North Carolina* ordered a mammoth bathtub that measured 7 feet, 1 inch in length and 3 feet, 5 inches in width. Its proud manufacturer, J. L. Mott Iron Works, had a photo taken of the 2,000 pounds of porcelain that ran in the February edition of *Engineering Review*. The editor described the piece as having "pondlike dimensions" and saw "no reason why it should not be transferred from the *North Carolina* into the White House."

The photo, in all probability shot at Mott's plant in Trenton, New Jersey, shows four grown men sitting comfortably inside the empty tub as if it were a king-size Jacuzzi. A story that is now common folklore began to circulate: Taft had the oversize tub installed at 1600 Penn because he got stuck in the previous one, which hardly adds up, considering the porcelain beast had been ordered prior to his inauguration.

properly diagnose the nasal disorder, leaving the chief in a miserably languid state during most workweeks. Taft "did not and could not function in alert fashion," according to Watson. "Often, when I was talking to him after a meal, his head would fall over on his breast and he would go sound asleep for 10 or 15 minutes. He would waken and resume the conversation, only to repeat the performance in the course of half an hour or so."

The letters of Captain Archibald Butt corroborate the fatigue-related symptoms. The bodyguard once described a road trip in which "his great bulk would lunge from side to side as the car turned or jolted over street-car tracks and crossings" but "he would never wake." In 2003, a medical journal unearthed a case-cracking daytime photo of the somnambulant president, positioned upright but with eyes shut. Zoom in, and you might see crumbs from a cheese biscuit in his 'stache.

//

ROCKY MOUNTAIN PUNCH

In a 1909 interview with *Ladies Home Journal*, the first lady said that alcohol "will be served at dinners," enough of a quote to stir the old temperance pot and get lobbyists to raise the volume on discussions about Prohibition. But dry days were too far ahead for anyone to care, as Mrs. Taft gladly broke out the champagne punch. The slightly revised recipe below dates back to the 1860s, courtesy of the Union Army's Colonel James Foster, who would recommend this one for larger crowds.

---

sliced lemons and oranges (3 of each)

2 tablespoons sugar

1 quart rum

1 pint curaçao

5 bottles champagne

large chunk ice

Presoak the lemons, oranges, and sugar in the rum and curaçao for 4 hours. Then strain the rum and curaçao into a large bowl. Add the champagne to the mixture, and drop a large chunk of ice in the center of the bowl. Decorate the top of the ice with the fruit slices. Drink.

//////////////// **Serves 20** ////////////////

A PASSIONATE SCHOLAR

MARCH 4, 1913–MARCH 4, 1921

Woodrow Wilson

DEMOCRAT

28

Curious that Woodrow Wilson, the son of a Presbyterian minister, would grow up to sign his love letters "Tiger," a signature meant to either acknowledge the mascot of his Ivy League alma mater or perhaps the kitten costume he donned in the bedroom.

We don't know the extent of Wilson's sexual proclivities, only that the twice-married academic kept an open mind and open heart. His religiosity has been compared to that of Jimmy Carter's: a deeply personal commitment to faith sans the fire and brimstone. His intellect smacked of the same meticulous

Easy, Tiger.

Vulcan-like logic seen in Barack Obama. And, judging from volumes of personal letters, Wilson possessed a superhuman caliber of horniness that the White House had never before seen.

A passing glance at old photos might lead one to suspect otherwise. In black-and-white, the former president of Princeton University—where he attended undergrad and later became a faculty member—comes across as a miserable stiff. He looked like the kind of uptight banker who gets off on denying loans to customers. In the PhD's defense, he hated posing for the camera. Perfectly understandable, given the long jaw, donkey ears, and beak nose. "In portrait photography people had to sit still and not smile," said John Milton Cooper Jr., author of the supersize *Woodrow Wilson: A Biography*. "It's very easy to look and say, 'This guy was a stern, priggish sort of guy,' but that's not Woodrow Wilson at all. He had an extremely healthy sex drive."

You needn't remind Ellen Axson Wilson of said libido. Married to the ugly professor for nearly three decades, Ellen received stacks of love letters, even during the twilight of their marriage, despite his supposed fling with a woman whom he met in Bermuda in 1908. (No matter how wonderfully she'd fill out a swimsuit, the shapely Ellen opted not to vacation in the isles with her husband; she preferred, rather insanely, to "stay with the house, like the fixtures.") But forget the side action for a minute: Wilson wrote his wife practically every day when out of town. One piece of correspondence, postmarked almost ten years after their honeymoon, revealed an everlasting affection. Or at least that he preferred her on top. "When you get me back you'll smother me, will you, my sweet little lover?" Wilson wrote in 1894 while touring the lecture circuit. "Are you prepared for the storm of lovemaking with which you will be assailed?"

If medical examiners didn't know better, the president might have screwed her to death. But she suffered a more tolerable fate. In 1914 Ellen was taken by Bright's disease, and Wilson felt lost without a woman by his side. He confided in an advisor that he "had no heart in the things he was doing," a comfort to no one, considering Wilson's agenda included maintaining American neutrality in World War I. Capital gossips knew what was up. Ellen Maury Slayden, a congressman's wife, wagered a friend five pounds of chocolate that the widower would remarry before the end of his first term. "Why not?" Slayden disputed. "He is a youngish man, and we have reason to believe rather leans to the ladies."

Less than a year after the funeral, Wilson found a new mate. On December 18, 1915, and against the wishes of his advisors—concerned with public perception, as Ellen had only just begun to rot—President Wilson tied the knot with a buxom forty-three-year-old jeweler's widow named Edith Bolling. No word if Slayden got her chocolate.

Chances are, the newlyweds did not wait until the big night for consummation. Throughout their months-long courtship, during which time they had become secretly engaged, the president's security detail noted a bounce in his step after visits to his fiancée's residence. But was it always a humpfest? Seven months before the wedding day, Tiger and Edith spent what sounded like a frustrating two hours in the back of a limousine, curtains drawn. "For God's sake, try to find out whether you really love me or not," Woody wrote the following morning. "You owe it to yourself, and you owe it to the great love I have given you, without stint or measure."

A pity the chauffeur could never repair those claw marks in the backseat.

> ## "Are you prepared for the storm of lovemaking with which you will be assailed?"

//

CHAMPAGNE COCKTAIL

The next time your partner won't put out in the back of a limo, ice down a bottle of bubbly. Dr. Max Lake, an Australian surgeon and winemaker, concluded after years of study that champagne's 13 percent alcohol content and typically luxurious surroundings were not the sole reason for its seductive effects—rather, drier varietals, Lake contends, emit a subtle aroma that is nearly identical to sex pheromones. Roll up the partition and try this mixture.

1 sugar cube

dash of Angostura bitters

1 bottle dry champagne

orange twist

Drop the sugar cube and bitters in a champagne flute and let soak. Add the champagne and garnish with the orange twist. Sip.

// **Serves 1** //

SCANDALOUS

MARCH 4, 1921–AUGUST 2, 1923

Warren G. Harding

29

REPUBLICAN

█ f there is one thing you should know about Warren G. Harding, our nation's twenty-ninth president, it is that he nicknamed his penis "Jerry." This fact is revealed in letters to his mistress—the one whose vagina he christened "Seashell," as opposed to the one thirty years his junior. Or the one he impregnated. Or the other one he impregnated, then shipped off to a sanitarium. Or, for that matter, the Ohio prostitute who gave the country's future leader gonorrhea.

Who better than this sleazy, hard-partying Republican whiskey aficionado to steer the country through the early years of Prohibition?

THE EIGHTEENTH AMENDMENT

Before the Great Depression, the courts maintained a strict interpretation of the Constitution's Commerce Clause (Article I, Section 8), particularly in its powers to regulate interstate trade. Supreme Court justices felt it was not Uncle Sam's place to restrain the pursuit of dollars and happiness. So, to outlaw manufacture and sale of booze across state lines, prohibitionists couldn't just pass a law by a simple majority. Anti-saloon lobbyists had to approach the issue as if they were freeing the slaves or guaranteeing women's right to vote (which, consequently, didn't happen until months after this Prohibition nonsense).

The goody-goody temperance movement resurged in the 1910s and gained frightening momentum in Congress. The Eighteenth Amendment, outlawing the manufacture and sale of alcoholic beverages, passed with ease through both houses over the 1917 holidays and, despite President Woodrow Wilson's veto attempt, was ratified two years later. The body of law officially went into effect on January 17, 1920—the year Harding was elected to office. (See "The Eighteenth Amendment.")

The religious right had a remarkable stronghold in the political arena, piously implicating drink for inner-city crime, home-wrecking, the abuse of women—you name it. Not even Harding, the landslide president-elect whose popular vote tally doubled that of his Democratic rival, would dare repeal this conservative legislation supported by the Anti-Saloon League and William Jennings Bryan's Jesus freaks—two constituencies vital for anyone hoping to stay in federal politics. Besides, the new commander in chief was too wrapped up in his own party, not the Republican one.

Harding kept a fully stocked sidebar. The former Ohio newspaperman was a fiend for hard liquor, chasing tail, and five-card stud—a model hypocrite, he voted in favor of Prohibition during his one term in the U.S. Senate. And, in the Oval Office, he swilled behind closed doors; meanwhile, the rest of the country struggled to sneak a measly flask of hooch home to the family.

IN 1920, THE NEWFANGLED PHRASE "SMOKE-FILLED ROOM" DESCRIBED A familiar setting for Harding (see "A Chicago All-Nighter"). Along with his better half, Florence, the power couple hosted poker nights for nearly twenty years. Twice a week, they invited members of the elite to both their home in Marion, Ohio, and, when Harding was a senator and finally president, their homes in Washington. Harding's card games entailed "air heavy with tobacco smoke," recalled Alice Roosevelt Longworth (Teddy's daughter), and "trays with bottles containing every imaginable brand of whiskey." Everyone drank, including Florence, who suffered from a kidney ailment. One evening, the party was joined by the pet monkey of a newspaper publisher; the long-tailed animal poured a bottle of brown all over Harding's white suit.

Sauerkraut and knockwurst made the rounds at the poker table, something of a clumsy precursor to barroom finger foods at a time when people were still adjusting to evenings at home rather than at nightclubs. "When [Prohibition]

A CHICAGO ALL-NIGHTER

At the Republican National Convention of 1920, it took delegates five whole days to pick a nominee.

On the next-to-last day, a group of balding men with bad breath and cigars screwed into the corners of their mouths were holed up inside magazine publisher George Brinton McClellan Harvey's fourth-floor suite at the Blackstone Hotel. "Republican officials wandered in and out during the course of the evening," according to John Dean's *Warren G. Harding*, "and Harvey's group attracted attention because there was plenty of liquor [and] good food." The dark horse among candidates, Harding came out the victor in the convention's final hours. (Colleagues agreed with Senator Frank Brandegee's assessment that Harding was "the best of the second-raters.") The developments from that fabled evening inspired one reporter to introduce the phrase "smoke-filled room" to the American lexicon.

first came in, we grumbled, shrugged our shoulders, and decided to use the stock we had," Longworth wrote in her memoir. "I don't think that we foresaw in the slightest degree the great bootlegging industry that was to develop." In the short time before illegal gaming and drinking parlors with alleyway peep slots colonized underground nightlife, socialites added "BYO" on invitations in an effort to conserve their own personal stock.

Sharing booze was still the custom in smaller circles, especially for those wanting out of the public eye. Back at the poker table, whenever Harding or one of the guests required another scotch and soda, there was no need to get up. "Duchess," Harding would call to his wife. "You are lying down on your job." One card player remembered an obedient yet sickly Florence, shuffling from the wet bar to her guests with a "withering" neck and "ankles thickly swollen."

Yep, the first lady put up with a lot of crap. With "unusually large, strong, powerful, crushing" hands on a "delicate body," as described by her staff, Florence prepared gastro-pornographic treats such as hickory nut cake, lemon almond cookies, and waffles with dried beef gravy. For years, her husband inhaled the latter on two or three mornings a week with sausage, eggs, coffee, and a cigar. At the White House, the potbellied president and Duchess slept in twin beds. A Bible rested on their nightstand while Harding's womanizing ran rampant.

The rumors date back to Ohio. Long before a career in Washington, the statesman allegedly contracted a case of gonorrhea from a prostitute at the Red Bird Saloon. While courting Florence in the 1890s, Harding supposedly hid the dried beef gravy with her parents' next-door neighbor, Susan Pearl McWilliams, which resulted in pregnancy. (McWilliams left Ohio to quietly give birth in Nebraska.) Harding also apparently knocked up an Augusta Cole, whom he subsequently committed to Battle Creek Sanitarium. (The pregnancy was terminated.)

One Florence Harding biographer accounted for a total of seven alleged mistresses, the most publicized of whom was Nan Britton. A starstruck fangirl thirty years Harding's junior who adorned her bedroom with news clippings of the politician, she claimed to have borne Harding's second illegitimate child. Britton self-published an autobiography, *The President's Daughter*, four years after the chief's death. In it she details how Harding set her up with a clerk position at the U.S. Steel Corporation and had the Secret Service hand-deliver child support payments to her doorstep. The exposé was never corroborated with reliable sources.

One affair of Harding's, however, lasted for years and has the, ahem, *hard* evidence to back it up. Carrie Phillips, wife of his Ohio friend Jim Phillips, would invite the senator into her bedroom while her husband was at work and, on one occasion, when Florence was admitted to the hospital for her kidney disorder. Harding, wrapped up in work as always, used his time to write Carrie cheesy letters, some of which extend more than thirty-five pages. "I am extremely in love with you this morning," read one note from the spring of 1908. "I want you . . . and I wanted to feast my eyes, to intoxicate them in glorious breasts and matchless curves and exquisite shapeliness. And I wanted to fondle and feel of beauty and superbness . . . the 'Oh, Warren! Oh, Warren!' when your body quivers with divine paroxysm and your soul hovers for flight with mine." In other letters, Warren nicknamed his penis ("Jerry is standing up beside me while I write you") and referred to Carrie's vagina as "Seashell."

So how, after slaving over a waffle iron in the morning and trays of whiskey at night, could the Duchess deal with a husband who seemingly broke his vows at every

A Bible rested on their nightstand while Harding's womanizing ran rampant.

opportunity? She kept it to herself. "Most of the pain in this world is located in the hearts of women," Florence jotted on her desk calendar. "Maybe women are forced into mute acceptance of disloyalty, faithlessness, and humiliation because this is, after all, a man's world."

IN HIS MERE TWO AND A HALF YEARS AT THE HELM, MORE CRIME AND corruption shrouded Harding's office than perhaps any administration in U.S. history. The everlasting supply of whiskey in the White House for "when he entertained his most intimate man friends," housekeeper Elizabeth Jaffray recalled, was all thanks to a backroom frat collectively known as "the Ohio Gang." The shady crew followed the president-elect to Washington, where many took up jobs at the Department of Justice and practically ran an entire bootlegging operation.

Several members of Harding's cabinet conspired in underhanded dealings, from looting the Veterans' Bureau's supplies for personal profits to the exploitation of U.S. Navy oil reserves for corporate interests. Albeit hardly on the level, they weren't all members of the Ohio Gang. That bootlegger's cartel was spearheaded by Harry Daugherty, Harding's presidential campaign manager who was appointed U.S. attorney general. Despite Prohibition going into effect in 1920, select distillers were able to peddle "medicinal liquor" through a legal loophole—permits provided by Daugherty's Justice Department in exchange for bribes and kickbacks.

THE OHIO GANG

AND OTHERS

WARREN G. HARDING
President of the
United States

ALBERT B. FALL
Secretary of the Interior
ONE YEAR IN PRISON
Ⓐ Ⓔ

HARRY M. DAUGHERTY
U.S. Attorney General
CASE DISMISSED (HUNG JURY)
Ⓑ Ⓒ Ⓔ

CHARLES R. FORBES
Director of the Veterans' Bureau
TWO YEARS IN PRISON
Ⓓ

**EDWARD L.
DOHENY**
Owner, Pan-American
Petroleum and
Transport Company
**ACQUITTED OF
ALL CHARGES**
Ⓐ Ⓔ

HARRY SINCLAIR
Owner, Mammoth Oil
**NINE MONTHS
IN PRISON**
Ⓐ Ⓔ Ⓕ

JESS SMITH
Aide to Attorney General
**COMMITTED SUICIDE
(NO AUTOPSY)**
Ⓑ Ⓒ Ⓔ

**HOWARD
MANNINGTON**
Campaign contributor
**REFUSED TO TESTIFY
ON GROUNDS OF
CONSTITUTIONAL AUTHORITY**
Ⓑ

GASTON MEANS
Detective,
Bureau of Investigation
**TWO YEARS
IN PRISON**
Ⓑ Ⓖ

**GEORGE
REMUS**
"King of the
Bootleggers"
**TWO YEARS
IN PRISON**
Ⓑ Ⓔ

**COL. THOMAS
W. MILLER**
Alien Property
Custodian
**18 MONTHS
IN PRISON**
Ⓒ Ⓓ Ⓔ

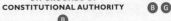

CRIMINAL ACTIVITY CODE

Ⓐ Conspiracy to exploit drilling
rights of U.S. Navy oil reserves

Ⓑ Bootlegging

Ⓒ Transferring of funds relating
to deposition of alien property

Ⓓ Conspiracy to defraud
U.S. government

Ⓔ Bribery

Ⓕ Contempt of court

Ⓖ Perjury

Daugherty alone may have permanently wrecked Harding's reputation as a public servant, although the president was never implicated in any of the administration's wrongdoings. Within a decade after the chief's fatal heart attack in 1923, two highly disputed tell-alls turned into bestsellers—Britton's *The President's Daughter* and *The Strange Death of President Harding* by Ohio Gang member Gaston Means—and revealed details related to Harding's philandering and supposed unlawful activity. (Given that these scandals didn't come to light until after the fifty-seven-year-old's unexpected death in the middle of his term, luck was on his side.)

To protect their namesake, surviving members of the Harding family restricted public access to presidential papers for nearly three decades. But the knee-jerk effort backfired. Without access to thousands of documents, journalists relied on what information was available—i.e., hometown gossip and half-truth trash—to retell the Harding story, a legacy that was soured by gangster cronies and a confidant named Jerry who couldn't say no.

VANILLA PUNCH

To battle the knockwurst and other hearty fare served in the Harding White House, it wouldn't have killed the president to try something light and sweet.

ice

1 tablespoon sugar

dash lemon juice

2 ounces brandy

a few drops vanilla extract

lemon peel

Pour the ice, sugar, lemon juice, and brandy into a tumbler. Shake well. Strain into a cocktail glass and add the vanilla extract. Garnish with the lemon peel. Serve with a straw.

Serves 1

THE UNKNOWN COMIC

AUGUST 2, 1923–MARCH 4, 1929

Calvin Coolidge

REPUBLICAN

30

Presidents are often remembered for their great oratorical moments. For Abraham Lincoln, it was the Gettysburg Address. John F. Kennedy's inaugural speech inspired generations. Dwight D. Eisenhower's forewarning of the military-industrial complex still resonates today. As for Calvin Coolidge, his legacy is rooted in his silence, which was legendary. Hence his nickname, "Silent Cal."

Voters knew what they were in for. After Warren G. Harding's corrupt administration, the people longed for a low-key president to simmer down Washington. Such was Vice President Coolidge, who assumed office at age fifty-two when Harding died in August 1923. (Coolidge was reelected in 1924.) Harding was a panty-sniffing, whiskey-smuggling sleaze-bag. Coolidge, by contrast, remained faithful to his wife, Grace, whom he had wed in 1905, and abided anti-drinking laws no matter how childish he found them. The president "did not believe in [P]rohibition any more than did the rest of sensible citizens," according to U.S. Secret Service agent Edmund Starling's 1946 autobiography, "but he observed it strictly while in the White House."

Coolidge maintained the lifestyle of the average hospital patient. Striving for eleven hours of sleep each night, the beady-eyed New Englander slipped into his pajamas by 10 p.m. He was also prone to afternoon naps, and the well-rested president caught flack for his somnolence. One evening, he attended the Marx Brothers' musical *Animal Crackers*. Onstage, a hawkeyed Groucho spotted the president in the audience and acknowledged his presence in true wisenheimer fashion: "Isn't it past your bedtime, Calvin?"

At photo ops, Coolidge flashed the obligatory smile and, against his better half's wishes, cut out early. Grace would be forced to make small talk in his absence. However, on occasions when he felt like opening his trap, Coolidge exhibited an excruciatingly dry sense of humor—a high-pitched nasal voice with an astringent delivery often lost on colleagues and constituents. To Coolidge's credit, some zingers were worthy of a vaudeville sketch; others made no sense whatsoever. But his acerbic nature was always a mainstay, and, perpetually in damage-control mode, the first lady frequently apologized for her condescending husband. One can see why:

☞ "Is the country still there?" he routinely asked an aide after waking from his naps.

☞ Before the White House and his three years as Massachusetts's forty-eighth governor, Coolidge spent five (nonconsecutive) years as a state legislator. During one session, a long-winded congressman harangued fellow representatives about supporting some notion, and he began almost every sentence with "It is." When the lecture was over, Coolidge, recognized by the floor, stood up and responded, "Mr. Speaker, it isn't." Then, he returned to his seat.

☞ Alice Roosevelt Longworth once asked Coolidge why he bothered with dinner parties if he hated dealing with crowds so much. His response: "Well, a man must eat."

☞ In 1918, shortly after Coolidge's gubernatorial election, a newspaper reporter named Bill stopped by unannounced to congratulate the governor-elect. As Coolidge made his way down the stairs to greet Bill, a family member asked, "Cal, aren't you going to give Bill a drink?" Silent Cal snatched two keys from his pocket, opened a closet door with one key and, inside the closet, unlocked a trunk with the other. He opened the trunk and carefully removed a bottle of liquor from the bottom. Then, he tediously pulled the cork from the bottle and took an empty glass. Bill waited as Coolidge poured a small drink, stuffed the cork back into the bottle, placed the bottle back into the trunk, closed the trunk, locked the trunk, and locked the closet door. A short time after, another reporter, this one named Jim, stopped by to pay his respects. Again, a relative gestured for Coolidge to offer Jim a drink. Coolidge smirked, then repeated the agonizing routine.

☞ In the hours leading up to one of those dreaded public events, Coolidge stopped by the White House kitchen to express gratitude for their hard work. Perspiring staffers were simultaneously preparing hors d'oeuvres and serving the first family's six canines. "Mighty fine-looking dog food," the president said.

☞ When an author approached the president with the prospect of writing his biography, Coolidge replied, "Better wait 'til I'm dead."

☞ At a campaign stop in 1924, reporters asked the incumbent if he would comment on reelection chances, Prohibition, and the state of world affairs. "No," Coolidge repeatedly answered. "No. No." The mob dispersed. "Now, remember," Coolidge shouted at the backs of their heads, "don't quote me."

3 FACTS YOU MIGHT NOT KNOW ABOUT
Calvin Coolidge

He liked to sleep for eleven hours a night.

He was made an honorary Sioux chief.

He was president of the United States.

THE CLOVER CLUB COCKTAIL

While Coolidge was sleeping, the Clover Club in Philadelphia held meet-ups at the Bellevue-Stratford hotel. As far back as the 1880s, the informal men's club, populated mostly by attorneys and aspiring comedians, named a cocktail after itself. Before Prohibition, the Clover Club Cocktail turned up in bar columns and New York City hot spots. Jeannette Young Norton managed to preserve the recipe in her 1917 collection *Mrs. Norton's Cook-Book*.

2 ounces gin

juice of ½ lemon

½ teaspoon sugar

1 ounce grenadine

1 egg white

clover mint for garnish

Combine all the ingredients in a tumbler and shake well. Strain into a glass. Top with the clover mint.

// **Serves 1** //

LOCK, STOCK, AND BOOTLEGGER'S BARRELS

MARCH 4, 1929–MARCH 4, 1933

Herbert Hoover

REPUBLICAN

Herbert Hoover once said that the day's finest hour—cocktail hour—was "the pause between the errors and trials of the day and hopes of the night." Before his appointment as secretary of commerce in 1920, the millionaire philanthropist traveled the world and collected nice things. Screw the expensive antiques and precious china picked up along the way. His prized possession must have been the outstanding wine cellar from the estate of California sena-tor Leland Stanford, the founder of

Concealing hooch was not only customary; it was required.

Hoover's alma mater. Sadly, Hoover did not have the opportunity to make a dent in the late senator's collection. To save face during the era of Prohibition, Hoover's wife, Lou Henry, gave away their remaining stock in 1919. Talk about charity.

Oh, the devastation for Hoover to see his collection wind up somewhere other than his liver; but weep not for the secretary. At a time when buying alcohol was forbidden, the cabinet member made perfectly legal pit stops on the way home from the Department of Commerce. Every day at 6 p.m. Hoover paid a visit to the Belgian embassy for gin and vermouth, stirred.

In 1928, however, cocktail hour for President-elect Hoover was nonexistent. "Mr. and Mrs. Hoover were keenly aware that, as public figures, they were subject to increased scrutiny," said an archivist at the Herbert Hoover National Historic Site. "So they avoided any appearance of impropriety." And yet, during Prohibition, impropriety was in vogue. If you were once a law-abiding lush, by the mid-1920s you more than likely turned into a full-blown alcoholic. Concealing hooch was not only customary; it was required. And since beer and wine were hardly flask-friendly, hard liquor occupied the breast pockets and ankle socks of America—the contents of which (Canadian whiskeys, harsh ryes, bathtub gins) were in need of drastic improvement.

Enter the twentieth-century bartender, who transformed illegal mouthwash into concoctions that were tolerable enough to swallow. Gone were the days of casually eyeballing measurements into relatively clean glasses. Speakeasy culture introduced flowery liqueurs, fruity mixers, and meticulous recipes to mask the fumes of distilled toilet water. Ridiculous outfits provided a theatrical, almost Disneyland vibe. And let us not forget the gimmickry! At the Merry-Go-Round in midtown Manhattan, patrons drank bootlegged liquor while mounted on carousel horses that took eleven-minute laps around the bar. The amount of vomit accrued on the floorboards is unknown.

Merry-Go-Round
Restaurant & Bar,
146–148 E. 56th St.

THE ST. VALENTINE'S DAY MASSACRE

On February 14, 1929, four unidentified men dressed as police officers gunned down seven members of George "Bugs" Moran's crew. At the crime scene, a beer depot on Chicago's North Side, cops counted more than one hundred empty bullet casings. Newspapermen did not hesitate to sensationalize. "The roar of the shotguns mingled with the rat-a-tat of the machine gun," the New York Times reported, "a clatter like that of a gigantic typewriter."

Committed to campaign promises made to advocates of Prohibition, Hoover did not partake in the Roaring Twenties' shenanigans, but he certainly read about them. Club owners made a figurative killing—squeezing customers $1 for ten cigarettes, $10 for a pint of whiskey, and $2 for soda backs—and their mobster wholesalers literally killed. Territorial disputes erupted into a gangland war epidemic, which proponents of temperance somehow interpreted as reason to keep anti-drinking laws in place. Brilliant deduction, teetotalers: Homicide rates continued to spike, prisons overpopulated, and, in 1929, the St. Valentine's Day Massacre took the national spotlight, glorifying bootlegger-related violence (see box).

Saloonkeepers and crooked bureaucrats colluded with underworld factions. Chicago Police Commissioner William F. Russell declared "a war to the finish" against gangsters and bribed officials. He ordered the removal of secret buzzer systems and questionable doorways while conducting militant speakeasy raids. It was this sort of urban combat that kept Hollywood genre writers employed for decades and enabled Hoover to become the first president to reference crime in an inaugural address. Corruption on the streets, he argued, "is only in part due to the additional burdens imposed upon our judicial system by the Eighteenth Amendment." In May 1929, he established a National Commission on Law Observance and Enforcement, whose eleven members concluded that the repeal of Prohibition could very well end the bloodshed. The martini-loving president knew it in his heart to be true, but his hands were tied. Progressives attacked. "Mr. Hoover stands revealed as the driest body this side of the Sahara," wrote syndicated columnist Heywood Broun. "He is for the Methodist Board of Morals lock, stock, and bootlegger's barrels."

A wooden public persona and the stock market crash of 1929 largely wrecked Hoover's chances for a second term. The Hoovers kept their personal lives out of the public eye, even though revealing a human side could have boosted reelection chances. (Friends and colleagues who spent time with the president in smaller circles remembered him as chatty and a joke-teller.) But failing to repeal the Eighteenth Amendment was surely a factor.

In October 1931, almost one year before Franklin D. Roosevelt won by a landslide in the presidential election, Hoover threw out the first ball at the World Series in Philadelphia's Shibe Park. He was booed. "We want beer!" the crowd chanted at the president. "We want beer! We want beer!" (Looking back on that day years later, Hoover joked, "You know, there were a number of thirsty people present with no patience for constitutional process.")

After Roosevelt took office and Prohibition was repealed, Hoover returned to the sideboard. He had two martinis at the day's finest hour until his personal physician recommended he cut back to one. Hoover relented, but not before switching to the largest martini glass he could find.

//

RAMOS GIN FIZZ

In 1880s New Orleans, bartender Henry C. Ramos reeled in Big Easy tourist dollars with this frothy number that, according to the *Kansas City Star*, transformed his Imperial Cabinet Saloon into "the most famous gin fizz saloon in the world." The hot spot didn't last, of course, as soon as Prohibition shrouded the land. But, had the law allowed, a gin-loving Hoover surely would have approved.

---

1 tablespoon powdered sugar

3 to 4 drops orange flower water

juice of half a lime

juice of half a lemon

1½ ounces Old Tom or Plymouth gin

1 egg white

crushed ice

2 tablespoons 1 percent milk or heavy cream

1 ounce seltzer water

Pour all the ingredients except the seltzer into a tumbler. Shake until there is a bubble-less, smooth consistency. Strain into a glass. Top with the seltzer. Give a light stir before serving.

//////////////// **Serves 1** ////////////////

AMERICAN HERO, AWFUL BARTENDER

MARCH 4, 1933–APRIL 12, 1945

Franklin D. Roosevelt

32

DEMOCRAT

There are obvious reasons why C-SPAN's Historians' Presidential Leadership Survey has consistently listed Franklin Delano Roosevelt as one of the top three commanders in chief. He put the kibosh on the Great Depression with his New Deal program. His "arsenal of democracy" prevailed over Nazi Germany. He restructured federal government to protect the little guy instead of Big Business. Yet during an unprecedented four terms, for a total of twelve years as president, Roosevelt accomplished an even greater feat, making perhaps the most sensible, heroic, and utterly compassionate executive decision by anyone to reside at 1600 Pennsylvania Avenue.

He repealed Prohibition.

It was an unavoidable issue for the former New York governor. The dastardly body of law had been in full force for far too long, about fourteen years, and annual alcohol consumption had taken a nosedive to less than a gallon per person. After the 1929 stock market crash, people were dying of thirst and avoiding the local speakeasies for fear of police brutality. America needed a real political hero to put bread and booze in the mouths of thirteen million unemployed citizens.

When Roosevelt stepped into office in 1933, fascism was on the rise in Europe, and the Great Depression was crushing the nation. And yet the new president made it a top priority to see that, first and foremost, average citizens could get their hands on liquid happiness—legally.

On March 9, 1933, five days after his inauguration, Roosevelt had Congress convene in a special session to re-legalize booze. A number of special interest groups were pushing for Prohibition's repeal to boost the economy and tax revenues, and the academic community, aka "wet intellectuals," believed that hooch benefited medical studies. One of these believers was Dr. Samuel Harden Church, president of the Carnegie Institute of Technology in Pittsburgh, who praised liquor as "one of the greatest blessings that God has given to men out of the teeming bosom of Mother Earth."

Repeal was an essential pillar to Roosevelt's 1932 presidential campaign, and when the fifty-one-year-old moved into the White House, he kept his word. On December 5, 1933, at 5:32 p.m., Congress amicably passed the Twenty-first Amendment. As the ink from Roosevelt's ratification signature was still drying, he said, "I believe this would be a good time for a beer."

And freedom reigned. "The country is deluged," one scholar accounted. "Barrel-houses have consequently sprung up all over the state . . . Long distance beer trucks cross and re-cross the country with huge trailers, running from a Pueblo [Colorado] brewery to points between Dallas, Texas, and South Dakota." In Chicago, nightlife had "a host of new evils," according to the Juvenile Protective Association, including the exploitation of women. No, not Jell-O wrestling contests, but "girl hostesses" who coerced bar patrons into emptying their pocketbooks. The JPA also claimed that "parents are having to prosecute proprietors of school-supply and lunch rooms for selling liquor to their children." Meanwhile, Chicago must have had the highest turnout for school lunches in U.S. history.

Schenley Distillers Corporation, as a publicity stunt at their Delaware plant, had a worker strap on safety goggles and shatter the chains from stacks of kegs. A few years later, brewers leaned on members of Congress to pass a bill that would legalize the curbside sale of beer. Yes, the president had unlocked the gates to a paradise of potentials, but, as much as one would like to believe that Roosevelt's push for repeal was an utterly selfless act, public outcry wasn't the sole reason for his signing the Twenty-first Amendment. This was personal.

"Before dinner we usually had martini cocktails made by the President's own hands," according to cabinet member Robert H. Jackson's memoir *That Man: An Insider's Portrait of Franklin D. Roosevelt*, "but any impression that the President was given to any considerable amount of drinking . . . is a mistake. I never knew him to take more than a couple of cocktails, nor did he want anyone about him who drank to excess. He aimed for two cocktails before dinner and then perhaps a smidgen afterward."

Jackson is, of course, applying a bit of whitewash. When the first family vacationed at their summer home on Canada's Campobello Island, Roosevelt would go boating and fishing (read: get blasted). When the workweek was up, the president would retreat to his Hyde Park mansion in New York and invite Hollywood luminaries, as well as other lefty weekend warriors. You couldn't talk about the war or politics at said gatherings; you just had to endure FDR's eccentric bartending skills. A variety of recipes for his Plymouth martinis have been documented, all in a rather disapproving context. Some guests didn't like the combined garnish of olives and lemon peels. Others dismissed his choice of fruit juices. Supreme Court Justice Samuel Rosenman would dump his beverage into a flowerpot no matter what the mixture, but the most common criticism? Too much vermouth.

FDR's sons would pressure him into using different gin-vermouth ratios. Jimmy suggested a 3-to-1; Elliot pushed for 4-to-1; Johnny advocated a stout 6-to-1. "They were not that strong," grandson Curtis told the History Channel in 2005. "He'd throw in a little gin at the end . . . He'd also put in two or three drops of absinthe, changing the taste of a martini to where many people—and this is recorded—say 'the president made the worst martinis I've ever tasted.'"

ROOSEVELT MAY HAVE BEEN HOBBLED BY POLIO, BUT HIS DISEASE MUST not have been the sole purpose for that wheelchair. During the war, the president opened the liquor cabinet to White House guests "every single night," according to historian Doris Kearns Goodwin. ("It was important to him to relax," she said.) FDR smoked a pack of cigarettes every day, right up until his health took a turn for the worse. In response to conservatives who called him a "dictator" for his big government philosophy, the White House threw a Roman toga costume party for his fifty-second birthday. He wore a knock-off version of Julius Caesar's civic crown and, as the evening unfolded, probably popped a wheelie.

As for the first lady, Eleanor Roosevelt's two uncles were such lushes that the family couldn't invite company to the house. As a result, she rarely touched the stuff. In the 1920s, she preached about drinking responsibilities—not exactly the type of discourse that FDR would entertain. Perhaps Eleanor did not realize the ways in which the bottle assisted the president on the job, specifically with foreign policy. In 1938, when King George and Queen Elizabeth paid a visit to the U.S., FDR had a cocktail shaker chilled and waiting in the library. (Three years before the U.S. entered World War II, and the cunning Roosevelt was already cultivating the English.) Prime Minister Winston Churchill visited the White House for two to three weeks at a time during the war, and the English bulldog pulled all-nighters accompanied by snifters of brandy and cigars.

"Before breakfast, [Churchill] preferred a tumbler of sherry, and he would have that as his eye-opener," recalled White House butler Alonzo Fields. "For lunch, he started drinking scotch and soda, and he'd drink scotch and soda until he'd take a nap. And at dinner, he had to have his champagne and ninety-year-old brandy." The president ruggedly engaged in the Brit's benders, or what the White House staff called keeping "Winston hours." To recuperate, FDR would sleep ten hours a night for three days in a row.

In later years, Elliot remembered his father telling him about the "three hundred and sixty-five toasts, one for every day in the year" during the famous Tehran Conference of 1943. Cigarette ashes smudged his lapels all week, but FDR didn't care. He was too busy practically double-fisting vodkas and champagne with Churchill and Joseph Stalin. He even told the Soviet leader that he wanted to market the Russian bubbly to Americans back home. And there is, of course, the legendary episode in which Roosevelt turned the dour

After FDR's toga party on January 30, 1934, a speechwriter would lightheartedly address Roosevelt as "Dear Caesar" in their written correspondence. The president eventually asked him to stop, according to historian Conrad Black, "fearing the press might get hold of such a letter and misconstrue it."

LUCY

Despite his nonexistent hip muscles, FDR got around. From staff member Missy LeHand to *New York Post* publisher Dorothy Schiff, Roosevelt had several alleged extramarital affairs, the most recognized of which was with his wife's assistant, Lucy Mercer. The tryst lasted two years before Eleanor discovered their love letters in 1918. ("The bottom dropped out of my . . . world," the first lady later admitted.) There was talk of divorce, but Eleanor supposedly refused, knowing that a breakup would ruin chances for a political future—although conflicting reports allude to possible interventions by either advisor Louis Howe or her mother-in-law, Sara Ann Delano Roosevelt.

The marriage continued, as did the hanky-panky. White House visitor logs indicate that between the summer of 1941 and winter of 1942, Mercer frequented the address at least eleven times, on occasion twice in one day.

Russian leader on to that great gift of democracy: the martini. Stalin politely finished his and said, "Well, all right, but it is cold on the stomach." This amounted to the only weakness that Stalin would show during the conference. Latter-day Soviet Premier Nikita Khrushchev would elaborate, declaring the martini "America's lethal weapon."

Clearly, FDR's boozing played an intrinsic part in international diplomacy and, ultimately, liberating the Western world from totalitarianism. No wonder there's a joint in Munich called the Roosevelt Bar.

HAITIAN LIBATION

When FDR was appointed assistant secretary of the Navy, he went to Haiti, where he learned to make "this deplorable invention," according to his son James Roosevelt in *Affectionately, F.D.R.* "If he continues serving this abomination, he won't have any friends."

1½ ounces orange juice

3 ounces dark rum

1 egg white

dash brown sugar

ice

Pour the ingredients into a frosted tumbler. Shake and strain into a rocks glass. Good luck.

/// **Serves 1** ///

STRAIGHT SHOOTER

APRIL 12, 1945–JANUARY 20, 1953

Harry S. Truman

DEMOCRAT

G rieving the loss of Franklin D. Roosevelt, who suffered a fatal stroke at the beginning of his fourth term, the average voter was fraught with uncertainty. And feelings were especially shaky after Vice President Harry Truman took the oath of office on April 12, 1945.

What to make of this accidental president, a Midwestern commoner who had peddled off-brand fedoras in a Kansas City haberdashery and made little impression upon his colleagues in the U.S. Senate for ten years? Truman was no insider. At the 1944 Democratic National Convention, Roosevelt selected the meek senator as his running mate as more or less a token of goodwill toward conservative factions within the party.

At first glance, Truman looked like the kind of guy one would cut off in traffic without hesitation. He did not possess a smidgen of FDR's panache, the people thought, and no way could he settle the Pacific theater of World War II, let alone union strikes and inflation issues. Bureaucrats called him "Back Porch Harry," a snide comment in reference to his plebeian demeanor. Amusingly, in the decades to come, revisionists would praise the failed retailer as one of the most resolute and gutsy men to ever rest his keister in the Oval Office chair. But, before Back Porch Harry jump-started modern civil rights legislation and dropped nukes on Japan, he would require a stiff one. On the afternoon

Harry and Bessie
never missed
a sunset.

of Roosevelt's death, when the sixty-year-old received a message to call White House Press Secretary Stephen Early "right away" to discuss his imminent inauguration, the vice president poured himself a shot before dialing.

A **PEEK INTO TRUMAN'S MEMOIRS REVEALS THE MISSOURI NATIVE OFTEN** worked up his nerve with the help of bourbon, or, as family physician Philip D. Reister put it, "He'd get in his cups." At 5 a.m., Truman's routine began as always: a reasonable breakfast that included a piece of toast, fruit, an egg, and maybe a strip of bacon. Afterward, he took a two-mile walk. Then, he returned home for a shower and an ounce of Old Grand-Dad "to get the engine going." In retirement, this daily habit continued with the intent to battle low blood pressure. Even *Truman*, David McCullough's cinder block of a biography, could not crack the case on that one. "Whether the bourbon was on doctor's orders, or a bit of old-fashioned home medicine of the kind many of his generation thought beneficial to the circulation . . . is not known," the author wrote. "But it seemed to agree with him."

Bourbon seemed to agree with Truman in most settings. At the 1948 DNC, columnists from the *New York Herald Tribune* remembered that moments before accepting the presidential nomination for a second term, Truman "took a pull on a half-bottle of liquid that was in his pocket." (One would assume the president of the United States wouldn't have to wrestle with the burden of carrying his own flask!) In 1947, in the face of White House restoration critics, he ordered the addition of a veranda to the South Portico—he and the first lady needed a sunset cocktail spot.

As a senator, Truman held meetings with committee members in "the Dog House," an inner office in his space on the Senate Office Building's second floor. The middle-aged man cave was sparsely furnished—nothing but ratty leather chairs, a fridge, bottles of whiskey, and landscape portraits of the Civil War. As president, Truman downed more bourbon while attending to his "favorite form of paperwork" at the card table. But on nights when he was particularly stressed, Truman ditched after-hours poker. Staff sometimes found the president in bed by 8 p.m.

Truman biographer William P. Helm watched the president toss back five whiskeys like water. "Not once did I ever see him under the slightest influence of liquor," Helm said. Others witnessed similar superpowers on foreign soil. While attending the Potsdam Conference in the summer of 1945, an economist from the U.S. Treasury Department remembered one Saturday afternoon walking into Truman's temporary residence and finding seated at the piano "an alert small man in shirtsleeves with a drink on the corner of the piano." Leaning against the instrument were Secretary of State James F. Byrnes and five-star admiral William D. Leahy, both without suit jackets and belting out lyrics to a ragtime number. "I can't say the singing was very high quality," recalled the economist, "but the piano playing was quite good."

In retirement, Truman upped his dosage of "a little H_2O flavored with bourbon," although his tolerance did not increase. As later revealed by Dr. Reister in 2001, it was one of those morning eye-openers that caused the former president's highly publicized spill in the upstairs bathroom of his Missouri home. On October 13, 1964, Truman's wife, Bessie, was at a bridge game when the eighty-year-old slipped on the bathmat and cracked his head against the sink, breaking his eyeglasses. Then he hit his chest against the tub, fracturing two ribs. A housekeeper heard the president's fall and rushed to dial an ambulance— shot of bourbon, STAT!

"OLD-FASHIONEDS"

In the Trumans' first week at 1600 Penn, butler Alonzo Fields would discover the meaning behind the president's pet name for his wife. According to Chief Usher J. B. West's *Upstairs at the White House*, "the Boss" ordered "two old-fashioneds" for herself and the president. Fields, no slouch with a muddler, arrived with chilled glasses filled with citrus peels, bitters, and whiskey. Bess took a sip, gave a sour smile, and passive-aggressively thanked him. The next evening, she asked Fields for two more "old-fashioneds" but made "a little drier."

"We don't like them so sweet," she explained.

Fields went light on the ingredients, only to find out later that the Boss was just as critical. "They're like fruit punch!" Bessie told usher West.

On the third evening, Fields made the below modification to the recipe. The bumpkin approved. "Now that's the way we like our old-fashioneds," she said.

---

bourbon

ice

Add the ingredients to a tumbler. Drink.

////////////// **Serves 1** //////////////

FIRST COUCH POTATOES

JANUARY 20, 1953–JANUARY 20, 1961

Dwight D. Eisenhower

REPUBLICAN

He was a prude. She was stingy. Together, they presided over a decade that has been roundly accepted as a prosperous, booming time for the United States—unless you were black, of course; or unless you lived in areas that were razed during the construction of the Interstate Highway System. A glance beyond the suburbia porn of the Fabulous Fifties might reveal a middle class that was so worn out from fighting in World War II and the Korean conflict, no one had the energy to care about civil rights or poverty. The Greatest Generation clocked in the necessary hours at the job and headed back to their families for casserole night.

Dwight David Eisenhower and his wife, Mamie, epitomized this kind of household. The celebrity five-star general enjoyed golf with corporate execs and nursed Chivas Regal like a geriatric Ward Cleaver. The coupon-clipping Mamie would not serve guests liquor before 6 p.m. ("Don't give them time to have more than one drink," she instructed staff.) At state dinners, wine was used for toasts only. The first couple, already grandparents, spent quiet evenings much like the rest of exhausted America: entranced by the hypnotic glow of television. Or they were loud evenings, depending on the TV volume.

Boob tubery was covered at the White House.

With a set in the West Sitting Hall and a second in the president's study, boob tubery was covered at the White House. On your average night, the general and first lady requested meals on TV trays, served in the West Hall, where they would watch the news, *I Love Lucy*, *You Bet Your Life*, and *Arthur Godfrey's Talent Scouts*.

Mamie's widely reported favorite was *As the World Turns*, CBS's daytime soap that belonged to a genre she found "touching, very true to life." Unlike Eleanor Roosevelt's civil rights activism or Bess Truman's charity work for the March of Dimes, Mamie limited her role of first lady to a domestic capacity. On the occasion that she left 1600 Penn for who knows what purpose (ran out of Mallomars? Beatnik orgy? Pray tell, Mamie!) and would miss an episode, a Secret Service agent was given orders to watch and take notes.

But Ike and Mamie weren't always in front of a TV. Sometimes they watched movies. In the family screening room, Eisenhower installed four giant armchairs with footstools in the first row. White House projectionist Paul Fischer noted Eisenhower's preference for westerns. *High Noon*, starring Gary Cooper, was in the rotation, but scratch any films featuring Robert Mitchum. The president wrote him off after the actor served two months in Los Angeles County jail for marijuana possession. "We would sometimes try to sneak Mitchum films on him," Fischer said, "but as soon as he saw Mitchum was in it, he got up and walked out."

The president was critical of more than just reefer. As smoking reached the apex of cool, Eisenhower quit cold turkey. In 1949, the general suffered lower

INTRODUCING...
HOME ENTERTAINMENT AS NEVER BEFORE
In Your House as in the White House

President Dwight D. Eisenhower

The All-New Sensation from
UNITED ELECTRICAL CORPORATION

HIS & HERS
TELEVISION SETS

SUPERIOR RECEPTION, STUNNING DISPLAY,
STATE-OF-THE-ART SOUND AND RELIABILITY

First Lady Mamie Eisenhower

"JUST LIKE WHAT IKE LIKES!"

AVAILABLE FOR PURCHASE AT BETTER RETAILERS. MADE IN AMERICA.

abdominal pains and laid off the four-packs-per-day habit for a stint. The stint turned permanent. "If I had lived for ten days without a cigarette," Eisenhower wrote in *At Ease: Stories I Tell to Friends*, "I could get along without them for another ten days, ten years or ten decades." He tested his willpower by keeping cigs in pockets and at his desk. At meetings, Eisenhower "made it a practice to offer a cigarette to anyone who came in," he told a friend. "I lighted each while mentally reminding myself as I sat down, 'I don't have to do what that poor fellow is doing.'"

His scotch consumption, however, increased after a September 1955 heart attack hospitalized the president for nearly two months. Previously, as son John recalled, Eisenhower drank five ounces daily. Then his valet "would bring him a short one just before dinner." After the attack, personal physician Howard McCrum Snyder, who kept meticulous records of presidential intake, noted that "several scotches" became the norm.

In 1961, the Eisenhowers retired to their farm and installed an RCA Victor color television in the master bedroom. The former president kept a *TV Guide* in his lap and hogged the remote control, which drove his old lady nuts. "His switching back and forth between his favorites and Mamie's every ninety seconds or so was a habit that upset Mamie," according to grandson David. He'd compulsively flip between *Rawhide, Donna Reed, Perry Mason,* and back to *Rawhide.* "Ike," Mamie snapped, "make up your mind."

//

EGGNOG

The Dwight D. Eisenhower Presidential Library and Museum has a notebook filled with newspaper clippings of the daredevil first couple's recipe favorites. Here's one for eggnog that they enjoyed before bungee-jumping off the veranda.

12 egg yolks

1 pound sugar

1 quart bourbon

1 quart whole milk

1 quart whipping cream

nutmeg shavings for garnish

Drop the egg yolks into a mixer and beat on a low setting. Gradually pour in the sugar while beating. Still beating, slowly add the bourbon over an excruciating 30-minute span. Stop the mixer and add the milk and whipping cream. Place the mixture in the freezer for 30 minutes. When serving, garnish with the nutmeg shavings.

// **Serves 25** //

THE CARNAL ADVENTURES OF
JFK
AND HIS HIGHLY INFLUENTIAL
VICE PRESIDENT,"JJ"

JANUARY 20, 1961–NOVEMBER 22, 1963

John F. Kennedy

35

DEMOCRAT

L ike some mythical rock star enjoying both his first chart-topping record and his cocaine addiction, John F. Kennedy had problems remembering the names of his sexual conquests. As problems go, this was a bit like having too much money, or too many friends. But it was a dilemma nonetheless. Kennedy's standard opening line for those occasions when he would come across an old fling was the catch-all "Hello, kid," which no doubt sounded less cheesy when delivered in his Boston accent. And time was precious in his pants-dropping schedule. "We have only fifteen minutes," he said to an attractive college student while on the 1960 campaign trail. One mistress joked that while he was in bed, Kennedy kept one eye on his wristwatch. Always a charmer.

Kennedy's indiscretions were not limited to his 1,036 days as president. From losing his virginity at age seventeen to a prostitute in Harlem, to rendezvousing with movie actresses as a senator, to skinny-dipping in the White House indoor pool with interns nicknamed Fiddle and Faddle, sex was both his life force and his main vice. During a meeting with British prime minister Harold Macmillan in December 1961, Kennedy over-shared that if he did not slip the presidential sausage to a woman once every three days, he would get a splitting headache. "I can't get to sleep unless I've had a lay," the satyromaniac once admitted, for some reason, to a United States ambassador. Does the fact that said ambassador was a woman make his comment more or less sleazy? And did he consider taking his problem to a medical professional?

It was pretty stressful for anyone working in the White House at that time. A purported champion of civil rights and world peace whose intense diplomacy during the Cuban Missile Crisis protected the country from nuclear annihilation—even as he concealed a severe illness from the public—JFK remains an inspirational figure in American history. How could the youngest man elected president perform under the pressures of the Cold War and the agonies of Addison's disease? Popeye the Sailor Man had his cans of spinach. For Kennedy, it was poontang.

AN AIDE ONCE ASKED THE PRESIDENT IN CONFIDENCE IF HE UNDERstood the root of his sex addiction. "I don't know, really," Kennedy answered. "I guess I just can't help it." Perhaps the behavior was learned from his womanizing father, Joseph Kennedy Sr., a business magnate and renowned bootlegger who owned a piece of Hollywood. Despite a reputation for being a devious swindler with mafia ties, Papa Joe provided for his family. In 1929, he established a trust fund that would distribute more than $1 million to each of his children when they reached the age of twenty-one. By 1949, each of the Kennedy children was to receive more than $10 million.

Kennedy Sr. dispensed the gift of sagacity and Buddhist-like wisdom as well: "Dad told all the boys to get laid as often as possible," JFK once said of his father. No wonder he turned into one of the twentieth century's most successful cocksmen. In his twenties, Kennedy cranked up the sexual odometer. In 1938, when his twenty-one-year-old penis—lovingly named "JJ"—was circumcised, he reported back to an old prep school roommate that little JJ "has never been in better shape or doing better service." At some point during these adolescent escapades, Kennedy picked up a case of nonspecific urethritis. It went untreated; consequently, he dealt with constant flare-ups for the rest of his life. (Even as late as April 14, 1961, approximately seventy-two hours prior to the Bay of Pigs invasion, the president ordered a doctor to the White House to examine a "burning" sensation and "occasional mucus" when he peed.)

"Dad told all the boys to get laid as often as possible."

Packing a flamethrower in his shorts was not Kennedy's primary ailment. Since his days at Choate, he suffered from bouts of colitis, one of many symptoms related to Addison's disease. These included chronic back pains that underwent heavy testing and under-the-radar care from several specialists. "There was a hole in his back that had never closed up after the operation," one friend said. "You could look into it and see the metal plate that had been put into his spine." Over the years, Kennedy struggled to climb flights of stairs, let alone endure the physical demands of back-to-back campaign stops. There was one upside to the medical attention: During longer hospital stays, the patient received visits from young women who were supposedly his "cousins."

At twenty-four, Kennedy was appointed ensign at the Office of Naval Intelligence. While working at a position in the capital that was presumably orchestrated by his father (no way could rancid JJ pass the physical exam!), Kennedy fell in love with one Inga Arvad, a Dane who was four years his senior. Turn-ons? She had blond hair, blue eyes, and the curves Kennedy men loved. Turn-offs? She *might* have been a communist spy and was admired by the Führer. "Inga Binga," as Kennedy called her, won a beauty contest in 1930s Berlin and was adored by leading members of the Nazi Party. Hitler, channeling his inner Hefner, called her a "perfect example of Nordic beauty."

During World War II, when she worked at a Washington newspaper, federal agents tapped Ms. Binga's phone line, listening in on numerous calls to her horny boyfriend. "A titillated J. Edgar Hoover was delighted at hearing Jack's voice with Inga's," according to Herbert Parmet's *Jack: The Struggles of John F. Kennedy.* (Which party titillated Hoover is subject to debate.) When word spread that the ensign might be shacked up with the enemy, Joseph Kennedy Sr. made arrangements to split up the lovebirds and save the family the potential shame of a military discharge. His son was deployed to Panama and, eventually, the Pacific theater. "[Some] son of a bitch had transferred me to sea duty," JFK complained to Arvad, "and I'm going to find out who it was."

THAT TRANSFER MIGHT HAVE BEEN THE BEST THING THAT COULD HAVE happened to the sailor with the dirty dick.

When the Japanese destroyed his torpedo boat in 1943, Kennedy famously rescued his fellow crew members. He left the war with impenetrable confidence, a Harvard pedigree, a celebrated family, and a "bumper crop of lightly combed brown hair," according to the *Saturday Evening Post,* that "always makes him look as though he had just stepped out of a shower." He was a sure shot for Congress.

Yet Kennedy's 1953 marriage to Jacqueline Bouvier and the glare of the public spotlight hardly stopped him from fooling around. How could this devastatingly handsome trust-fund baby give up one-night stands? He "didn't have to lift a finger to attract women," *New York Times* writer Gloria Emerson said. "They were drawn to him in battalions."

The most famous enlisted member in said battalion was Marilyn Monroe. In *The Dark Side of Camelot,* Seymour Hersh puts the start of the JFK-Monroe affair sometime during his first term in the senate (1953–58). By the time Kennedy launched his presidential bid in 1960, the actress "was in love with JFK," an Associated Press reporter told Hersh. Somewhat at odds with Hersh's assessment, Monroe biographer J. Randy Taraborrelli gathered that the pair had one or two romps at best. Regardless of how often they schtupped, historians and muckrakers commonly agree upon one getaway location for mattress action: the Santa Monica residence of Peter and Patricia Lawford, Kennedy's brother-in-law and younger sister.

White House Tours

Regardless of frequency, the tryst did not end well. According to Senator George Smathers, a friend and campaign manager of Kennedy's, the president told Monroe—she of the famous naked pictorials and failed marriages—"You're not really first lady material." Historians consider these words the greatest understatement uttered in all of 1962.

Even with highly publicized flirtations (see "Lip Service"), JFK somehow managed to never get busted. At times, it seemed as if the entire White House staff had pitched in to help the adulterous president cover his tracks.

"There was a conspiracy of silence to protect his secrets from Jacqueline and to keep her from finding out," wrote White House kennel keeper Traphes L. Bryant. "The newspapers would tell how First Lady Jacqueline was off on another trip, but what they didn't report was how anxious the president sometimes was to see her go." After Kennedy sipped daiquiris and took naked swims with beautiful women, a clean-up crew swept in to remove any leftover jewelry, hairpins, or underwear. Again, the early '60s were a tense time for those in government.

The left coast provided more efficient means to score tail with less worry. On occasions when JFK spent weekends at Frank Sinatra's place in Palm Springs, Ol' Blue Eyes renamed the star-studded entourage "the Jack Pack." ("That was not a weekend you brought the kids into," daughter Tina Sinatra said.) There were, of course, other choice venues for making whoopee. The Sands Hotel in Las Vegas was an old standby for Beefeater gin martinis and chasing showgirls around a suite, and Lawford's digs in Santa Monica still befitted as a reliable hump pad. His brother-in-law kept it short about "Jack and his broads" in *His Way*, Kitty Kelley's unauthorized Sinatra biography. "I'm not proud of this," Lawford said. "All I will say is that I was Frank's pimp and Frank was Jack's. It sounds terrible now, but then it was a lot of fun."

Surely one highlight took place at 1600 Penn when Lawford and Kennedy gave a dose of amyl nitrite to either Fiddle or Faddle (who can keep track?) and watched as the intern suffered a panic attack. They were both too chicken to try the poppers themselves, but Kennedy dabbled in more than his share

> # "You're not really first lady material."

of psychedelics. One night, at the height of the Cold War, Jack smoked three marijuana cigarettes with Mary Pinchot Meyer, the ex-wife of a CIA official and—shockingly—a Kennedy mistress who visited the White House two to three times a week when Jackie was out of town. When offered a fourth joint, the president begged off. "Suppose the Russians did something now," wondered the bloodshot-eyed leader of the free world. Apparently, one can deal with a Soviet ripple in the Cold War when stoned—just not *that* stoned.

LIP SERVICE

On May 29, 1962, not three months before Monroe's death, Lawford's agent shoved Monroe onto the stage at Madison Square Garden during a Democratic fund-raiser, which doubled as JFK's forty-fifth birthday celebration. The first lady was traveling overseas when the heavily intoxicated, and still sultry, actress fumbled through her iconic "Happy Birthday, Mr. President." Afterward, Kennedy expressed his gratitude to those in attendance. "Thank you," he said. "I can now retire from politics after having had, ah, 'Happy Birthday' sung to me in such a sweet, wholesome way."

NO MATTER HOW MANY MÉNAGES À TROIS KENNEDY RACKED UP, HIS back pain would not subside. (Whether all this hanky panky was the smartest activity for a man with a bad back is another question.) Dr. Max Jacobson, MD, ran a quack practice on Manhattan's Upper East Side. A chemically dependent celebrity clientele paid visits to "Dr. Feelgood" for "pep pills" and "vitamin injections," aka 30 to 50 milligrams of pure amphetamine. Singer Eddie Fisher called him "my god." Surely not by coincidence, Aretha Franklin's "Dr. Feelgood" on her 1967 debut album contains the lyrics "that man takes care of all my pains and my ills." Ostensibly, it was Kennedy's Hollywood network that connected the good doctor and the president during the 1960 presidential campaign.

Thanks to Dr. Feelgood's questionable meds, Kennedy was able to withstand televised debates against Vice President Richard M. Nixon. (Crutches, the other alternative, would have not been a good look—although next to the unshaven, slumping Nixon, who knows?) By the summer of 1961, the president was hooked—as was Jackie. After all, when your husband is on a mission to bone half of the planet, it's probably best to enjoy whatever convenient escapes

RING-A-DING-DONG

In December 1962, Kennedy and a few cronies crashed Bing Crosby's estate in Palm Springs. A United States Secret Serviceman claimed to witness aide David Powers "banging a girl on the edge of the pool." Meanwhile, Kennedy sat on the other side of the pool and chatted up airline stewardesses with foreign accents. "Everybody was buckass naked," U.S.S.S. Agent Larry Newman said.

Hours later, Powers went inside the house and grabbed as many of Crosby's suits as he could. Then he ran back outside and jumped into the swimming pool for the sole purpose of ruining the Old Groaner's wardrobe. "The president thought that was pretty funny—laughed and about fell out of the chair," Newman added. "The only difficulty was Bing Crosby didn't think it was funny."

are within your grasp. Jacobson was flown into Washington more than thirty times—three to four times a week. At one point, JFK even asked the doctor/drug dealer to move into the White House. By 1962, a suspicious Attorney General Robert Kennedy thought it wise for his older brother to quit the intravenous doses of speed. "I don't care if it's horse piss," the president replied. "It works."

As it turned out, Bobby's instincts proved correct. A former nurse of Jacobson's later called the doctor "a butcher" and revealed that he had been self-administering his own meds. ("His speech was often slurred," she said.) In 1975, the New York State Department of Education revoked Dr. Feelgood's license to practice medicine. (Was the nickname a giveaway?) In 2002, Dr. Jeffrey Kelman reviewed JFK's medical records and concluded that the president "was being treated with narcotics all the time," with the opiate-based codeine sulfate and procaine, a common dental anesthetic. "He was tired because he was being doped up." Bonus rounds of meds included Bentyl, cortisone, penicillin, Ritalin, and Transentine.

To think, it was not venereal disease, drugs, communist spies, the Imperial Japanese Navy, jealous husbands, or an enraged Jackie that would ultimately bring Kennedy down—just an assassin's bullet fired by a moron (or morons) in Texas.

//

DEALEY PLAZA

Four miles from the Kennedy family compound in Hyannis Port, restaurant proprietor David Keville opened the Compound Bar and Grille in 2013 and listed a controversial drink on its bar menu. The "Dealey Plaza," named after the downtown Dallas district where Kennedy was assassinated, drew criticism for its insensitivity toward the neighboring Massachusetts dynasty.

According to the *Cape Cod Times*, Keville agreed that the name was "a bit macabre" and pointed the finger at his alcohol distributor, United Liquors, for their wrongdoing in coming up with the shock-valued cocktail. A spokesperson for United denied the accusation. So who is truly to blame here? Another conspiracy looms.

(The *Times* mentioned only part of the recipe, which is no longer available, but thanks to Brooklyn barkeep Emily L. Blackman for reluctantly figuring out the rest. "Jack's sorority girls would love it," she said.)

---

ice

1½ ounces Smirnoff Sorbet Light Raspberry Pomegranate

1 ounce cranberry juice

1 ounce ginger ale

3 ounces Prosecco

lime wedge

Throw the ice in a highball glass. Add the Smirnoff and cranberry juice. Top with the ginger ale and Prosecco. Garnish with the lime.

// **Serves 1** //

THE TEXAS WHITE HOUSE

NOVEMBER 22, 1963–JANUARY 20, 1969

Lyndon B. Johnson

36

DEMOCRAT

I n another life, Lyndon Baines Johnson could have been an S&M dungeon master, as he took pleasure in having others submit to him in the most humiliating circumstances. Speechwriter Richard Goodwin had the unfortunate experience of being summoned into a toilet stall for dictation while his terrifying boss moved his bowels. After shattering a cocktail glass against a wall in his office, LBJ watched one of his secretaries get on her knees with paper towels to soak up the sherry-stained carpet. And in the House Office Building bathroom, it was not uncommon to find the then–senate majority leader holding his penis, aka "Jumbo," and "shaking it, as if he was showing off," according to one account, and asking, "Have you ever seen anything as big as this?"

These were, as hack pop psychology would have it, the actions of a giant ball of insecurity—a Texas hayseed rebelling against a society worlds more refined than that from whence he came. The hill country native and Southwest Texas State Teachers College alum had the brains and balls—just not the sophistication—to successfully navigate to the top of Capitol Hill (and, through a stroke of fate, into the White House). It was a steep climb. Johnson always had his guard up, especially as vice president. His Sta-Comb hair grease and Texas twang comforted the likes of good ol' boy congressmen but drew negative attention from Ivy Leaguers. Members of John F. Kennedy's "Camelot" cabinet pet-named the veep "Uncle Rufus Cornpone" behind his back. During JFK's black-tie functions, at which the *Washington Post*'s Ben Bradlee noted "the crowd is always young" and "the women are always gorgeous," Cornpone stood out like a thumbprint on Waterford crystal. At one occasion that lasted until 4 a.m., Vice President Johnson attempted the twist, sending both himself and his dance partner to the hardwood floor. "He lay on her like a lox," one guest said.

One place to avoid further embarrassment was United States Capitol rooms S-211 and S-212, Johnson's private office space. Since his days as a lowly congressman representing Texas's Tenth District, the Machiavellian redneck could count floor votes better than Rain Man. As Senate Majority Leader, he lit one cigarette after another at his desk while telephoning members of Congress to bully his way for whatever bill was on deck. When he invited a colleague to his office for cocktails, staffers were instructed to make his scotch and soda significantly weaker than his guest's, which held, at minimum, 2 or 3 ounces of whiskey. Cutty Sark was preferred; Wild Turkey worked in a pinch. "His drinks could have no more than an ounce of liquor in it," secretary Ashton Gonella said, "and if there was more than an ounce, you were in trouble."

In 1955, the forty-seven-year-old suffered a serious heart attack and had no choice but to quit his three-packs-a-day habit, cold turkey. This was a devastating disciplinary action. "I'd rather have my pecker cut off," the senator told his doctor. In the White House, the cook tried to shrink his Golden Corral buffet–size dinners to portions resembling those of a normal human being. One night, she left a message on the dinner table. "Mr. President," Zephyr Wright's note read, "you always tell me you want to lose weight, and yet you never do very much to help yourself. Now I am going to be your boss for a change. Eat what I put in front of you, and don't ask for any more and don't complain."

He would have to fly 1,600 miles to feel like a king. Not that he got any more polite.

INSIDE LBJ'S RANCH HOUSE NEAR THE PEDERNALES RIVER, SIXTY MILES west of downtown Austin, in one of the recliners sat a pillow embroidered with the words "This is my ranch and I do as I damn please."

The thirty-sixth president spent the equivalent of one of his five years working at "the Texas White House." Technological advances in long-distance phone lines, jet aircraft, satellite, and microwaves made the telecommute possible, and they also set the precedent for more hardheaded, vacation-happy presidents who owned ranch land. On the Pedernales, Johnson lived like Dom DeLuise's Caesar in *History of the World, Part I.* There were no treasure baths, but White House Press Secretary George Reedy remembered LBJ going on "a wild drinking bout" without the press corps or the snobbery of Camelot snickering behind his back. "He was not an alcoholic or a heavy drinker in the commonly accepted sense of those words," the press secretary said. "But there were occasions when he would pour down scotch and soda in a virtually mechanical motion." If LBJ behaved robotically

> ## "This is my ranch and I do as I damn please."

with the liquor provisions, then at the breakfast table he was the Terminator. A typical morning meal consisted of orange juice, cantaloupe, scrambled eggs, bacon, venison sausage, hominy grits, popovers, and coffee.

"Please," appealed Illinois governor Adlai Stevenson during one sleepover, "let's skip lunch."

Had Johnson taken his breakfast companion's advice, he might have lived long enough to see *The Dukes of Hazzard.* (Johnson would die in 1973 at age sixty-four from a heart attack, and judging from his lax dietary restrictions, one can see why. Hickory-smoked spareribs and baked beans aren't exactly an ideal deterrent for myocardial infarctions.) Clocking in at six-foot-four and 225 pounds, the cholesterol king had suits tailored full and long and with wide lapels to hide that bowling ball of a belly. Cowboy boot heels made up for the long stride in his slacks. An alteration request, made on a famously crude phone call, details his preference for a roomy crotch area. "Down where your nuts hang is always a little too tight," he told pants mogul Joe Haggar Jr. in 1964. "See if you can't leave me about an inch where the zipper—*belch*—ends round under back to my bunghole."

Back at the ranch, when it was time to give reporters a tour of the rolling hills of the Texas property, Johnson slid behind the wheel of a white Lincoln Continental convertible. The president wouldn't stay on the road. "His Lincoln-Mercury supplier in Austin said he destroyed the things," said Russ Whitlock, superintendent at the Lyndon B. Johnson National Historic Park. "He was constantly going out there to haul one of his cars back when he knocked the oil pan out or ruined the suspension." The auto dealer recommended a jeep that was better suited for outings across the pastures; Johnson showed no interest. Instead, he ordered a Lincoln customized with mud-grip tires and reinforced with a steel pan on the bottom. Secret Service agents trailed behind in a sedan with a portable scotch bar, not unlike the kind "you'd see on a ship or a motor home," according to Whitlock. Sometimes, agents would take the station wagon and keep a cooler full of water, liquor, and beer in the trunk.

"Their job was to open and close gates and keep the drinks refilled," Whitlock said. "They had to learn to get the combination right." By day's end, LBJ would be back at the ranch house in time for the 6 o'clock news and accompanied by his amour, scotch and soda in a Styrofoam cup. The first lady, Claudia Alta "Lady Bird" Johnson, would whip up a platter of crackers with cheddar cubes and venison sausage on toothpicks.

AN INFINITE KNOWLEDGE OF THE INS AND OUTS OF CAPITOL HILL allowed President Johnson to push through groundbreaking legislation, particularly a package that commenced the Great Society. But the Vietnam War forever tainted his legacy, and he knew it. On March 31, 1968, Johnson announced to the American people on live TV that he would "not seek" and would "not accept . . . another term as your president." In his final

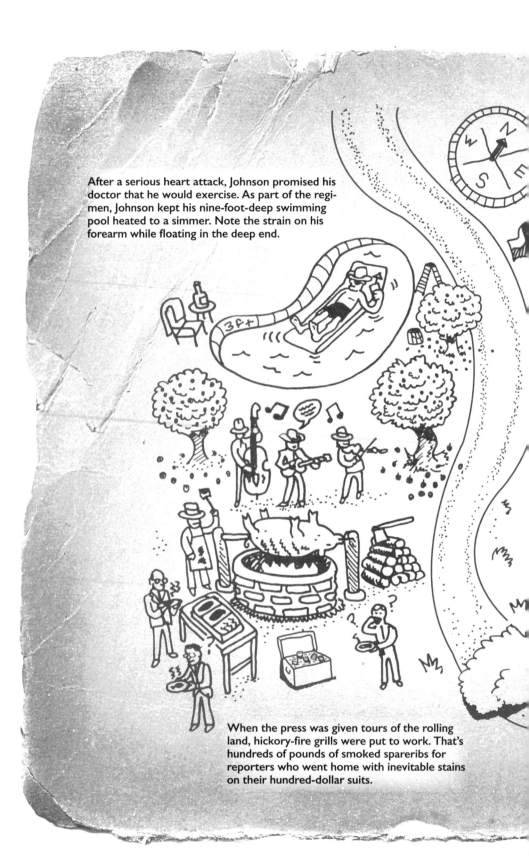

After a serious heart attack, Johnson promised his doctor that he would exercise. As part of the regimen, Johnson kept his nine-foot-deep swimming pool heated to a simmer. Note the strain on his forearm while floating in the deep end.

When the press was given tours of the rolling land, hickory-fire grills were put to work. That's hundreds of pounds of smoked spareribs for reporters who went home with inevitable stains on their hundred-dollar suits.

Before the guesthouse was completed, secretaries and company slept in the five bedrooms on the second floor of the main house. Johnson made "frequent nocturnal visits," according to Robert Caro's *Master of the Senate*, which relates one night that "a good-looking girl was sleeping" upstairs. Two staffers, bunking in an adjacent room, overheard LBJ's unmistakable footsteps and "the door to that room open and shut." Downstairs, Lady Bird was catching z's.

On a whim, Johnson would helicopter guests and himself across the hills to Lake Travis for a spin on an 18-foot speedboat.

"When you saw that arm come out and that Styrofoam cup stick out," said one Secret Service agent, "you knew the old man was ready for a refill."

year at the helm, his approval rating lingered as low as 36 percent.

After his final day in office, LBJ fired up a cigarette on the Air Force One flight to the ranch. It was his first since 1955. For the next five years of his life, "he began drinking more heavily than in the White House," said Mark K. Updegrove, director of the LBJ Presidential Library in Austin. "He would drive around in his Lincoln convertible, have a scotch and soda, and watch the antelope and the deer and the sunset and the Pedernales."

CENTRAL TEXAS SANGRIAS

When Lady Bird Johnson was buried next to her husband in 2007, grandson Lyndon Nugent paid respects at the family cemetery. "I guess this is adiós, Nini, at least for now," he said. "Perhaps we'll be able to ride the ranch again some day with our sangrias in hand." Here's a mixture that the first lady would probably inhale without protest.

6 ounces frozen concentrate limeade

6 ounces frozen concentrate orange juice

water

1 liter grapefruit soda, chilled

1 bottle red wine

orange and lemon slices for garnish

Dilute the concentrates with two cans of water. Add the grapefruit soda and wine. Freeze until slushy. Pour into a pitcher. Garnish with the fruit.

////////// **Serves 12 to 16** //////////

ALL THE PRESIDENT'S MEDS

JANUARY 20, 1969–AUGUST 9, 1974

Richard M. Nixon

REPUBLICAN

37

O n the morning of October 27, 1970, Richard Nixon positioned himself behind a desk inside the Department
of Justice's Bureau of Narcotics and Dangerous Drugs.
Clad in a dark suit with an American flag lapel pin and his hair
greased back in his signature 1950s-sitcom-dad style, the president sat before snapping photographers and rolling news cameras.

To his left was a display of confiscated bricks of marijuana, cocaine, heroin, uppers, downers, and stacks of dollar bills. Nixon, professedly concerned "for the lives of hundreds of thousands of young people all over America," signed the Comprehensive Drug Abuse Prevention and Control Act, enabling the attorney general to hire three hundred federal agents and enforce drug laws "far beyond, for example, heroin," according to Nixon. "It will cover the new types of drugs, the barbiturates and amphetamines that have become so common."

And so began the war on drugs in the United States.

The legislative package did not exclusively set out to crack hippie skulls—some funding went toward treatment centers in impoverished areas—but you have to wonder. Even before his 1968 presidential campaign, Nixon touted himself as the law-and-order candidate, a pro-establishment conservative who had the nerve and know-how to mollify race riots in Los Angeles and bring "peace with honor" to the war in Vietnam.

He winced at the countercultural movement, and the feeling was mutual. There had never been a greater ideological divide between the White House and youth. The Fab Fifties were long gone, as was an innocent nation's blind faith in government. Women bore children at rock festivals—maybe not the best environment for a birth, but who wants to miss Sha Na Na? An X-rated movie, *Midnight Cowboy*, won the Oscar for Best Picture. (Alas, Ron Jeremy did not win Best Actor.) At the 1972 Democratic National Convention, a longhair boasted at the top of his lungs that he was the first "fucker ever to cast a vote on acid!" And in the White House was a middle-aged square widely known as "Tricky Dick," the scourge of drug-addled college campuses across the land. The new town sheriff appeared nothing but a deceitful hawk, making a desperate and delusional grasp for Archie Bunker's fabled good old days.

As America later learned, courtesy of Nixon's secret audio recordings of White House conversations, the president didn't just hate pot—he also hated Jews! "You know it's a funny thing," Nixon told Chief of Staff H. R. Haldeman in 1971, "every one of the bastards that are out for legalizing marijuana is Jewish. What the Christ is the matter with the Jews, Bob? What is the matter with them? I suppose it's because most of them are psychiatrists."

That last part is admittedly true, but no other president could have used a shrink more. Nixon's enigmatic psyche (read: batshit insanity) resulted from a medley of Oval Office anxieties mixed with everyone-is-against-me paranoia and a bad temper. To ward off the self-torment, Nixon went against doctor's orders and mixed pre-scription cocktails, sending him into nightly stupors. (Anthony Summers's feather-ruffling *The Secret World of Richard Nixon*

The Fab Fifties were long gone.

suggests the president may not have even had a prescription for the pills in the first place.) The law-and-order candidate gained a reputation in Washington as a sad, slurring troglodyte, of perennial five o'clock shadow, who gargled whis-keys on the rocks and drunk-dialed colleagues until passing out in a wingback chair. Staffers nicknamed him "Our Drunk" or "Our Drunken Friend" behind his back. Nevertheless, Don Fulsom, a former White House press corps mem-ber who wrote the children's bedtime story *Nixon's Darkest Secrets*, recalled a moderate intake by the president. "His drink of choice was the martini, but he also went for scotch," Fulsom said. "One time on a trip, Nixon ordered a scotch. He told the waitress that he doesn't like the taste of it, but this way he won't order too many." Fulsom attributes the combination of said scotch with the contents of the Oval Office desk drawer—a sleep aid called Seconal and 1,000-milligram capsules of the antipsychotic Dilantin—as the reason that Nixon earned those "Drunk" nicknames. ("Tricky Dick" sprung from down-and-dirty politics decades before the Watergate scandal.)

"One beer would transform his speech into the rambling elocution of a Bowery wino," Haldeman wrote. "It didn't take a whole lot of gin to get him sloshed," noted advisor John Ehrlichman. At a White House dinner on December 17, 1973, Senator Barry Goldwater listened to a president who resembled "a tape with unexpected blank sections." But Nixon's drunken state was far more dangerous than your standard point-and-laugh scenario with an embarrass-ing relative. Fulsom's book goes into detail about Nixon's physical abuse toward his wife. And this drunk was, after all, the leader of the free world in a nuclear age. A Secret Service agent, on duty at Nixon's winter retreat in Key Biscayne, remembered a heated and intoxicated Nixon shouting, "Bomb the shit out of them!" into a telephone. Rumors circulated among Secretary of State Henry Kissinger's staff of "that drunken lunatic" who could "blow up the world."

What seed could have been planted in such an intelligent and capable individual that would drive him into madness? Rick Perlstein's epic *Nixonland* reveals insecurities that blossomed at a young age. At Whittier College, the seventeen-year-old felt alienated from the polished, wealthy student body, who christened themselves "the Franklins," a nice, rich-sounding name. In bitter rebellion, the Quaker farm boy formed with outliers "the Orthogonians," an organization of awkward un-beauty that prided the lesser privileged "beans, brains, and brawn" on campus.

Resentment and endurance drove this complicated and crazed Nixon to greatness, from what classmates hailed as his "iron butt" marathon study sessions in the law school library; to grudgingly winning poker games while in the Navy; to enduring two devastating defeats on the national stage—first the presidency to John F. Kennedy in 1960, then California's gubernatorial race to Pat Brown in 1962. Eventually, the Orthogonian would have his day. "Nobody else had the iron-assed will to do what needed to be done," Perlstein wrote, "to wait out the dozens and dozens of poker hands it would take before you had the cards you needed to *really* be able to collect the only bounty that mattered, in 1968."

Unfortunately for Nixon, the bitter loser demeanor he spent a lifetime cultivating ultimately bested him. Rather than hand over those secret audio recordings that would have implicated him in the burglarizing of the Democratic Party Headquarters at the Watergate Hotel, he resigned in disgrace. Making his exit on August 9, 1974, the president flashed two V-for-Victory signs to members of the press on the South Lawn. The gesture was, no doubt, also directed at the hippies cheering at home—many of whom authorities would eventually lock up for possession of barbiturates and amphetamines, all part of a mass incarceration that had been set into motion by this overmedicated anti-Semite with a five o'clock shadow.

//

PINK RUSSIAN

When Helen Gahagan Douglas rivaled Nixon for his California senate seat in 1950, the incumbent's team distributed flyers calling her "pink right down to her underwear"—a sexist jab and accusation of Communist sympathy.

ice

1 ounce strawberry cream liqueur

½ ounce Kahlúa

½ ounce vodka

dash of milk

Shake the ice, liqueur, Kahlúa, and vodka in a tumbler. Strain into a rocks glass over ice. Top off with the milk.

/////////////// **Serves 1** ///////////////

MEMORIES OF JERRY

AUGUST 9, 1974–JANUARY 20, 1977

Gerald R. Ford

38

REPUBLICAN

Throughout his twenty-five years in the U.S. House of Representatives, nine months as vice president, and 896 days in the White House, Gerald R. Ford was as accommodating as they come.

Generally perceived as an unassuming and down-to-earth president, Ford toasted his own English muffins and picked up after his golden retriever on the South Lawn in his morning bathrobe. The man's man from Grand Rapids was a happy-go-lucky American who, when compared to his vindictive and temperamental predecessor, Richard M. Nixon, also passed for clinically sane.

Ford asked that the nation refer to 1600 Penn as "the residence" rather than its more traditional and intimidating handle, "the Executive Mansion." One week into office, he danced to a cover band rendition of Jim Croce's "Bad, Bad Leroy Brown" at a White House dinner thrown for King Hussein of Jordan. Honestly, how could you not love this guy?

"He was a friend to everyone who met him," Kansas senator Bob Dole said of his 1976 running mate. "He had no enemies."

In addition to warming the hearts of policymakers on both sides of the aisle, the thirty-eighth president maintained an almost filial connection to his White House press corps. His modesty and kindness inspired loyalty from several members of the news media, especially those who knew him before a disgraced Nixon left office, and Ford's so-called accidental presidency went into effect. Prior to assuming the top spot, he had less than one year under his belt as Tricky Dick's veep—and was *appointed* to the position of vice president, mind you, not elected. (Plenty of Beltway personalities were more than qualified to serve in December 1973, but, presumably after a nail-biting round of cootie catcher, Nixon selected the unobtrusive Ford to fill the shoes of his previous number two, Spiro Agnew, who had resigned in the wake of a bribery scandal.)

Point being, Ford was never voted into high office, yet his relatable image and bipartisan alliances reestablished confidence in the federal government after Watergate. Good times were well-documented along the way. "He was the only fun president that I ever met," *New York Times* Washington correspondent John Herbers said. "He was more intimate than any of the others."

He was also a supplemental insurance company's worst nightmare. One morning, upon his arrival at Salzburg Airport in Austria, the former University of Michigan football star famously tumbled down the stairs of Air Force One. Another time, on a golf course in Palm Springs, California, Ford drove an electric cart into the side of a shack. ("I'm just one big clumsy sonofabitch," he told Secret Service agent Dennis Chomicki.) The media ate it up. Press secretary Ron Nessen explained how, during Ford's vacation ski trips, TV crews would station themselves on the more challenging slopes and turns in gleeful anticipation of his next pratfall. By now, Chevy Chase's *Saturday Night Live* impersonation of a clumsy Ford has arguably eclipsed the former president in public imagination.

One slapstick stunt, however, remained off the record for decades. In 1974, the president spent his first Christmas break in Vail, Colorado, where for the

It *did* look awfully like an ottoman.

better part of two weeks he congregated with family and esteemed locals. On Sunday, December 30, members of the press corps invited the world leader to a holiday reunion at their rented condo, a no-frills cocktail hour for the chief and the correspondents who had trailed him since Agnew stepped down. Upon his arrival at No. 3J at the Village Center apartments, Ford "made a bee-line for the kitchen," according to reporter Thomas DeFrank's memoir *Write It When I'm Gone*, "asking, 'Who needs a drink?'"

With martini in hand, the president puffed his tobacco pipe among friends and melted into the couch for a half hour. (He and his wife, the world-famous alcoholic Betty, were scheduled for a dinner with the owner of a ski equipment company.) Ford was so comfortable and off his guard, DeFrank observed, that the president set his "loafer dead in the center of a two-pound wheel of brie on the coffee table . . . As he stood up, the cheese stuck to the bottom of his shoe for a heart-stopping instant—before quietly plopping back onto the plate. He never knew."

FOR SUCH A NICE GUY, IT SEEMS REMARKABLE THAT FORD WOULD BE THE target of not one, but two assassination attempts.

Not three weeks after one of Charles Manson's homicidal minions pulled a gun on the president in Sacramento, a woman named Sara Jane Moore, unrelated to the Helter Skelter tribe but perfectly suitable for a walk-on in *One Flew Over the Cuckoo's Nest*, tried to assassinate Ford in downtown San Francisco.

The Ford motorcade fled the scene to safety, hitting the SFO tarmac in no time. Accompanied by photographer David Hume Kennerly, chief of staff Donald Rumsfeld, speechwriter Robert Hartmann, and a regiment of Secret Service agents, the president hopped onto Air Force One and into a private compartment. Having narrowly escaped getting his head blown off, he naturally went looking for cocktails—standard procedure in the top-secret security manual. Ford took his first big gulp, and the remaining passengers followed suit. "What had happened sunk in," Nessen, who was also present, told the *San Francisco Chronicle* in 2006. "[Q]uite a few martinis were consumed on the flight back."

Flying the friendly skies...

Safely en route to Washington, Kennerly, with Groucho Marx timing, approached the man whose fate had nearly been sealed and asked, "Other than that, Mr. President, how did you like San Francisco?"

Ford didn't need an assassination attempt as an excuse to suck down gin at 33,000 feet. On Air Force One, the president "always had two large martinis before meals," *New York Times* correspondent Maggie Hunter wrote, "and two scoops of butter pecan ice cream for dessert." The same rules applied on Air Force Two. In April 1974, he gave a regrettable "late-night, highball-lubricated interview" to the *New Republic*'s John Osborne, who prodded the vice president on which Nixon cabinet members he would keep if he became president.

On another flight, DeFrank recalled Ford dashing up the aisle, "gleefully cackling in full frat-boy mode" while wearing a T-shirt with the words *KEEP ON STREAKING* across the chest. Thankfully, he was wearing pants.

//

CHARLESTON LIGHT DRAGOON'S PUNCH

Around 1961, Ford curated food and cocktail recipes from fifty colleagues for his *Republican Congressional Cookbook*, including this South Carolina concoction that "is just as good made in less terrifying proportions."

4 cups sugar

4 quarts brandy

juice of 24 squeezed lemons

1 quart Jamaican rum

4 quarts black tea

½ pint peach brandy

sparkling water

peel of 6 lemons for garnish

Mix all the ingredients except the sparkling water in the order given. Top with the sparkling water before serving. Cut the lemon peel into thin slices or curls for serving.

// **Serves 80** //

BROTHER'S KEEPER

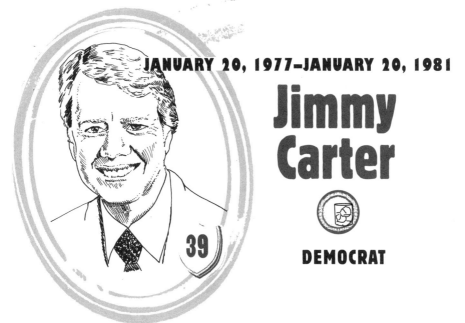

JANUARY 20, 1977–JANUARY 20, 1981

Jimmy Carter

39

DEMOCRAT

Patti McGuire was Playmate of the Month in Playboy's November 1976 issue. The centerfold spread begins on page 121, where, clad in baby doll pajamas, the twenty-five-year-old brunette flashes her tan-lined derrière in front of a jukebox. Two pages later, Miss November is seen in a full-frontal nude shot as she drinks a milkshake through a straw and leans against the coin-operated music player. Oh, and if you happened to miss the in-depth interview with Jimmy Carter, Georgia peanut farmer and Democratic presidential nominee in the 1976 election, flip back to page 63. It's opposite the Budweiser

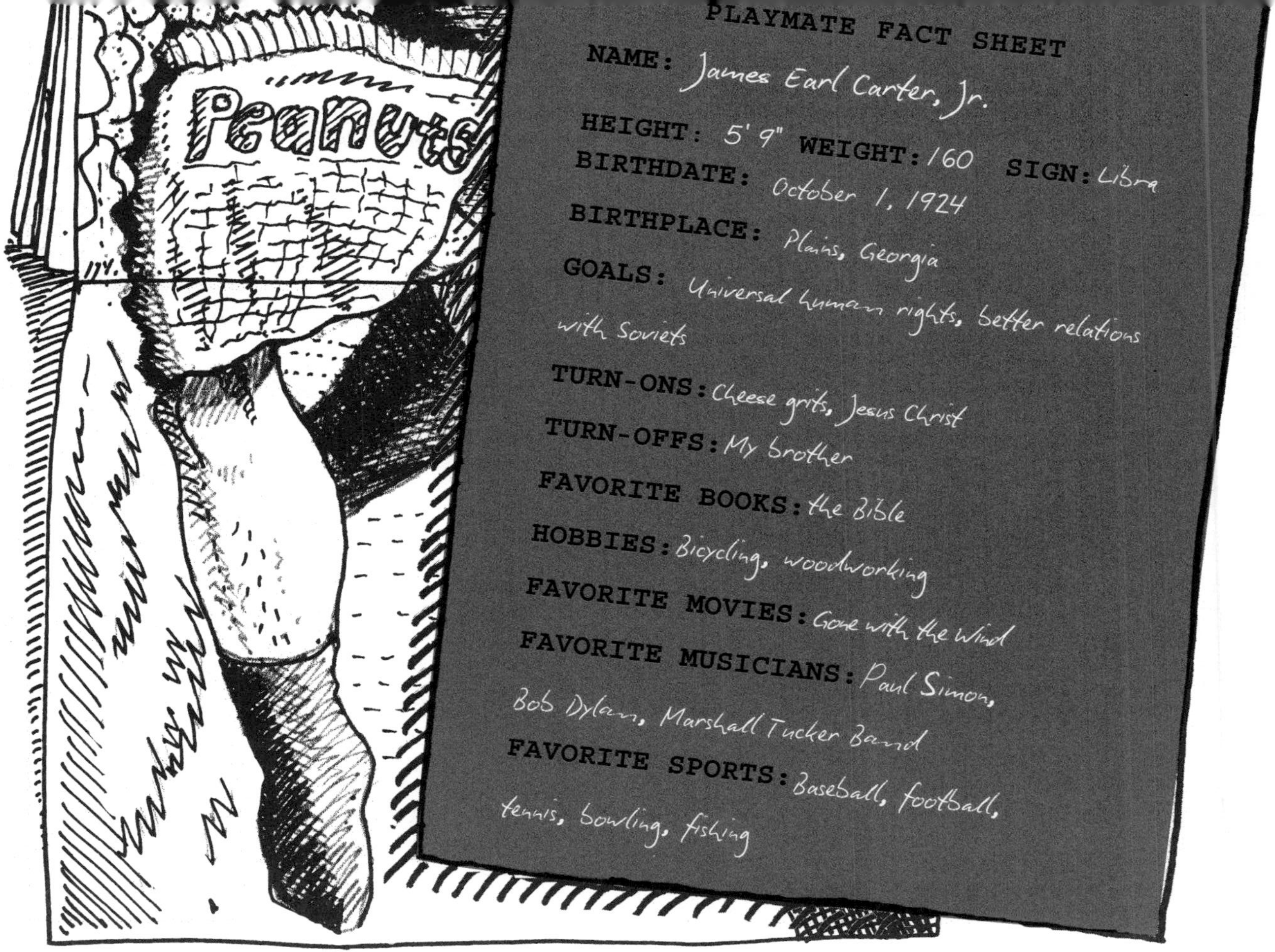

PLAYMATE FACT SHEET

NAME: James Earl Carter, Jr.

HEIGHT: 5'9" WEIGHT: 160 SIGN: Libra

BIRTHDATE: October 1, 1924

BIRTHPLACE: Plains, Georgia

GOALS: Universal human rights, better relations with Soviets

TURN-ONS: Cheese grits, Jesus Christ

TURN-OFFS: My brother

FAVORITE BOOKS: the Bible

HOBBIES: Bicycling, woodworking

FAVORITE MOVIES: Gone with the Wind

FAVORITE MUSICIANS: Paul Simon, Bob Dylan, Marshall Tucker Band

FAVORITE SPORTS: Baseball, football, tennis, bowling, fishing

ad, touting itself "The King of Beers for 100 years."

The *Playboy* interview sent a ripple through conservative pockets of America. The fact alone that he'd permit *Playboy* scribe Robert Scheer to hitch a ride on his campaign plane was off-putting to churchgoing communities, but the

"I've committed adultery in my heart many times."

contents of the interview may have caused a few Ned Flanders types to black out in their pews. Carter, a devoted Southern Baptist and happily married for thirty years, admitted to having sexual fantasies. "Christ said, 'I tell you that anyone who looks on a woman with lust has in his heart already committed adultery,'" Carter told Scheer. "I've looked on a lot of women with lust. I've committed adultery in my heart many times. This is something that God recognizes I will do—and I have done it—and God forgives me for it. But that doesn't mean that I condemn someone who not only looks on a woman with lust but who leaves his wife and shacks up with somebody out of wedlock."

Carter barely snagged the election from incumbent Gerald Ford. In the end, Bible-beaters had little to worry about in terms of his potential for lechery or indulgence. The thirty-ninth president led a straight-laced life. Partial to buttermilk before booze, the mild-mannered Christian innocuously sipped scotch with water before dinnertime. On wedding anniversaries, flutes of champagne touched his lips. Frozen margaritas numbed his tongue during a trip to Mexico. But one wouldn't find a hidden flask in his toilet tank or reels of Super 8mm porn behind his shoe rack. White House receptions would not serve hard liquor to guests. At times, Carter would abstain completely.

If Scheer's Q&A revealed anything, it was that the interview subject would not cast a stone at those who did not spend weekends memorizing verses from the New Testament. The Carter White House welcomed multiplatinum recording artists—and iconic potheads—for afternoon visits and overnight stays. In 1978, the Ambassador to Weedville himself, Willie Nelson, performed on the South Lawn to honor a NASCAR celebration hosted by First Lady Rosalynn Carter. (Her husband, meanwhile, was away at Camp David, trying to mitigate a peace settlement between Egypt's Anwar al Sadat and Israeli Prime Minister Menachem Begin—less fun.) That evening, Nelson and his then-wife Connie were set for a sleepover in the Lincoln bedroom. Before bedtime, Shotgun Willie took his braided ponytails to the rooftop, where, along with one of the president's sons (and a Secret Service escort), Nelson fired up "a big fat Austin torpedo."

Another time, one of David Crosby's band members supposedly roasted a bone inside the West Wing. "One of us, and I will not say who, lit a joint in the Oval Office," Crosby was quoted in Dave Zimmer's *Crosby, Stills & Nash: The Authorized Biography.* "Just to be able to say he'd done it, you know?" According to the president's daily diary, the band's visit lasted five minutes—long enough for a gang of five to burn a skinny one—though in a 2014 *Rolling Stone* profile, a sober Crosby backpedaled on the story. When gesturing toward a framed photo taken during the visit, the Grammy Award winner indicated a member of his entourage in the background. "That guy wanted to light up a joint in the Oval Office," he said. "Even I thought that was a stupid idea."

For the best example of Carter's tolerance of others, look no further than his relationship with his little brother, a plainspoken gas station owner with a penchant for piss beer and raunchy comments in mixed company. Billy Carter was a grown man who, in the middle of the night, once swallowed a cup of bait that he presumed was bourbon and who bragged to the press during his brother's presidential campaign that he now would "drink liquor out of a cup instead of out of the bottle." He also criticized the candidate's supposedly newfound scotch habit as a city-slicking front. ("I've never trusted a scotch drinker.")

New York Times columnist William Safire called Billy Carter "America's favorite redneck, Southern version of Archie Bunker." Billy, twelve years younger than Jimmy, became a nuisance to the administration, from sounding off in *Penthouse* magazine that he was "more popular" than the president "because I get along with folks," to accepting a supposed $220,000 loan from Libyan dictator Muammar Gaddafi, to capitalizing every which way possible on the family name. Falls City Brewing Company of Louisville, Kentucky, gave him an endorsement deal for Billy Beer, a notorious flop of a six-pack enterprise that Billy anticipated would transform him into "the Colonel Sanders of beer."

President Carter, exhibiting a rare graciousness found in the Dalai Lama and Virgin Mary, did not take action against his brother. He offered forgiveness.

RAISING THE DRINKING AGE

JANUARY 20, 1981–JANUARY 20, 1989

Ronald Reagan

REPUBLICAN

It might not come as a surprise to learn that Ronald Reagan was unhip to eighties pop culture. The former California governor and Hollywood star, whose credits included host of CBS's General Electric Theater *and pitchman for Boraxo powdered hand soap, took the oath of office at sixty-nine—four years after the traditional retirement age—making him the oldest man ever elected to the presidency.*

Deep into the era of Madonna and Springsteen, and a full generation after the rock and roll revolution, he preferred listening to Frank Sinatra. As a hopped-up MTV nation practiced 360-degree head spins to Run DMC and stayed up past midnight for *Late Night with David Letterman*, Reagan's idea of a good time consisted of horseback riding at his Santa Barbara ranch and slurping bowls of something called hamburger soup. The senior citizen was an avid collector of California vintage wines, even though he didn't imbibe all that much. Perhaps it was to set an example? While campaigning for a second term, President Lame-O believed that youths should cut out drinking altogether.

In 1984, Reagan signed the National Minimum Drinking Age Act, prohibiting teens across America from downing alcohol. The bill, sponsored by New Jersey senator Frank Lautenberg, was not a federal mandate. Rather, it offered individual states a choice: Raise the drinking age from eighteen to twenty-one, or lose 10 percent of federal highway funds each year thereafter. All fifty states, plus the District of Columbia, complied.

The bipartisan legislation would have been a coup for any politician. While holding true to his small-government credo, Reagan won support from the nonprofit juggernaut Mothers Against Drunk Driving. The senate bill's passage was one of many reasons the seventy-three-year-old achieved a historical landslide reelection—525 electoral votes to Democratic opponent Walter Mondale's 13.

//

JELLY BEAN MARTINI

White House staff kept bowls of the president's favorite snack, jelly beans, at his desk and on Air Force One. Reagan claimed they helped ward off his craving for cigarettes. Here's a disgusting, albeit less boring, use for the confectionery treat.

1 cup jelly beans

12 ounces vodka

handful of powdered sugar

8 ounces Cointreau

ice

handful of jelly beans (use white or clear)

4 lemon peels

Mix the jelly beans with the vodka in a closed container. Let sit for several hours. Strain the liquid through a coffee filter into a new container. Discard the used jelly beans. Wet the rim of martini glasses with water and coat with the powdered sugar. Place the glasses in the freezer for 5 minutes. Shake the vodka and Cointreau in a tumbler with ice. Strain into the chilled glasses. Drop a handful of fresh jelly beans into the glasses. Garnish with the lemon peel.

///////////// **Serves 4** /////////////

1933

The Twenty-first Amendment repeals Prohibition nationwide. States can now regulate the sale, transport, and manufacture of alcoholic beverages. The amendment is ratified by thirty-six states, the majority of which set the minimum age for purchase and possession at twenty-one.

1935

Ohio hikes the age to purchase beer from sixteen to eighteen.

Post-Prohibition Drinking-Age Legislation:
A TIMELINE

1966

Mississippi (finally) ratifies the Twenty-first Amendment and sets the age at eighteen.

1971

Primarily for voting rights, ratification of the Twenty-sixth Amendment constitutionally recognizes eighteen as the age of majority. Several state legislatures respond by lowering the drinking age from twenty-one to eighteen. "If he is responsible enough to serve as a platoon leader," one Michigan senator says, "you can't tell him he's not responsible enough to drink."

1981

Concern grows over alcohol-related teen driving accidents. Following suit with eleven other states, Massachusetts raises the age requirement to twenty.

1983

Rock and roll dies in the Garden State after the drinking age is upped to twenty-one. "Places closed left and right," one club owner recalls. "A lot of the bands that played primarily the New Jersey rock club circuit retired."

1948

Kansas regulates the sale of liquor but "forever prohibits" rights to public establishments. (Unless they belong to a private club, barflies have to wait until the law gets repealed in 1986.)

1961

Illinois passes a bill that bumps the age to twenty-one for both men and women; previously, only women were allowed to drink at eighteen. The next day, nineteen-year-old Virginia Wantroba partakes in a lawsuit claiming that, if the law were enforced, she would suffer "irreparable injury."

1984

The age requirement is now twenty-one in nineteen states. Despite undercurrents of big government at work, Reagan supports the bill to raise ages for all fifty states and end "a national tragedy involving transit across state borders," he says.

1984

Reagan signs the National Minimum Drinking Age Act to resolve what he calls the "crazy quilt of different states' drinking laws." The bill requires all fifty states to raise ages to twenty-one in the next two years or lose a percentage of federal highway funds.

THE VOMITING INCIDENT

JANUARY 20, 1989–JANUARY 20, 1993

George H. W. Bush

REPUBLICAN

41

On January 8, 1992, auto industry executives and the first lady accompanied President George Herbert Walker Bush on a tour of the Far East. There, President Bush paid a visit to the prime minister and emperor of Japan.

It might very well have been the most sensational episode of his entire single term.

THE TRIP WAS A NICE BREAK FROM HIS REELECTION CAMPAIGN BACK IN THE U.S....

. . . DESPITE A VICIOUS FLU BUG THAT HAD BEEN CIRCULATING AMONG REPORTERS AND WHITE HOUSE AIDES.

AROUND 3 P.M., BUSH AND U.S. AMBASSADOR TO JAPAN MICHAEL H. ARMACOST PLAYED A ROUND OF DOUBLES TENNIS WITH EMPEROR AKIHITO AND CROWN PRINCE NARUHITO AT THE IMPERIAL PALACE.

THE AMERICANS LOST.

THAT EVENING, PRESIDENT BUSH AND THE FIRST LADY PREPARED FOR A DINNER IN THEIR HONOR, HELD INSIDE PRIME MINISTER KIICHI MIYAZAWA'S HOME. BUT THE SIXTY-SEVEN-YEAR-OLD WAS NOT FEELING WELL.

BEFORE DINNER, BUSH ATTEMPTED TO PARTICIPATE IN A RECEIVING LINE AT MIYAZAWA'S RESIDENCE.

WILL YOU PLEASE EXCUSE ME?

IT WOULD BE A SLAP IN THE FACE TO THE JAPANESE TO CANCEL NOW.

YOU BETTER TAKE MY TIE, SIR.

135 DIPLOMATS AND OFFICIALS ATTENDED THE FOUR-COURSE DINNER, WHICH INCLUDED COLD SALMON WITH CAVIAR, CLEAR SOUP WITH MUSHROOMS, MEDALLIONS OF BEEF WITH PEPPER SAUCE, AND PASSION FRUIT ICE CREAM. TOASTS WERE EXCHANGED AN HOUR INTO THE AFFAIR.

THEN, BUSH TURNED WHITE.

PERSONAL PHYSICIAN DR. BURTON LEE LOOSENED BUSH'S TIE TO GIVE HIM SOME AIR. WHEN LEE UNZIPPED BUSH'S TROUSERS, THE PRESIDENT REGAINED CONSCIOUSNESS.

BURT, WHAT THE HECK ARE YOU DOING DOWN THERE?

THE MUSIC STOPPED. JAPANESE TV CAMERAS SURROUNDED THE TABLE. EVERYONE PUT DOWN THEIR FORKS AND RUBBERNECKED. A USSS AGENT ATTEMPTED TO DISPERSE THE CROWD.

WHERE'S THE AMBULANCE?

I THINK THE PRESIDENT IS GOING TO BE FINE!

MIYAZAWA CRADLED BUSH'S HEAD FOR A MOMENT.

WHY DON'T YOU ROLL ME UNDER THE TABLE, AND I'LL SLEEP IT OFF WHILE YOU FINISH THE DINNER.

PALE AND EXHAUSTED, BUSH WALKED OUT OF MIYAZAWA'S HOUSE WITH USSS AGENTS. EVERYONE APPLAUDED AS HE STOOD UP.

BARBARA REMAINED AT THE DINNER AND CONTINUED TO EXCHANGE TOASTS WITH MIYAZAWA.

I CAN'T EXPLAIN WHAT HAPPENED ... I'M BEGINNING TO THINK IT IS THE AMBASSADOR'S FAULT. HE AND GEORGE PLAYED THE EMPEROR AND THE CROWN PRINCE IN TENNIS TODAY, AND THEY WERE BADLY BEATEN.

WE BUSHES AREN'T USED TO THAT. SO HE FELT WORSE THAN I THOUGHT...

BACK IN THE U.S., BUSH SPOKESPERSON MARLIN FITZWATER INFORMED THE PRESS THAT THE PRESIDENT SUFFERED FROM A CASE OF GASTROENTERITIS.

IT'S A SIMPLE CASE OF THE FLU.

THE PRESIDENT IS HUMAN.

HE GETS SICK.

THE NEXT DAY, REPORTERS ASKED VICE PRESIDENT DAN QUAYLE IF HE HAD BEEN PREPARED TO ASSUME THE POWERS AND DUTIES OF THE PRESIDENCY.

THAT DIDN'T EVEN CROSS MY MIND...

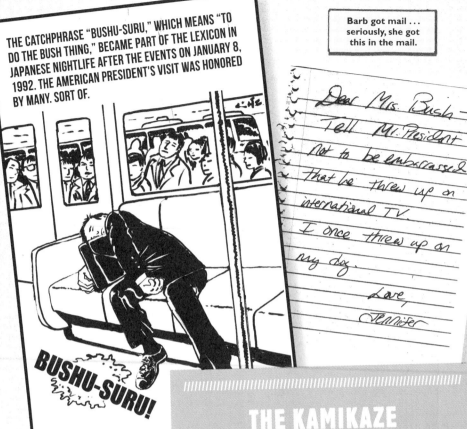

THE CATCHPHRASE "BUSHU-SURU," WHICH MEANS "TO DO THE BUSH THING," BECAME PART OF THE LEXICON IN JAPANESE NIGHTLIFE AFTER THE EVENTS ON JANUARY 8, 1992. THE AMERICAN PRESIDENT'S VISIT WAS HONORED BY MANY. SORT OF.

BUSHU-SURU!

Barb got mail . . . seriously, she got this in the mail.

Dear Mrs. Bush—
Tell Mr. President not to be embarrassed that he threw up on international TV. I once threw up on my dog.
Love,
Jennifer

THE KAMIKAZE

The late '80s and early '90s were a shitty time for bartending culture. A new generation of yuppies had been borne out of a decade more focused on drugs than drinks. And so what Tom Cruise didn't teach everyone in *Cocktail*, your unqualified TGI Fridays staffer made up for with this sour disaster.

1 ounce triple sec
1 ounce vodka
1 ounce lime juice
lime slice for garnish

Pour ingredients into a tumbler. Shake well, not that it matters. Strain into a cocktail glass. Garnish with the lime.

Serves 1

SLICK WILLY

JANUARY 20, 1993–JANUARY 20, 2001

William Jefferson Clinton

42

DEMOCRAT

Bill Clinton's election marked a changing of the guard in the United States. After spending a dozen years in the White House, Republicans were cast into the wilderness; at the same time, the centrist Democrat moved his own party rightward. Perhaps most importantly in terms of cultural progression, Clinton was the first baby boomer to make it to the White House, ushering out the Greatest Generation and their Don Draper–boozing. With this child of the '60s, America was given its first leader to admit to

"One more stop, boys!"

past marijuana use. But Clinton's main vice, as everybody knows, has never been chemical—rather, the sexual favors of curvy white women.

The week following Clinton's inaugural ceremony in 1993, smoking was banned at 1600 Penn. The omission of matches and ashtrays would prove a challenge to visitors and employees who were accustomed to the throat-choking habits of yesteryear. For a quick fix, senators crouched in doorways; in the winter, lobbyists shivered in the carport. As for Clinton, an amateur cigar aficionado, this president discovered another use for tobacco—with assistance from an enthusiastic twenty-two-year-old named Monica Lewinsky.

For her part, the Beverly Hills–bred intern once kidded that her aspiration was to become "the assistant to the president for blow jobs." As the world learned through a multimillion-dollar investigation launched by the insanely creepy independent counsel Ken Starr, America's #1 Intern more or less achieved her dream. Clinton's tongue-wagging horniness as commander in chief, as well as during his prior governorship in Arkansas, dominated newspaper headlines for the latter half of the 1990s, and Starr's bizarre probe culminated in a report for nearly every boob groped, skirt lifted, and lover's spat associated with the sexual résumé of the president.

The Starr Report, 211 steamy pages of testimonies and evidence submitted to Congress in 1998, figured Lewinsky and Clinton's affair at an eighteen-month span. The Lewis and Clark College undergrad, a whopping six and a half years older than the president's daughter, scored an internship at the White House in 1995. Thereafter, she allegedly gave the president oral sex on several occasions. These liaisons mostly occurred within the confines of a hideaway room adjacent to the Oval Office—a far more tasteful locale for an afternoon delight than, say, atop the flower beds in the Rose Garden.

EVEN BEFORE AMERICAN HOUSEHOLDS CAME TO KNOW CLINTON AS "Slick Willy," his affairs with gut-busting cuisine attracted much of his publicity. As president-elect, the 230-pound reformed hillbilly stuffed his face with fast food and what the *New York Times* termed "the stuff with fat in it." Favorites included "jalapeño cheeseburgers, chicken enchiladas, barbecue, cinnamon rolls and pies." In the White House, a former pastry chef recalled that "[h]e could eat five or six pork chops."

You'd think this was a man suffering from a common case of the munchies, but the president's appetite required no herbal stimulant. Marijuana wasn't really his bag. During his first presidential campaign, Governor Clinton notoriously admitted that, as a Rhodes scholar in the 1960s, he "experimented . . . a time or two" but "didn't inhale." While the two subsequent presidents were admitted former drug users, at the time, Clinton's weed admission was earth-shattering, marking the Woodstock generation's arrival to power. (More crucially, his admission gave life to approximately four billion hackneyed Jay Leno jokes.)

Clinton's main vice, as everybody knows, has never been chemical.

While her husband was cramming his mouth with various fried foods, First Lady Hillary Rodham Clinton promoted one of those first lady eat-healthy campaigns. Did the president lose at least *some* weight in effect? Sure. But in November 1995, when the United States underwent a shutdown of the federal government—the White House alone cut 90 from its staff of 430—the commander in chief needed an outlet to calm his nerves. And it's possible that the McDonald's drive-thru was no longer an option. At least, that's the laziest excuse one could conjure for a sex fiend who, according to a former member of the governor's security detail, did not consider fellatio an adulterous act—or so Clinton concluded after he "researched the subject in the Bible." And Clinton's carnal needs did not, apparently, extend to his wife. Arkansas State Trooper and gossipmonger Roger Perry recalled an evening during which an angered Hillary shouted, "I need to be fucked more than twice a year!" at the top of her lungs.

And really, why have sex with your wife when you have young interns eager for the work? In a tale as familiar to American history as George Washington and his stupid cherry tree, during the government shutdown Monica Lewinsky began giving the president peeks of her underwear and casually meandering past the Oval Office doorway as an excuse for Clinton to summon her in for small talk. This covert act, purported to look unintentional, was previously orchestrated via phone calls with Clinton on prior evenings. (Many of those calls escalated into phone sex.) As the forty-second president would chat up Lewinsky and reel her into his office, so the plan went, passersby in the hallway would think little of their water-cooler banter. And yet, moments later in the inner sanctum of the Oval Office, Clinton and Lewinsky redefined the thirty-minute break at 1600 Pennsylvania Avenue. To wit: kissing, fondling, blow jobs, and ruining a perfectly good size-12 blue dress from the Gap. Exactly what a child of Beverly Hills was doing shopping at the Gap was never fully established—but then, it was the '90s.

Lewinsky's testimony in the Starr Report approximates that the two messed around a total of twelve times; however, they never engaged in sexual intercourse. ("That was kind of a little bit of a letdown for her," said one of her high school friends, armed with the gift of understatement.) During blow job #1, set in Clinton's private study, Lewinsky remembered that the president "was talking on the phone" to a congressman as she went to task. When he finished the call, Clinton requested that the intern stop her labor. (She wanted him "to complete," but "he needed to wait until he trusted me more.") It was at this same BJ session that Clinton eyeballed a cigar in a "sort of naughty way." Lewinsky took notice. "We can do that, too, sometime," she recalled telling the president.

Five months later, they put the stogie to use, which was the moment, according to Lewinsky's authorized biography, that "she realized she had fallen in love."

OF COURSE, LEWINSKY WAS NOT CLINTON'S FIRST AFFAIR. BEFORE Monica, he was famous for possibly putting the moves on one Paula Jones, who met Clinton when he was governor of Arkansas and she was a typist for the Arkansas Industrial Development Commission. Within hours of meeting her, Clinton allegedly sat next to her on a couch and yanked his pants down to his knees. "He had boxer shorts and everything," Jones said, "and he exposed hisself" and "wanted me to kiss it.

"He was saying it in a very disgusting way," Jones continued, "just a horny-ass way that just scared me to death." (This would mark the first time in our nation's history that the phrase "horny-ass" was used to describe our leader, and was covered as if news.) Nonetheless, a mere eighteen months later she sought out her alleged assailant, who was now president. The pair supposedly sat in the same inner office where Clinton and Lewinsky would swap spit years later, and, as Jones recalled, "it got physical."

A state trooper leaked a version of the events back in Arkansas to *The American Spectator*, and they were part of its January 1994 cover story— "His Cheatin' Heart"—an exposé on the president's scandalous behavior. Embarrassed and upset by the right-wing magazine's yellow journalism, Jones wanted to sue for defamation; her husband and attorneys thought it better to file a civil suit against the president for sexual harassment. And so it began the firestorm that engulfed the news media. But in February 1999, the same man who "didn't inhale" or "complete" beat Starr's investigation. While roundly deny-ing and eschewing allegations related to "sexual relations" with Lewinsky, Clinton was acquitted of congres-sional impeachment charges. And yet, the August prior, he admitted on national television to having "a rela-tionship with Miss Lewinsky that was not appropriate."

Slick Willy elaborated on his craft in the 2005 autobiography *My Life*. "I was unsure of exactly what the curious definition of sexual relations meant," the former president wrote. "In the deposition, I was trying to protect my family and myself from my selfish stupidity. I believed that the contorted definition of 'sexual relations' enabled me to do so." As for Jones's "spurious" allegations, Clinton added that she settled out of court for "a large amount of money and no apology."

History was made in the events that unfolded from *Clinton v. Jones*. Never before—not even that time JFK went skinny-dipping at Bing Crosby's house—had a commander in chief's penis made such a public spectacle.

///

ZIPPER DROPPER

Newspaper reporters and late-night comedy writers weren't the only ones whose jobs became more interesting during the Clinton sex scandal. Denizens of the service industry squeezed out a few Slick Willy–inspired barroom gimmicks to boost sales and inappropriate relations at bachelorette parties.

⅓ ounce white crème de cacao

⅓ ounce crème de menthe

⅓ ounce coffee-flavored liqueur

ice

Pour the ingredients over ice in a rocks glass.

//////////////// **Serves 1** ////////////////

THE DEMON LOOKING BACK

JANUARY 20, 2001–JANUARY 20, 2009

George W. Bush

43

REPUBLICAN

Despite leaving behind a federal budget surplus, relative world peace, and a prosperous economy, Bill Clinton and his impeachment hearings sent parts of the country on a soul-searching detour. It veered away from fiscal and social progress and onto a path led by a simpleminded born-again Christian who didn't touch booze or flagrantly cheat on his wife; a self-proclaimed "compassionate conservative" who, as governor of Texas, spent hundreds of millions of dollars to see tougher punishments enforced on drug users. Before that, as managing general partner of a Major League Baseball team, he designated

A Connecticut
Yankee in boots
and spurs.

"alcohol-free zones" at the Texas Rangers ballpark.

A nation's moral redemption—i.e., getting the fishy taste of Bill and Monica out of its mouth—was in demand just enough to elect George W. Bush to the Oval Office. Elect him without the popular vote and the questionably legal interference of the Supreme Court—but elect him nonetheless. Good call, America! In the two terms that followed, Bush ignored warnings that resulted in the largest terrorist attack ever staged on home soil, went to war with the wrong country, allowed a major city to sink, and watched haplessly as the entire economy nose-dived.

Through it all, however, he remained fit, amiable, and sober.

But once upon a time Bush wasn't so uptight in regard to boozing, whoring, and drugs. When the firstborn son to a future president and third generation of a Republican political dynasty attended Yale University—class of '68—he did not partake in Vietnam teach-ins or revel in the psychedelic golden age of rock and roll. Although born in Connecticut, the East Coast WASP began to cultivate a macho honky-tonk persona that was completely divorced from his American royalty reality, to say nothing of the era's countercultural mind-set. ("I don't remember any kind of heaviness ruining my time at Yale," Bush told GQ magazine.) By the time he entered Harvard Business School in 1973—after being rejected from University of Texas Law School—the C+ student swaggered down the hallways in shitkickers and spit tobacco into a Styrofoam cup, seemingly the grandchild not of Senator Prescott Sheldon Bush, but of Ty Cobb.

At Yale, Bush was your stereotypical douchebag frat boy. Jumping on the coattails of creepy traditions such as branding fraternity letters into the flesh of Delta Kappa Epsilon brethren—"There's no scarring mark," he argued, "only a cigarette burn"—the man who would later open the Guantanamo Bay detention camp made his presence known among campus degenerates. He minored in history with a major in rabble-rousing and spent time as a male cheerleader holding a cool old-timey megaphone. Classmates and his father's spies recalled W.'s incessant binge-drinking; he attended class with Jack Daniel's on his breath and, as the Kennebunkport Police Department would document in the coming years, enjoyed driving a car while plastered. On one occasion, young Bush got so stinking drunk at a frat house that "he literally rolled back to the dorm." A friend suggested that liquor was not the only item in the medicine cabinet. "If he didn't use marijuana at that point," classmate Tom Seligson said, "then he wasn't alive."

Bush was also a playboy. After graduating, he meandered from pilot training in Georgia to the oil-well business in west Texas. A colleague remembered that the Ivy League preppy fancied himself "God's gift to women." Bush had his share of barroom lays; in a drunken tizzy, he even promised one conquest that she would be his wife.

"So, what's sex like after fifty, anyway?" the future president asked one of his mother's friends during a cocktail party, while he was on holiday break at Yale. Had Barbara Bush heard Chevy Chase or Rodney Dangerfield utter this remark in a film, she no doubt would have laughed until she peed herself; her son, however, got chewed out.

IN 2001, BUSH BRAGGED ABOUT BEING "A BETTER MAN BECAUSE OF YALE," though he was noticeably mute regarding the years that followed. In the early part of the 1970s, he lived in a Houston apartment complex called the Chateaux Dijon, which was something like Melrose Place, with tenants who had their names etched on the backs of their belts. Come evening, he frequented a nightspot called the Mileau for bottled Budweiser and—allegedly!—toots of cocaine. Bush would later vaguely refer to this time as his "reckless" years.

Christmas 1972 was unfortunate enough to omit from the family photo album and, even worse, make it into Oliver Stone's 2008 biopic: An intoxicated Bush, with his fifteen-year-old brother, Marvin, riding shotgun, drove from a friend's house back to his parents' without incident—with the exception of his audibly dragging a neighbor's trash cans down the block. A fight broke out in the living room.

He attended classes with Jack Daniel's on his breath.

"I hear you're looking for me," Dubya barked at his disappointed father. "You want to go mano a mano right here?" (Always the killjoy, Barbara broke up the fisticuffs between Junior and Poppy, depriving the world the satisfaction of learning that George H. W. Bush kicked the living shit out of his loser son.) In the same year, according to an unnamed source in J. H. Hatfield's much-disputed biography *Fortunate Son*, the wannabe pugilist got himself arrested for possession of cocaine. "George damn sure wasn't the first rich kid who got caught with a little snow," the source said, "and because of his family's connections, had his record taken care of by the judge." Apparently, an arrangement was made for Bush Junior to agree to a temporary position as counselor at an inner-city youth center. (Woe betide the troubled youth who got George W. Bush as their counselor.)

This was not his last run-in with the cops. In September 1976, police clinked the thirty-year-old Bush for driving under the influence—an arrest made near the family summer home in Kennebunkport, Maine (and swept under the rug). Less than a year later, he went on a weeklong drinking binge after discovering a longtime friend had been diagnosed with leukemia. It was on the seventh day that the silver-spooned alkie, eyes bloodshot and body aching from dehydration, stared at himself in the mirror and saw "the demon looking back."

Around this time, Bush married librarian Laura Lane Welch, who would passive-aggressively scatter bookmarked titles about alcoholism around the house. "She suggested it was either me or Jim Beam," Bush said on A&E's Biography Channel. "At some point in time I had to make a decision."

The dark hour of sobriety came during a celebratory fortieth-birthday weekend with friends at the Broadmoor Hotel in Colorado Springs. Once again, a hungover Bush found a hellion staring back at him from a hotel bathroom mirror. ("It's your reflection, George," his wife probably said. "Remember our talk about the way mirrors work?") He swore off drinking then and there; for

the rest of his life, he would manage to swallow nonalcoholic beer on NFL Sundays. (His White House stocked the Netherlands-brewed Buckler.) In August 1999, when Bush's "reckless" past returned to haunt his bid for the Republican presidential nomination, he confessed to a previous life of alcoholism. Yet he would never fully admit to usage of marijuana, "because I don't want some little kid doing what I tried," he later told Doug Wead, a former aide of his father's who secretly recorded their conversations. Lord knows, youth across America have always turned to George W. Bush as a trendsetter.

As for nose candy, Bush told Wead, "I haven't denied anything." Could he be any clearer? Obviously, this man never used cocaine for a single minute.

In November 2000, less than a week before the presidential election, a report surfaced about his September 1976 DUI arrest. The GOP frontrunner responded on the campaign trail. "I've said I've made mistakes in the past," Bush said. "People know that. They've thought about that. They're making their minds up now."

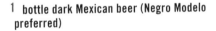

MICHELADA

The Lone Star State prides itself on this beer cocktail, a hearty hangover remedy with which Dubya was surely more than familiar in 1970s Houston. Recipes vary, but your best bet is this classic approach.

juice of ½ lime
kosher salt
ice
2 dashes Worcestershire sauce
1 dash Tabasco sauce
pinch black pepper
1 bottle dark Mexican beer (Negro Modelo preferred)

Coat the rim of a frosted mug with the juice from the lime, then add salt. Fill with ice, then squeeze the rest of the lime juice into the mug. Add the sauces and pepper. Pour the beer on top. Stir slowly. Drink.

/////////////// **Serves 1** ///////////////

THE CHOOM GANG

JANUARY 20, 2009–

Barack Obama

DEMOCRAT

High school was probably the least stressful four years of Barack Obama's life. This was, of course, thirty years before falling subject to an outpouring of unfounded and arguably racist conspiracy theories, ranging from the location of his actual birthplace to his undercover work for terrorist organizations. But long before the crazies lunged out of the backwoods of America, senior year at the prestigious Punahou prep school basically ruled. Never mind that 1979 was the year of atrocities such as the Iran hostage crisis, Star Trek: The Motion Picture, and the inexplicable popularity of the beanbag chair. In a postcard Honolulu

Mount Tantalus, 1979

aloha

backdrop, the kid then known as "Barry" and a few classmates—collectively known as "the Choom Gang"—managed a mental escape from global uncertainty and the dilapidation of American culture by way of pickup basketball games, banging tunes, and chest-bursting bong rips. If Bill Clinton's election brought the baby boomers to power, Obama's 2008 victory over old man John McCain marked yet another generational shift: Here was a president who attended high school at the same time as the *Dazed and Confused* crowd. The stoners had risen.

Could there be a more luscious climate than the Hawaiian Islands to choom oneself silly in a parked Volkswagen bus while cranking up the stereo to the tunes of Blue Öyster Cult, Aerosmith, and Stevie Wonder? David Maraniss asked Obama's high school friends similar questions for the 2012 book *Barack Obama: The Story*. Tom Topolinski, sworn Choom Gang member, tripped down memory lane about not only the "never panicked, never fazed" beloved Barry but the specific rules of their smoke-outs, as well. It should come as no surprise to learn that, even as a teen, this covert nerd required smoke circle procedures.

Everybody knew rule number one: "TA"—"total absorption"—because "wasting good bud smoke was not tolerated," according to Topolinski. Forget to inhale the entire hit? Forfeit the next turn in the smoke circle. (Not that the rules always applied to Barry, known for shouting "Intercepted!" when intentionally breaking up a perfectly sound rotation of puff-puff-give.) Another effective method to conserve kush was taking "roof hits," i.e., rolling up car windows, clouding the vehicle and, when the bowl cashed, taking in the last remnants of "sweet-sticky Hawaiian buds" by puckering lips to the ceiling. Every corner sack of precious cheeba could not go to waste, despite relatively affordable rates provided by their weed dealer, a "freakin' scary" long-haired pizza shop employee who lived in a bus inside an old warehouse. (Later, the scary pizza guy would be reunited with Obama, when he grew up to become Vice President Joe Biden.)

The future president exhibited more benevolent leadership at weekend pickup basketball games. In the streetball "Hack League," players engaged in the usual smack talk and flagrant fouls, but Obama, the "cool head, main thing," would not get physical on the court; he argued his way out of double-dribbles and charging calls. And Choomers kept environmental awareness. After killing brain cells on Mount Tantalus with bottles of St. Pauli Girl and reefer, they somehow managed to clean up after themselves. The Gang was harmless, "more *Animal House*-y and more fun," recalled another Punahou alum.

Unlike Bill Clinton's "didn't inhale" cop-out or George W. Bush's 1976 DUI arrest that was swept under the rug, Obama's tryst with Mary Jane was hardly a matter he shied away from. In his 1995 autobiography, *Dreams of My Father: A Story of Race and Inheritance*, published after he was elected the *Harvard Law Review*'s president—a position previously held only by white people—the author admitted to pot usage in high school, as well as "a little blow when you could afford it." As a high-profile U.S. senator, Obama did not change his tune. "When I was a kid, I inhaled," he drily told the American Society of Magazine Editors in 2006. "That was the point."

Heroin never made it into his bloodstream. *Dreams of My Father* describes a "potential initiator" named "Micky" who worked at a local delicatessen. One afternoon, Micky was "shaking like a faulty engine" as he "pulled out the needle and the tubing" in the back of the store. "I'd looked at him standing there," Obama wrote, "surrounded by big slabs of salami and roast beef, and right then an image popped into my head of an air bubble, shiny and round like a pearl, rolling quietly through a vein and stopping my heart." Like any good stoner, he seemed much more taken with the hoagies than the heroin.

After high school, Obama enrolled for two years at Los Angeles's Occidental College, "mainly because I'd met a girl from Brentwood while she was vacationing in Hawaii," he wrote. The student association produced weekly events

known as Wet Wednesdays, Thirsty Thursdays, and Fried Fridays. (Better to have kids get schnockered on campus than somewhere else, was the thought process.) But Obama's partying began to wind down. "It wasn't a big druggie scene," said Susan Keselenko, who edited the student newspaper. "If someone passed him a joint, he would take a drag," according to friend Vinai Thummalpally, who would later become an Obama fund-raiser. "[B]ut he would not even do as much as other people on campus." Others remember the Oxy freshman engaging in casual debates on the dormitory couches. As the "Kashmir" chords rang through the hallway, a politically minded Obama "would point out the negatives of a policy," dormmate John Boyer said. "[He would] illuminate the complexities of an issue the way others could not."

"I inhaled. That was the point."

When Obama transferred to Columbia University, where he would finish his B.A., he completed his transition into the levelheaded, health-conscious bore who would later save the United States from economic collapse and inherit Dubya's mess abroad. Sadly, the Choom member's most enjoyable buzzes in a hectic first four years in office were probably a Guinness on St. Patrick's Day at a D.C. pub and—*yawn*—the July 2009 "beer summit" publicity stunt with Henry Louis Gates Jr. and Sergeant James Crowley. (White House staff iced down Bud Light, Red Stripe, Blue Moon, and the nonalcoholic Buckler, which was consumed, oddly, by wildman Biden.) Alas, Barry, the dazed and confused, pot-loving, coke-dabbling pride of the Choom Gang, was dead. The Gap-shopping, henpecked soccer dad Barack was here to stay.

MARIJUANA-INFUSED MARTINI

Honor the Choom Gang's roots with this ganja-infused refreshment. It might taste awful, but after 20 minutes, who cares?

⅛ ounce finely chopped marijuana

12 ounces gin

ice

3 cups simple syrup

3 cups lime juice

Bake the cannabis in the oven at low heat (200 degrees) on a pan for 1 hour. Then, combine the gin with the baked weed inside a lidded container. Shake well, then store at room temperature. After 3 days, strain the liquid into a cocktail glass with the ice, simple syrup, and lime juice. Stir.

/// **Serves 12** ///

So: Who Partied the Hardest?

HOW WOULD YOU EVEN MEASURE SUCH A THING? ON THE AFTERNOON OF December 5, 1933, members of Congress must have felt delighted when the newly ratified Twenty-first Amendment ended Prohibition and Franklin D. Roosevelt quipped, "I believe this would be a good time for a beer." But does a man's personal politics qualify him for the party award? What of his penchant for martinis and cheating on the first lady? Would they somehow endow FDR with a higher rating than, say, Chester A. Arthur, who, albeit a faithful husband and moderate drinker, hosted gatherings at his Manhattan apartment and the White House as if he ran an after-hours saloon? History is subjective. Customs change. One would have to consider several facets before evaluating which, if any, president gets top prize here.

For starters, define "party." Are we talking about one's capability to consume the most cocktails in one sitting, or the person who is more likely to dance a jig while using a lampshade for a top hat? Does it make a difference if he indulges for stress relief rather than juvenile curiosity? How about if a commander in chief prefers benzos to bourbon? After all, liquor cabinets and wine cellars are not the only means of escape. Richard Nixon ate prescription pills as if they were Skittles, and he was a spastic nine-year-old. John F. Kennedy toked weed while the Soviets were planning for the apocalypse. A college-age Benjamin Harrison rebelled against his parents by—*gasp!*—puffing on cigars. Woodrow Wilson and William Jefferson Clinton were in a seemingly constant pursuit of orgasm.

Ultimately, there's just no comparing one to another. At least, that's what I concluded after attempting to formulate an intricate point system not unlike C-SPAN's Historians' Presidential Leadership Survey. Rather than prodding academics to rank each president from one to ten in categories such as "Crisis Leadership" and "Economic Management," I tallied scores with nonsense such

as "Ability to Consume Mass Quantities," "Psychedelic Experimentation," and "Hosting Skills." It didn't work. Why penalize William Howard Taft for having a teetotaler lifestyle when he could snort a pork loin up his nostril faster than the lot of 'em? And just because James Buchanan woke up barely hungover doesn't necessarily mean he was such a ball on the night prior. Though, I suppose, if you wanted to place bets on who could win a marathon boozing session, my money's on the alkie with the most body mass. Here's looking at you, Uncle Jumbo.

It's no secret that the presidency is a crazy, demanding job. Young politicians might let loose as they rise in the ranks—in smoke-filled hotel rooms where elbows are rubbed and on barstools in taverns where votes are won—but, after the inaugural reception and early wave of generous news coverage, rarely does the honeymoon continue. There are too many things to do. There are too many people watching. For some, the party was over the day they entered office. For others, that's when they leaned on their indulgences the most. With stakes so high—assassination attempts, financial crises, threats of nuclear annihilation—it's a wonder that any of these guys made it out of the White House alive, much less sober.

B. A.

PARTY APPENDIX

PRESIDENT	🍺 Beer	⚡ Drugs	🍾 Champagne	🚬 Cigarette	🃏 Cards	💋 Lips
GEORGE WASHINGTON (1789–1797)	🍺			🚬		
JOHN ADAMS (1797–1801)	🍺			🚬		
THOMAS JEFFERSON (1801–1809)			🍾			💋
JAMES MADISON (1809–1817)			🍾	🚬		
JAMES MONROE (1817–1825)			🍾			
JOHN QUINCY ADAMS (1825–1829)	🍺					
ANDREW JACKSON (1829–1837)	🍺			🚬		
MARTIN VAN BUREN (1837–1841)	🍺		🍾			
WILLIAM HENRY HARRISON (1841)				🚬		
JOHN TYLER (1841– 1845)			🍾			💋
JAMES K. POLK (1845–1849)						
ZACHARY TAYLOR (1849–1850)				🚬		
MILLARD FILLMORE (1850–1853)						
FRANKLIN PIERCE (1853–1857)	🍺		🍾	🚬		
JAMES BUCHANAN (1857–1861)	🍺		🍾			
ABRAHAM LINCOLN (1861–1865)						
ANDREW JOHNSON (1865–1869)						
ULYSSES S. GRANT (1869–1877)	🍺			🚬	🃏	
RUTHERFORD B. HAYES (1877–1881)						
JAMES A. GARFIELD (1881)				🚬		
CHESTER A. ARTHUR (1881–1885)	🍺		🍾	🚬		
GROVER CLEVELAND (1885–1889; 1893–1897)	🍺			🚬		💋

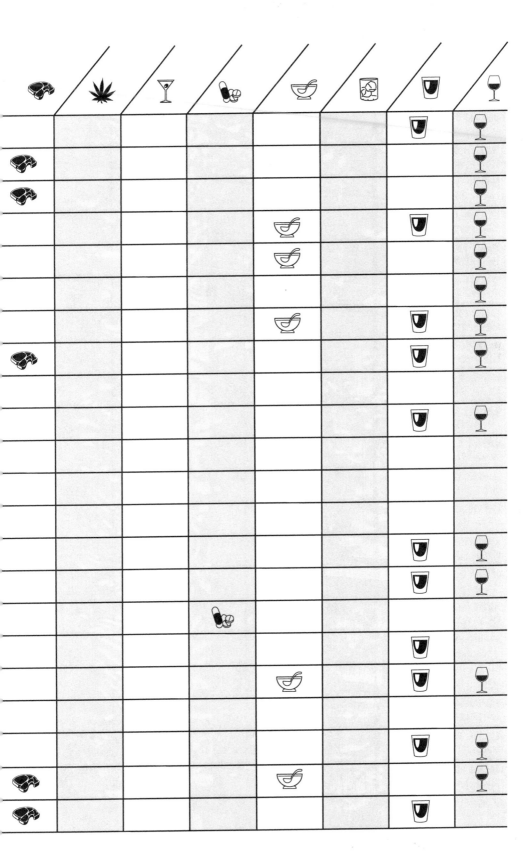

PRESIDENT	🍺	⚡	🍾	▬	🗋	👄
BENJAMIN HARRISON (1889–1893)				✓		
WILLIAM McKINLEY (1897–1901)				✓		
THEODORE ROOSEVELT (1901–1909)						
WILLIAM HOWARD TAFT (1909–1913)						
WOODROW WILSON (1913–1921)						✓
WARREN G. HARDING (1921–1923)	✓		✓	✓		✓
CALVIN COOLIDGE (1923–1929)				✓		
HERBERT HOOVER (1929–1933)				✓		
FRANKLIN D. ROOSEVELT (1933–1945)	✓		✓	✓		✓
HARRY S. TRUMAN (1945–1953)						
DWIGHT D. EISENHOWER (1953–1961)				✓		
JOHN F. KENNEDY (1961–1963)	✓	✓	✓	✓		✓
LYNDON B. JOHNSON (1963–1969)	✓			✓		✓
RICHARD M. NIXON (1969–1974)						
GERALD R. FORD (1974–1977)	✓			✓		
JIMMY CARTER (1977–1981)						
RONALD REAGAN (1981–1989)				✓		
GEORGE H. W. BUSH (1989–1993)						
WILLIAM JEFFERSON CLINTON (1993–2001)				✓		✓
GEORGE W. BUSH (2001–2009)	✓				✓	✓
BARACK OBAMA (2009–)	✓			✓	✓	

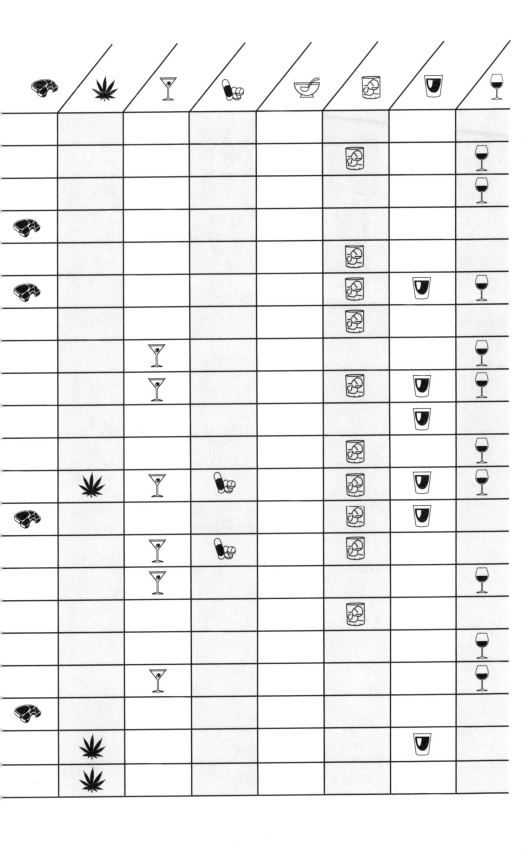

ADDITIONAL RECIPES

As if more of these are necessary to assist in prematurely eroding the liver. Then again, you *were* promised 44 . . .

///

HOT TODDY

On March 26, 1841, William Henry Harrison's personal physician recorded the dying president's condition as "slightly ailing"—clearly a downplay, given that the patient was prescribed a grab bag of goodies that included brandy, castor oil, cupping therapy, laudanum, opium, wine, and their old-school version of Vicks VapoRub.

The next time you're feeling a hellacious chest cold coming on, consider this for a remedy instead. (Or go to the hospital. Whatever.)

hot water

2 ounces scotch

1 tablespoon honey

½ ounce lemon juice

lemon peel

cinnamon stick

Pour the hot water and scotch into a mug. Add the honey and lemon juice. Stir. Garnish with the lemon peel and cinnamon stick.

/// **Serves 1** ///

MARTINI IN A MILK BOTTLE

In yet another dubious hat tip to the dweeb in chief, some knuckleheads in 1970s San Antonio opened the Millard Fillmore Grammar School & Grille, a "public school atmosphere" that was "carried out with good humor and good taste," according to *Texas Monthly*. Naturally, the novelty restaurant—furnished with classroom desks for tables, pencil-writing tablets for menus, and cocktails in milk bottles—did not keep late hours. Here's an homage to the short-lived operation.

2½ ounces gin

½ ounce vermouth

lemon peel for garnish

Add the ingredients to a tumbler or mixing glass for shaking or stirring (your preference). Strain into a chilled milk bottle. Garnish with the lemon peel.

// **Serves 1** //

GIN RICKEY

Around the time James Garfield suffered a fatal gunshot wound, a bartender named George A. Williams inflicted a lethal two-part cocktail on the denizens of DC. Inside Shoomaker's, a tavern located right around the corner from the White House, Williams named his "gin rickey" after lobbyist and all-around good time Colonel Joseph Kyle Rickey. Initially, bourbon was used in the mixture, but eventually—and inexplicably—gin became its primary ingredient. In a short time, the gin rickeys got too big for Washington and became the toast of the East Coast.

2 ounces gin

½ ounce lime juice

lump of ice

seltzer

Pour the gin and lime juice over ice in a Collins glass. Top with the seltzer.

// **Serves 1** //

WHITE TRASH MIMOSA

I t's just a hunch, but Jimmy Carter's brother Billy probably would have approved of this one. According to Beltway-based mixologist Anthony Rivera, the makeshift cocktail hit the local scene around 2007, when a newly opened bar awaited its liquor license and had to temporarily make do with only beer and wine. Things got kitschy.

2 ounces orange-flavored Tang powder

water

1 bottle Miller High Life, aka "the Champagne of Beers"

ice

orange peel for garnish

Put the orange powder in a pint glass. Dilute with a smidgen of water to create a syrup-like consistency. Add the beer and ice. Stir slowly. Garnish and serve.

/// **Serves 1** ///

SOURCES

"A Large Bath Tub." *Engineering Review*. Vol. 19, 1909.

"A 'Loyal' Paper on the 'Loyal' Vice President: The Inaugural Humiliation." *The Cincinnati Gazette*, March 9, 1865. Reprinted *Daily Ohio Statesman*, March 11, 1865.

"A New York Mixer Taught How to Make Mint Juleps." *New York Sun*. Reprinted in *The Public Ledger*, page 4. Maysville, Kentucky. May 22, 1896.

Ackerman, Kenneth D. *Dark Horse: The Surprise Election and Political Murder of James A. Garfield*. Carroll and Graf Publishers, 2003.

———. Interview with Brian Abrams. January 18, 2014.

Algeo, Matthew. "Book Discussion on *The President Is a Sick Man*." C-SPAN2 BookTV. May 18, 2011.

———. Interview with Brian Abrams. February 18, 2014.

———. *The President Is a Sick Man: Wherein the Supposedly Virtuous Grover Cleveland Survives a Secret Surgery at Sea and Vilifies the Courageous Newspaperman Who Dared Expose the Truth*. Chicago Review Press, 2011.

Allgore, Catherine. *A Perfect Union: Dolley Madison and the Creation of the American Nation*. Henry Holt and Company, 2006.

Arkow, Phil. Vice president, SPERMFLOW. Interview with Brian Abrams. December 15, 2013.

Armstrong, Emma P. *The James K. Polk Cookbook: Treasured and Contemporary Recipes Honoring the Eleventh President of the United States*. James K. Polk Memorial Auxilar, 1978.

Arnett, Ethel Stephens. *Mrs. James Madison: The Incomparable Dolley*. Piedmont Press, 1972.

Baker, Russell. "Condition Is Good: Physician Sees President Back in Capital January 1." *New York Times*. October 10, 1955.

Barber, James D. "Adult Identity and Presidential Style: The Rhetorical Emphasis." *Daedalus*, Vol. 97, No. 3. *Philosophers and Kings: Studies in Leadership*. MIT Press, Summer 1968.

Bauer, K. Jack. *Zachary Taylor: Soldier, Planter, Statesman of the Old Southwest*. Louisiana State University Press, 1993.

"Big Game A-Plenty Awaits Roosevelt." *New York Times*. March 11, 1909.

Biggs, Barton. *Wealth, War and Wisdom*. John Wiley & Sons. December 17, 2010.

"Billy Carter Now Drinks from Cup." AP/*Lakeland Ledger*. October 24, 1976.

"Billy's Beer Is a Big Bust in Dusty Texas." UPI/*Boca Raton News*. June 2, 1978.

Blackman, Emily L. Barkeeper. Brooklyn, New York. Interview with Brian Abrams. June 15, 2014.

Blair, Joan and Clay Jr. *The Search for J. F. K*. Berkley Publishing Corporation. 1976.

Blake, Heidi. "The little blue pills that sent Abraham Lincoln into a rage." *Telegraph*. March 23, 2010.

Boller, Paul F. Jr. *Presidential Anecdotes*. Oxford University Press, 1981.

Bomboy, Scott. "Clearing up the William Howard Taft bathtub myth." National Constitution Center. Yahoo! News. February 6, 2013.

Borger, Julian. "The best perk in the White House." *Guardian*. June 3, 2004.

Borneman, Walter R. *Polk: The Man Who Transformed the Presidency and America*. Random House, 2008.

Brands, H.W. Interview with Brian Abrams (email). January 19, 2013.

——. *The Man Who Saved the Union: Ulysses Grant in War and Peace*. Doubleday, 2012.

Breslaw, Elaine G. *Lotions, Potions, Pills, and Magic: Health Care in Early America*. New York University Press, 2012.

Brinkley, Douglas G. "James Knox Polk." James Taranto, ed. *Presidential Leadership: The Best and the Worst in the White House*. Free Press, 2005.

Brodsky, Alyn. *Grover Cleveland: A Study in Character*. Macmillan, 2000.

Brooks, Daniel F. Director, Arlington Historic House, Birmingham, Alabama (retired). Interview with Brian Abrams. February 19, 2014.

Bryant, Traphes L. *Dog Days at the White House: The Outrageous Memoirs of the Presidential Kennel Keeper*. Ishi Press, 2010.

Bryk, William. "Dr. Feelgood: Past & Present." *New York Sun*. September 20, 2005.

Burks, Edward C. "Fillmore Society Lauds Whatsisname." *New York Times*. January 8, 1972.

———. "Society again sees that Millard Fillmore has his one day." *Eugene Register-Guard.* January 20, 1972.

Burleigh, Nina. *A Very Private Woman: The Life and Unsolved Murder of Presidential Mistress Mary Meyer.* Bantam Books, 1999.

Burner, David. *Herbert Hoover: A Public Life.* American Political Biography Press, 2005.

Burros, Marian. "Bill Clinton and Food: Jack Sprat He's Not." *New York Times.* December 23, 1992.

———. "Hillary Clinton's New Home: Broccoli's In, Smoking's Out." *New York Times.* February 2, 1993.

Burton, David Henry. *William Howard Taft: Essential Writings and Addresses.* Fairleigh Dickinson University Press, 2009.

Bush, Barbara. *Barbara Bush: A Memoir.* Scribner, 2003.

Bush Koch, Doro. *My Father, My President: A Personal Account of the Life of George H. W. Bush.* Grand Central Publishing, 2006.

Butt, A. W. *Taft and Roosevelt: The intimate letters of Archie Butt, Military Aide.* Doubleday, Doran, 1930.

Calhoun, Charles W. *Benjamin Harrison.* The American Presidents Series. Arthur M. Schlesinger, ed. Henry Holt and Company, 2005.

Campbell, Karlyn Kohrs. "Before the Rhetorical Presidency." Martin J. Medhurst, ed. *Presidential Rhetoric and Political Communication* (Book 19). Texas A&M University Press, 2008.

Cannon, Poppy, and Patricia Brooks. *The Presidents' Cookbook: Practical Recipes from George Washington to the Present.* Funk & Wagnalls, 1968.

Carey, Benedict. "West Wing Blues: It's Lonely at the Top." *New York Times.* February 14, 2006.

Carlson, Peter. "Revolutionary Spirits." *American History.* Vol. 45, Issue 2, June 2010.

Carman, Tim. "The rickey earns a place in D.C. history." *Washington Post.* July 14, 2011.

Caro, Robert. *Master of the Senate: The Years of Lyndon Johnson.* Vintage Books, Random House, 2002.

———. *The Passage of Power: The Years of Lyndon Johnson.* Alfred A. Knopf, 2012.

Chernow, Ron. *Washington: A Life.* Penguin Press, 2010.

Clarke, Patrick. Director, Wheatland. Interview with Brian Abrams. January 15, 2013.

Cleaves, Freeman. *Old Tippecanoe: William Henry Harrison and His Time*. American Political Biography Press, 1939.

Clinton, Bill. *My Life*. Vintage Books, 2005.

Cole, Tiffany. Assistant Curator for Research and Documentation, James Madison's Montpelier. Interview with Brian Abrams (email). September 30, 2013.

Collins, Gail. *William Henry Harrison*. The American Presidents Series. Arthur M. Schlesinger, ed. Henry Holt and Company, 2012.

———. *Woodrow Wilson: A Biography*. Alfred A. Knopf, 2009.

Cooper, John Milton Jr. Interview with Brian Abrams. March 6, 2013.

Crapol, Edward P. Author, *John Tyler, the Accidental President*. Interview with Brian Abrams. March 17, 2014.

Crook, Colonel W. H. *Memories of the White House: Personal Recollections of Colonel W. H. Crook*. Little, Brown and Company, 1911.

Curtis, Wayne. *And a Bottle of Rum: A History of the New World in Ten Cocktails*. Broadway Books, 2007.

Cutler, David M., and Grant Miller. *The Role of Public Health Improvements in Health Advances: The Twentieth Century United States*. Harvard University. February, 2004.

Dallek, Robert. *An Unfinished Life: John F. Kennedy, 1917–1963*. Little, Brown and Company, 2003.

Davis, Burke. *Old Hickory: A Life of Andrew Jackson*. The Dial Press, 1977.

Dean, John W. *Warren G. Harding*. The American Presidents Series. Arthur M. Schlesinger, ed. Henry Holt and Company, 2004.

DeFrank, Thomas M. *Write It When I'm Gone: Remarkable Off-the-Record Conversations with Gerald R. Ford*. G. P. Putnam's Sons, 2007.

"Dining Out." *San Antonio Light*. June 24, 1977.

Dixon, Elizabeth Lord Cogswell. "Journal written during a Residence in Washington during the 29th Congress. Commencing with the first of Decr., 1845." *Dixon Family Papers*, 1843–1864, Ms. 76582. Connecticut Historical Society.

Doenecke, Justus D. *The Presidencies of James A. Garfield and Chester A. Arthur*. American Presidency Series. University Press of Kansas, 1981.

Dowd, Maureen. "Woodrow Wilson, Stud Muffin." *New York Times*. December 7, 2013.

Drummond, B. Ayres. "Billy Carter Loses; Blames 'Antidrinking Vote.'" *New York Times*. December 7, 1976.

Eisenhower, David, and Julie Nixon Eisenhower. *Going Home to Glory: A Memoir of Life with Dwight D. Eisenhower, 1961–1969*. Simon & Schuster, 2010.

Eisenhower, Dwight David. *At Ease: Stories I Tell to Friends*. Doubleday, 1967.

Eisenhower, John S. D. *Zachary Taylor*. The American Presidents Series. Arthur M. Schlesinger, ed. Henry Holt and Company, 2008.

Emerson, Jason. *Giant in the Shadows: The Life of Robert T. Lincoln*. Southern Illinois University Press, 2012.

Epstein, Edward. "Ford escaped 2 assassination attempts / Both happened in California—one in capital, other in S.F." *San Francisco Chronicle*. December 27, 2006.

Executive Office of the President. "Congressional Budget Submission." WhiteHouse.gov. Fiscal Year 2014.

Felten, Eric. "An Icy Treat for Adults Only." *Wall Street Journal*. February 16, 2008.

———. "What Teddy Sipped." *Wall Street Journal*. February 18, 2006.

Fillmore, Millard. Announcement of death of Zachary Taylor. *Daily National Intelligencer*. July 11, 1850.

———. *The Early Life of Millard Fillmore: A Personal Reminiscence*. Salisbury Club, 1958.

———. "Millard Fillmore's Boyhood." *New York Times*. March 16, 1874.

Fishwick, Marshall W. "The Savant as Gourmet." *Journal of Popular Culture*. Vol. 32, Issue 1, Summer 1998.

Folk, Elyssa. "Bush mixes humor with humility in Commencement talk." *Yale Daily News*. May 22, 2001.

Ford, Gerald. *The Republican Congressional Cookbook*. Ford Library Museum. Mildred Leonard Papers, box 1. ARC Identifier 1113018.

Foster, Emily, ed. *The Ohio Frontier: An Anthology of Early Writings*. University Press of Kentucky, 2000.

Fromson, Daniel. "A Conversation with Derek Brown, Bartender and 'Booze Nerd.'" *The Atlantic*. March 29, 2011.

Fulsom, Don. Interview with Brian Abrams. September 29, 2012.

———. *Nixon's Darkest Secrets: The Inside Story of America's Most Troubled President*. St. Martin's Press, 2012.

Furman, Bess. "The Years at 1600 Pennsylvania Avenue." *New York Times*. October 26, 1958.

Garner, Dwight. "The Lure of Cocaine, Once Hailed as 'Cure-All.'" *New York Times.* July 19, 2011.

Garrett, William. *Reminiscences of Public Men in Alabama: For Thirty Years, with an Appendix.* Plantation Publishing Company's Press, 1872.

Geeslin, Phyllis D. President and CEO, Benjamin Harrison Presidential Site. Interview with Brian Abrams. May 14, 2014.

Geselbracht, Raymond H. "Oral History Interview with Philip D. Reister, Truman Family Physician." Overland Park, Kansas. June 20, 2001.

"Girl, 19, Battles Law Raising Drinking Age." *New York Times.* August 3, 1961.

Glass, Andrew J. "Culture in Carter's White House." *New York Times.* March 11, 1979.

Goitein, Annie. "Lincoln the Storekeeper." *Illinois History.* Northern Illinois University Libraries, 1995.

Gold, Robert. "Kennedy-themed Hyannis restaurant gets off to rough start." *Cape Cod Times.* June 5, 2013.

Gordon, Ernest B. *The Wrecking of the Eighteenth Amendment.* The Alcohol Information Press, 1943.

Gordon, Larry. "Occidental recalls 'Barry' Obama." *Los Angeles Times.* January 29, 2007.

Gordon-Reed, Annette. *Andrew Johnson.* The American Presidents Series. Arthur M. Schlesinger, ed. Macmillan, 2011.

Gould, Lewis L. Author, *The Presidency of William McKinley.* Interview with Brian Abrams. March 11, 2014.

Graff, Henry F. *Grover Cleveland.* Henry Holt and Company, 2002.

Gragg, Larry. "The Reign of King Mob, 1829." *History Today.* Vol. 28, Issue 4, April 1978.

Grant, Ulysses S. *Personal Memoirs of Ulysses S. Grant.* C. L. Webster, 1885–86; Bartleby.com, 2000.

Greenberg, David. *Calvin Coolidge.* The American Presidents Series. Arthur M. Schlesinger, ed. Henry Holt and Company, 2006.

Grimes, William. *Appetite City: A Culinary History of New York.* North Point Press, 2009.

———. *Straight Up or On the Rocks: The Story of the American Cocktail.* North Point Press, 2001.

Gunderson, Robert Gray. *The Log-Cabin Campaign.* University of Kentucky Press, 1957.

Haberman, Clyde. "A Forgotten Swearing-In, 123 Years Ago." *New York Times*. January, 21, 2005.

Haigh, Ted, a.k.a. Dr. Cocktail. *Vintage Spirits and Forgotten Cocktails: From the Alamagoozlum to the Zombie and Beyond. Deluxe Edition, Revised and Expanded.* Quarry Books, 2009.

Hailman, John. *Thomas Jefferson on Wine.* University Press of Mississippi, 2009.

Hall, Sherry. Site manager, Harding Home State Memorial. Interview with Brian Abrams. September 18, 2013.

Hall, Trish. "So Far, a Smoke-Free White House Is Drawing No Fire." *New York Times.* February 3, 1993.

Harrison, Caroline Lavinia Scott. "Statesmen's Dishes; and how to cook them." *The National Tribune.* 1890.

Hatfield, J. H. *Fortunate Son: George W. Bush and the Making of an American President.* Soft Skull Press, 2001.

Hayes, Rutherford B. "Memorandum for Garfield," January 17, 1881. Diary and Letters of Rutherford B. Hayes. Rutherford B. Hayes Presidential Center.

Herbers, John. Washington Bureau, *New York Times*, 1977–79. Interview with Brian Abrams. August 15, 2013.

Hersh, Seymour M. *The Dark Side of Camelot.* Little, Brown and Company, 1997.

Hess, Robert. "Bourbon Crusta Cocktail: The Cocktail Spirit with Robert Hess." *Small Screen Cocktails.* 2010.

Hess, Stephen. "Death of Gerald Ford: An Accidental President." *Independent UK.* December 28, 2006.

Hesson, Ted. "Bill Clinton: I Never Denied That I Used Marijuana." Fusion TV. December 3, 2013.

Hill, Mark Douglas. *The Aphrodisiac Encyclopaedia.* Random House, 2012.

Holt, Michael. *Franklin Pierce.* The American Presidents Series. Arthur M. Schlesinger, ed. Henry Holt and Company, 2010.

"Hoover Didn't Enjoy the Boos at 1931 Series Game." *Lewiston Evening Journal.* February 5, 1940.

Howard, Spencer. Archivist, Herbert Hoover National Historic Site. Interview with Brian Abrams (email). January 10, 2013.

Howe, George Frederick. *Chester A. Arthur: A Quarter-Century of Machine Politics.* Dodd, Mead, and Company Inc., 1935.

Hunter, Marjorie. "Ford, Arriving on Coast, Declares He Now Has 'Best of Both Worlds.'" *New York Times.* January 21, 1977.

——. "Top of the Line in Magic Carpets." *New York Times.* December 25, 1977.

Isaacson, Walter. *Kissinger: A Biography.* Simon & Schuster, 2005.

Isikoff, Michael. *Uncovering Clinton.* Crown Publishers, 1999.

Jackson, Robert. H. and John Q. Barret, ed. *That Man: An Insider's Portrait of Franklin D. Roosevelt.* Oxford University Press, 2004.

Jackson, Tutti. Research Services Department, Ohio Historical Society. Interview with Brian Abrams (email). October 28, 2013.

Jeffers, Paul H. *An Honest President: The Life and Presidencies of Grover Cleveland.* William Morrow, 2000.

Jensen, Richard J. *The Winning of the Midwest: Social and Political Conflict, 1888–1896,* Vol. 2. University of Chicago Press, 1971.

Joynt, Carol Ross. "Former White House Pastry Chef Recalls Bill Clinton's 'Scary' Appetite." *Washingtonian Magazine.* January 6, 2012.

Karabell, Zachary. *Chester Alan Arthur.* Henry Holt and Company, 2004.

Kelley, Kitty. *His Way: The Unauthorized Biography of Frank Sinatra.* Bantam, 2010.

Kellman, Laurie. "Bush Once Pleaded Guilty to DUI." Associated Press, November 3, 2000.

Kessler, Ronald. *In the President's Secret Service: Behind the Scenes with Agents in the Line of Fire and the Presidents They Protect.* Three Rivers Press, 2010.

Kirkpatrick, David D. "In Secretly Taped Conversations, Glimpses of the Future President." *New York Times.* February 20, 2005.

Klass, Rosanne. Applicant, Millard Fillmore Society. Interview with Brian Abrams. December 13, 2013.

Klein, Philip S. *President James Buchanan: A Biography.* Pennsylvania State University Press, 1962.

Kolata, Gina. "In Struggle with Weight, Taft Used a Modern Diet." *New York Times.* October 14, 2013.

Kovaleski, Serge F. "Old Friends Say Drugs Played Bit Part in Obama's Young Life." *New York Times.* February 9, 2008.

La Follette Jensen, Amy. *The White House and Its Thirty-Three Families.* McGraw-Hill, 1958.

Lachman, Charles. "America's Forgotten Presidential Sex Scandal." The Daily Beast. May 23, 2011.

———. *A Secret Life: The Lies and Scandals of President Grover Cleveland.* Sky Horse Publishing, 2011.

Landau, Barry H. *The President's Table: Two Hundred Years of Dining and Diplomacy.* Harper, 2007.

Leavitt, Judith Walzer, and Ronald Numbers. *Sickness and Health in America: Readings in the History of Medicine and Public Health.* University of Wisconsin Press, 1997.

Leech, Margaret. *In the Days of McKinley.* Harper & Row, 1959.

Lengel, Edward G. *Inventing George Washington: America's Founder, in Myth and Memory.* HarperCollins, 2011.

———. Editor in Chief, *Papers of George Washington,* University of Virginia. Interview with Brian Abrams. February 14, 2004.

Leuchtenburg, William E. *Herbert Hoover.* The American Presidents Series. Arthur M. Schlesinger, ed. Henry Holt and Company, 2009.

Loewen, James W. *Lies Across America: What Our Historic Sites Get Wrong.* New Press, 1999.

Longacre, Edward G. *General Ulysses S. Grant: The Soldier and the Man.* DaCapo Press, 2006.

Lyndon B. Johnson Presidential Recordings. "Johnson Conversation with Joe Haggar on August 9, 1964." WH6408.16. Conversation 4851. Miller Center, University of Virginia.

Mack, Robert C. Mixologist, Speakeasy 518, Albany, New York. Interview with Brian Abrams. January 6, 2014.

Madden, Richard L. "Issue and Debate; Legal Age for Liquor Argued Anew." *New York Times.* March 4, 1984.

Madison, Dolley. Letter to sister Anna. August 23, 1814. Dolley Payne Madison: An Exhibit. Virginia Center for Digital History.

"Mamie Eisenhower Still Not Used to Ike Being Gone." *The Lewiston Daily Sun*/AP. July 19, 1974.

"Mannington Here: Called to Capital." *New York Times.* April 9, 1924.

Margolis, Jay. *Marilyn Monroe: A Case for Murder*. iUniverse, 2011.

Marriott, Michel. "Taylor's Remains to Be Examined for Arsenic." *New York Times*. June 15, 1991.

May, Gary. *John Tyler*. The American Presidents Series. Arthur M. Schlesinger, ed. Henry Holt and Company, 2008.

Maynard, W. Barksdale. "The Governor, the First Lady, and the Other Woman." *New Jersey Monthly*. October 11, 2010.

McCormac, Eugene Irving. *James K. Polk: A Political Biography to the Prelude to War 1795–1845*. American Political Biography Press, 1995.

McCullough, David. *John Adams*. Simon & Schuster, 2008.

———. *Truman*. Simon & Schuster, 1993.

McHugh, Jane, and Philip A. Mackowiak. "What Really Killed William Henry Harrison?" *New York Times*. March 31, 2014.

Meacham, Jon. *American Lion: Andrew Jackson in the White House*. Random House, 2009.

———. *Thomas Jefferson: The Art of Power*. Random House, 2012.

Mencken, Henry L. "A Neglected Anniversary." *New York Evening Mail*. December 28, 1917.

———. "Melancholy Reflections." *Chicago Tribune*. May 23, 1926.

Merrill, Jane, and Chris Filstrup. *The Wedding Night: A Popular History*. Praeger, 2011.

Miles, Edwin A. "President Adams' Billiard Table." *The New England Quarterly*. Vol. 45, No. 1, March 1972.

"Millard Fillmore Grammar School & Grille." *Texas Monthly*. December 1977.

Miller, Nathan. *Theodore Roosevelt: A Life*. Quill/William Morrow; reissue edition, 1994.

Mitchell, Franklin D. *Harry S. Truman and the News Media; Contentious Relations, Belated Respect*. University of Missouri Press, 1998.

Moats, Sandy. "The Limits of 'Good Feelings': Partisan Healing and Political Futures during James Monroe's Boston Visit of 1817." *Proceedings of the American Antiquarian Society*. Vol. 118, No. 1. April 2008.

Morgan, Howard Wayne. *William McKinley and His America*. Kent State University Press, 2003.

Morris, Roy Jr. *Fraud of the Century: Rutherford B. Hayes, Samuel Tilden, and the Stolen Election of 1876.* Simon & Schuster, 2004.

Morton, Andrew. *Monica's Story.* Macmillan, 1999.

Nessen, Ron. *Making the News, Taking the News: From NBC to the Ford White House.* Wesleyan University Press, 2011.

———. White House Press Secretary, 1974–77. Interview with Brian Abrams. August 15, 2013.

Nixon, Richard M. "Remarks on Signing the Comprehensive Drug Abuse Prevention and Control Act of 1970." October 27, 1970. Gerhard Peters and John T. Woolley, eds. *The American Presidency Project.* University of California, Santa Barbara.

Obama, Barack. *Dreams of My Father: A Story of Race and Inheritance.* Three Rivers Press, 1995.

Okrent, Daniel. *Last Call: The Rise and Fall of Prohibition.* Scribner, 2011.

Olson, Dawn. Ranger, U.S. National Parks Service at Lindenwald. Interview with Brian Abrams. December 3, 2012.

Olver, Lynne. "American Presidents' Food Favorites." FoodTimeline.org, 1999.

Ott, Alex. *Dr. Cocktail: 50 Spirited Infusions to Stimulate the Mind and Body.* Running Press, 2012.

Ott, Katherine. Curator, Division of Medicine and Science at Smithsonian Institution. Interview with Brian Abrams. May 9, 2014.

"Our Fashionable Narcotics." *New York Times.* January 10, 1854.

Palmer, Robert. "City's Rock Clubs Fear Increase in Drinking Age." *New York Times.* March 11, 1985.

Parmet, Herbert S. *Jack: The Struggles of John F. Kennedy.* The Dial Press, 1980.

Pearson, Lee M. "The 'Princeton' and the 'Peacemaker': A Study in Nineteenth-Century Naval Research and Development Procedures." *Technology and Culture.* Vol. 7. No. 2. Johns Hopkins University Press, 1966.

Pember, P. Y. "The Tragedy of the United States Steamship 'Princeton.'" *The Independent,* Vol. 57, 1904.

Pendle, George. *The Remarkable Millard Fillmore: The Unbelievable Life of a Forgotten President.* Three Rivers Press, 2007.

Perlstein, Rick. *Nixonland: The Rise of a President and the Fracturing of America.* Scribner, 2008.

Perry, Mark. *Grant and Twain: The Story of a Friendship That Changed America.* Random House, 2004.

Pierce, Jane. Letter to son Benny. January 23, 1853. Franklin Pierce Papers. Accession Number: 1929-001. New Hampshire Historical Society.

Polk, James K. *Correspondence of James K. Polk,* Vol. 7. Wayne Cutler and Herbert Weaver, eds. University of Tennessee Press, 1989.

———. *The Diary of James K. Polk.* BiblioBazaar, 2008.

Preston, Dan. Editor, *Papers of James Monroe,* James Monroe Museum. Interview with Brian Abrams. March 13, 2014.

"Prohibition Repeal Is Ratified at 5:32 P.M.; Roosevelt Asks Nation to Bar the Saloon; New York Celebrates with Quiet Restraint." *New York Times.* December 5, 1933.

Reagan, Ronald. "Remarks on Signing a National Minimum Drinking Bill." July 17, 1984. Gerhard Peters and John T. Woolley, eds. *The American Presidency Project.* University of California, Santa Barbara.

"Reagan's Concept of America Hurts Party, Packwood Says." Associated Press. March 2, 1982.

Reed, Stephen B. Economist, Office of Prices and Living Conditions, Bureau of Labor Statistics. Interview with Brian Abrams. May 2, 2014.

Reeves, Thomas C. *Gentleman Boss: The Life of Chester A. Arthur.* Alfred A. Knopf, 1975.

———. Interview with Brian Abrams. October 29, 2013.

———. *A Question of Character: A Life of John F. Kennedy.* Prima Publishing, 1992.

"Remembering Gerald Ford." *Anderson Cooper 360.* CNN. December 27, 2006.

Remini, Robert V. *Andrew Jackson and the Course of American Freedom,* 1822–1832, Vol. II. Harper & Row Publishers, 1981.

———. *John Quincy Adams.* The American Presidents Series. Arthur M. Schlesinger, ed. Henry Holt and Company, 2002.

Ridgeway, James. "Dubya in 'Bama." *The Village Voice.* February 3, 2004.

Rivera, Anthony. "MxMo: The White Trash Mimosa." DoneLikeDundeeGoneLikeGandhi.com. July 12, 2011.

Rodrick, Stephen. "David Crosby: The Golden Years of Rock's Unlikeliest Survivor." *Rolling Stone.* February 19, 2014.

Roosevelt, James, and Sidney Shalett. *Affectionately, F.D.R.: A Son's Story of a Lonely Man.* Harcourt Brace, 1959.

"Roosevelt Plans for His Nile Trip." *New York Times*. December 6, 1909.

Roosevelt, Theodore. *African Game Trails: An Account of the African Wanderings of an American Hunter-Naturalist,* Vol. 1. Scribner, 1910.

———. *Hunting Trips of a Ranchman: Sketches of Sport on the Northern Cattle Plains.* Knickerbocker Press, 1885.

Roosevelt Longworth, Alice. *Crowded Hours.* Charles Scribner's Sons, 1932.

Rorabaugh, W. J. *The Alcoholic Republic: An American Tradition.* Oxford University Press, 1979.

Safire, William. "Billy the Problem." *New York Times*. January 15, 1979.

Sandburg, Carl. *Abraham Lincoln: Prairie Years, Volume 1.* New York. Harcourt, Brace and Company, 1925.

"Says Washington Was a Gambler, Distiller, Curser." *Lewiston Daily Sun*/AP. January 15, 1926.

Scarry, Robert J. *Millard Fillmore.* McFarland & Company Publishers, 2001.

"Scenes About the White House." *New York Times*. July 7, 1881.

Scheer, Robert. "*Playboy* Interview: Jimmy Carter; a Candid Conversation with the Democratic Candidate for the Presidency." *Playboy* magazine. November 1976.

Schmidt, "The Only" William. *The Flowing Bowl: When and What to Drink.* Charles L. Webster & Co., New York. 1892.

Schneider, Dorothy and Carl J. *First Ladies: A Biographical Dictionary.* 2nd ed. Facts on File, 2005.

Schultz, Ed. "Beer Diplomacy." MSNBC. *The Ed Show.* July 27, 2009.

Seager II, Robert. *And Tyler Too: A Biography of John and Julia Gardiner Tyler.* McGraw-Hill, 1963.

Seelye, Katharine Q. "Barack Obama, asked about drug history, admits he inhaled." *New York Times*. October 24, 2006.

Seigenthaler, John. *James K. Polk.* The American Presidents Series. Arthur M. Schlesinger, ed. Henry Holt and Company, 2004.

"7 Chicago Gangsters Slain by Firing Squad of Rivals, Some in Police Uniforms." *New York Times*. February 15, 1929.

Sferrazza Anthony, Carl. *Florence Harding: The First Lady, the Jazz Age, and the Death of America's Most Scandalous President.* William Morrow and Company, 1998.

Shaner, Arlene. "The Secret Surgeries of Grover Cleveland." New York Academy of Medicine. February 27, 2014.

Shlaes, Amity. *Coolidge*. Harper, 2013.

Sibley, Katherine A. S. *First Lady Florence Harding: Behind the Tragedy and Controversy*. University Press of Kansas, 2009.

Sievers, Harry J. *Benjamin Harrison: Hoosier Statesman*. University Publishers Incorporated, 1959.

Simpson, Brooks D. Author, *Ulysses S. Grant: Triumph Over Adversity*. Interview with Brian Abrams. April 8, 2013.

Smith, Marie. *Entertaining in the White House*. Macfadden-Bartell Corporation, 1967.

Smith Brownstein, Elizabeth. *Lincoln's Other White House: The Untold Story of the Man and His Presidency*. John Wiley & Sons, 2005.

Somervill, Barbara A. *Eleanor Roosevelt: First Lady of the World*. Compass Point Books, 2005.

Sotos, John G. "President Taft's Blood Pressure." Apneos Corporation. *Mayo Clinic Proceedings*. Vol. 81, Issue 11. November 2006.

———. "Taft and Pickwick: Sleep Apnea in the White House." *CHEST Journal*. Vol. 124, No. 3, September 2003.

Starling, Col. Edmund. *Starling of the White House*. Peoples Book Club, 1946.

Stein, Susan. Senior curator, Monticello. Interview with Brian Abrams. July 30, 2013.

Stephanopoulos, George. "Tapes Reveal Nixon's Prejudices Again." *ABC News*. March 22, 2002.

Stone, Andrea. "Lady Bird Johnson Buried Beside LBJ." *USA Today*. July 16, 2007.

Stroud, Kandy. "Jimmy Carter, Cheese Buff." *New York Times*. December 27, 1976.

Stryker, Lloyd Paul. *Andrew Johnson: A Study in Courage*. MacMillan & Co., 1936.

Suddath, Claire. "What Kind of Beer Is Served at the White House?" *Time*. July 30, 2009.

Sugar, Bert Randolph. *The Ultimate Book of New York Lists: Everything You Need to Know about the Greatest City on Earth*. Skyhorse Publishing, 2009.

Sugarman, Carole. "Oysters and Wild Turkey at President Tyler's Table." *Washington Post*. February 20, 1983.

Summers, Anthony. *The Arrogance of Power: The Secret World of Richard Nixon*. Penguin Books, 2001.

Swift, Will. *The Roosevelts and the Royals: Franklin and Eleanor, the King and Queen of England, and the Friendship That Changed History.* Wiley, 2009.

T., Jack. "Poppers? What are poppers?" PoppersGuide.com. July 26, 2012.

"Taft Eats Possum, Gives South Pledge." *New York Times.* January 9, 1909.

Taraborrelli, J. Randy. *The Secret Life of Marilyn Monroe.* Grand Central Publishing, 2010.

"Tests Lay Theory to Rest: Arsenic Didn't Kill Taylor." *Lexington Herald-Leader.* June 27, 1991.

"The Daily Diary of President Gerald R. Ford." A Day in the Life of a President Online Exhibit. Gerald R. Ford Presidential Library and Museum. Ann Arbor, Michigan.

"The Daily Diary of President Jimmy Carter." June 9, 1977. Jimmy Carter Library and Museum. Atlanta, Georgia.

"The Mangum Papers: Willie P. Mangum to Charity A. Mangum. July 10, 1850." Henry Thomas Shanks, ed. State Department of Archives and History, North Carolina.

"The Measure of a President." *New York Times.* October 6, 2008.

"The President's Fight for Life." *New York Times.* July 7, 1881.

"The Presidents." *The History Channel Presents.* A&E Home Video. May 31, 2005.

Thomas, Benjamin P. *Lincoln's New Salem,* by Benjamin P. Thomas; drawings by Romaine Proctor from photographs by the Herbert Georg studio, Springfield. University of Michigan Library. The Abraham Lincoln Association, 1934.

Thomas, Evan. *Ike's Bluff: President Eisenhower's Secret Battle to Save the World.* Little, Brown and Company, 2012.

Toobin, Jeffrey. *A Vast Conspiracy: The Real Story of the Sex Scandal That Nearly Brought Down a President.* Random House, 1999.

Trefousse, Hans L. *Andrew Johnson: A Biography.* W.W. Norton & Company, 1989.

Troy, Tevi. *What Jefferson Read, Ike Watched, and Obama Tweeted: 200 Years of Popular Culture in the White House.* Regnery Publishing, 2013.

"Truman Breaks Ribs in Fall at His Home." *New York Times.* October 14, 1964.

Truman, Margaret. *First Ladies: An Intimate Group Portrait of White House Wives.* Ballantine Books, 1996.

Tugwell, Rexford Guy. *Grover Cleveland.* Macmillan, 1968.

Unger, Harlow Giles. *John Quincy Adams.* Da Capo Press, 2013.

Updegrove, Mark K. Director, Lyndon Baines Johnson Library and Museum. Interview with Brian Abrams. January 10, 2013.

Van Ness, Cynthia. Director of Library & Archives, the Buffalo History Museum. Interview with Brian Abrams (email). December 13, 2013.

Vick, Dwight, and Elizabeth Rhoades. *Drugs & Alcohol in the 21st Century: Theory, Behavior and Policy.* Jones & Bartlett, 2010.

Waldo, S. Putnam. *The Tour of James Monroe.* 2nd edition. Silas Andrus, 1820.

Wallner, Peter A. "Book Discussion on *Franklin Pierce: New Hampshire's Favorite Son.*" C-SPAN Booknotes. October 25, 2004.

———. *Franklin Pierce: Martyr for the Union.* Plaidswede Publishing, 2007.

———. *Franklin Pierce: New Hampshire's Favorite Son.* Plaidswede Publishing, 2004.

———. Interview with Brian Abrams. December 7, 2012.

———. Interview with Brian Abrams (email). January 5, 2014.

"Was TR a Teetotaler?" *The Rough Writer.* The News of the Volunteers at Sagamore Hill. National Parks Service. August 2006.

Washington, George. *George Washington: Writings.* John H. Rhodehamel, ed. Library of America, 1997.

Watson, Robert P. *Affairs of State: The Untold History of Presidential Love, Sex, and Scandal, 1789–1900.* 1st edition. Rowman & Littlefield Publishers, 2012.

Wehner, Todd C. Department of Horticultural Science, North Carolina State University. Interview with Brian Abrams. May 14, 2014.

Weisman, Steven R. "Reagan Calls for Drinking Age of 21." *New York Times.* June 21, 1984.

West, J. B. *Upstairs at the White House: My Life with the First Ladies.* Warner Books, 1974.

Whitlock, Russ. Superintendent, Lyndon B. Johnson National Historic Park. Interview with Brian Abrams. January 21, 2013.

———. Interview with Brian Abrams. February 20, 2014.

Widmer, Ted. *Martin Van Buren.* Henry Holt and Company, 2005.

Wilson, Major L. *The Presidency of Martin Van Buren.* University of Kansas Press, 1984.

Wines, Michael. "Bush in Japan; Bush Collapses at State Dinner with the Japanese." *New York Times.* January 9, 1992.

Wondrich, David. *Imbibe!: From Absinthe Cocktail to Whiskey Smash, a Salute in Stories and Drinks to 'Professor' Jerry Thomas, Pioneer of the American Bar.* Penguin Group, 2007.

Yasko, James. Director of Education and Interpretation, The Hermitage. Interview with Brian Abrams (email). January 29, 2013.

Young, Dwight, and Margaret Johnson. *Dear First Lady: Letters to the White House— From the Collections of the Library of Congress and National Archives.* National Geographic Books, 2009.

Young Norton, Jeannette. *Mrs. Norton's Cook-Book: Selecting, Cooking, and Serving for the Home Table.* G.P. Putnam's Sons, New York. 1917.

Zimmer, Dave. *Crosby, Stills & Nash: The Authorized Biography.* Da Capo Press, 2000.

An earlier version of "The Unknown Comic" ran in *The Lowbrow Reader #9,* 2014.

An earlier version of "American Hero, Awful Bartender" ran in *Modern Drunkard Magazine,* June 2006.

ACKNOWLEDGMENTS

THIS WOULD HAVE NEVER HAPPENED HAD IT NOT BEEN FOR THE STROKES of genius from illustrator John Mathias, an artist I hope to work with forever. As for other big brains who deserve great thanks, the list is short: Jay Ruttenberg, publisher of *The Lowbrow Reader*, offered invaluable notes and suggestions from the book's inception; literary agent Lindsay Edgecombe and editors Maisie Tivnan and Sam O'Brien deserve praise for tolerating this mental case throughout; author and neighbor Robin Westen constantly reminded me of the healthier sides to obsession; Mara Altman, another author, gave emotional support during several trips to the Russian-Turkish Baths on 10th Street in Manhattan; and Charley Gerard shared his JSTOR password.